THE PROGENY

Center Point
Large Print

**This Large Print Book carries the
Seal of Approval of N.A.V.H.**

THE
PROGENY

TOSCA LEE

CENTER POINT LARGE PRINT
THORNDIKE, MAINE

This Center Point Large Print edition
is published in the year 2017 by arrangement with
Howard Books, a division of Simon & Schuster, Inc.

This book is a work of fiction.
Any references to historical events, real people, or real places are used fictitiously. Other names, characters, places, and events are products of the author's imagination, and any resemblance to actual events or places or persons, living or dead, is entirely coincidental.

The text of this Large Print edition is unabridged.
In other aspects, this book may vary
from the original edition.
Printed in the United States of America
on permanent paper.
Set in 16-point Times New Roman type.

ISBN: 978-1-68324-398-4

Library of Congress Cataloging-in-Publication Data

Names: Lee, Tosca Moon, author.
Title: The progeny / Tosca Lee.
Description: Center Point Large Print edition. | Thorndike, Maine : Center Point Large Print, 2017.
Identifiers: LCCN 2017008766 | ISBN 9781683243984 (hardcover : alk. paper)
Subjects: LCSH: Secret societies—Fiction. | Serial murderers—Fiction. | Large type books. | BISAC: FICTION / Suspense. | FICTION / Christian / Suspense. | GSAFD: Suspense fiction.
Classification: LCC PS3612.E3487 P76 2017 | DDC 813/.6—dc23
LC record available at https://lccn.loc.gov/2017008766

For Bryan.
Ours is my favorite story.

THE PROGENY

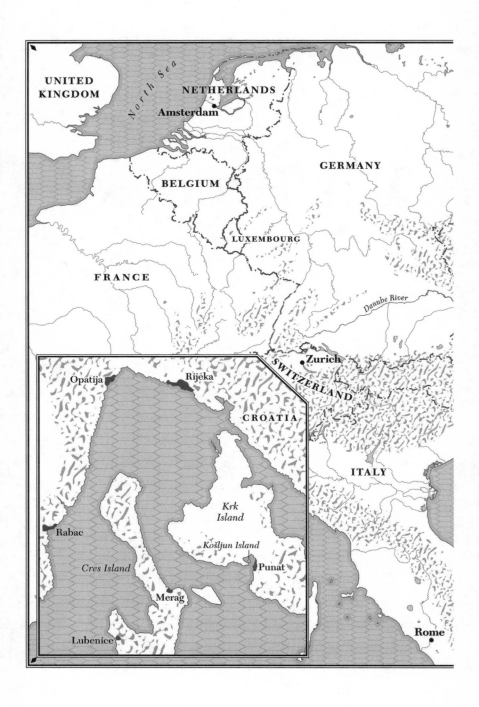

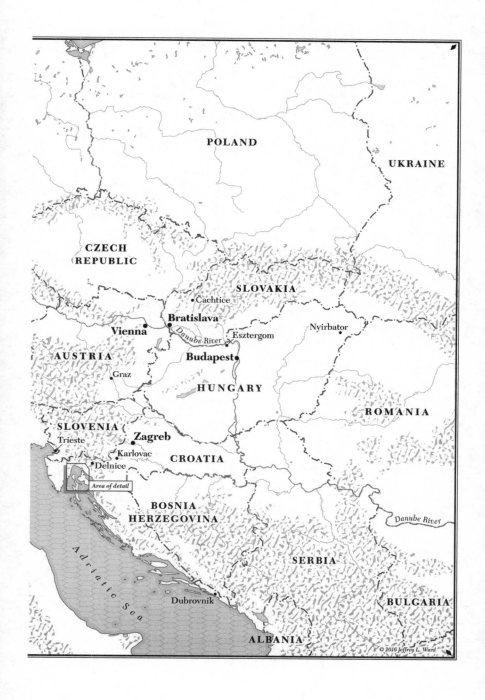

THE CENTER

No one speaks when you enter the Center for the final time. There's no need. You've gone through the counseling, tests, and a checklist of preparations to get the plastic bracelet you wear the day of treatment. The one that saves a life. They don't need to know why you're doing it anymore. Or that you lied about it all. Just the scratch of the stylus as you sign your name on the screen one last time.

A nurse takes me into a room and I lie down on the table. I give her the sealed packet—the only thing I brought with me. There's cash, meds, and an address inside, the one for "after." It's a thousand miles away. She'll pass it to the companion assigned to me. No point meeting her now.

I'm twenty-one years old and my name doesn't matter because it's about to be erased forever. I'm choosing to forget the ones I love, and myself, in the process.

They say your life flashes before your eyes when you die. But they don't tell you that every detail comes screaming back to life. That you taste each bite of every meal you savored, feel the shower of every rain you walked in . . . smell the hair against your cheek before that last, parting kiss. That you will fight to hold on to memory like a drowning person gasping for poisoned air.

Then everything you knew is gone. And you are still alive.

For now.

1

There's a figure standing by the window. Arms crossed, outlined against the fuchsia sky, looking out at what must be a spectacular sunset. When her chin lifts I wonder if she's seen something in the trees.

I push up from the cabin's lone sofa. An afghan with a giant moose stitched on it is tangled around my legs. It in no way coordinates with the moose valance in the kitchen or the fixture in the bathroom. Despite the name of the lake—Moosehead—I've yet to see a real moose anywhere since arriving here four weeks ago.

"You're awake." My caretaker, Clare, turns from the window. Her blond hair is pulled back in the loose ponytail she's worn every day since we arrived and she set up house. Going into town for groceries as I slept, taking me through two-hour assessments in the afternoon, complimenting my recent attempts at dinner, including the under-seasoned chicken casserole I made last night. It was the first time I'd tried it, I said, but I don't know if that's true.

"Yeah, finally."

My name is Emily Porter. I'm twenty-one years old and I am renting a cabin on a tiny island in

13

the north woods of Maine for reasons I no longer remember.

I go through this mental routine each time I wake, if only to assure myself I didn't get the lobotomy I joked about yesterday before sleeping—what, fifteen, twenty?—hours until just now. I don't even remember going to sleep. Nor do I remember where I lived before this, where I went to college, or the name of the high school with the blue lockers and squeaky gymnasium floor where I graduated. Including what happened to the garnet ring on my index finger as I accepted my diploma, or the name of the woman who gave it to me other than simply Mom.

Names, identifiers, faces up to age nineteen and everything in the two years since. All gone.

"A certain amount of postprocedure depression is normal. That will change, in time."

I slide my hand to the curve of my skull just above my left ear. To the stubby patch concealed by the longer hair above it. Not so stubby anymore. It could almost qualify for a military cut.

"As will that."

"Not fast enough." I flip the afghan off my legs, pop two pills from the bottle on the coffee table, already trying to decide what culinary disaster I'll create tonight. *Caretaker* is a misleading word; ever since I reached the two-week observation and recovery mark, Clare has seen to it that I cook, do laundry, find a job and my way around town as though I were already on my own.

"I'm thinking I should stay away from casseroles for a while. How do you feel about tuna quesadillas?" I get up and pad toward the kitchen, wash my hands. When she doesn't respond, I glance at her and say, "That good, huh?"

That's when I realize she's wearing the same blouse and skirt she wore the first day, the wooden tao cross hanging just below her collar. It looks like a capital *T,* which is what I thought it was the first time I saw it, for her last name: Thomas. And then I see the suitcase by the door.

A surge of panic wells up inside me.

"Today was my last day, Emily," she says quietly. "I was just waiting for you to wake."

"Oh." I put down the dish towel, finish drying my hands on my sweatpants. Look around me, lost.

Clare tilts her head. "We talked about it when you got up for a while this morning—remember?"

No. I don't remember. But I don't need to turn to see the calendar hanging on the fridge behind me, to follow the line of *X*s through each day in September to today—the twentieth—to know she's right.

"Are you sure you want to go now?" I say. "I mean, it's almost dark." I gesture to the window, already in shadow.

I'm not ready for this.

She comes to stand in front of me and lays her hands on my arms. Her left brow is angled a few degrees higher than her right. But instead of making her appear asymmetrical, which all faces are, it intensifies her gaze.

"You're doing fine, Emily. Your procedure was a success. You have your fresh start. It's time to live."

A fresh start. A weird concept when you don't know what you're starting over from.

She gives me a squeeze and shoulders her purse. "I could, however, use a lift to shore and into town."

"Right. Of course." I pull my jacket from the peg near the kitchen door. I knew this day was coming. Then why do I feel like I'm being abandoned?

I shove my feet into my boots and grab my keys, but the questions that came at me like a horde of insects those first few days—before Clare firmly counseled me to trust my decision—have come swarming back, louder than ever. I push them away, but when she meets me at the door there's something in her hand. An envelope.

The handwriting on the outside is mine.

She holds it out. "You wrote this before your treatment."

I take it slowly. It's sealed, my initials scribbled across the flap where it's stuck shut.

"Most patients choose to write a letter to reassure

16

their postprocedure selves. You can read it when you get back."

I nod, but a part of me wishes she hadn't shown it to me at all. I slide it onto the counter. "Okay."

Outside, we climb into the johnboat and I start the outboard motor. It takes all of five minutes for me to guide us into the dock two hundred yards away. I grab the flashlight from the boat, knock it with the heel of my hand when it sputters. The owner's beat-up Ford Bronco is waiting near the slip.

I ask what time her flight is as we turn onto Lily Bay Road, make small talk about the magnificent foliage around the lake. Finally ask if she ever saw a moose. No, she says, she never did.

Twenty minutes later we pull into the Food Mart at the top of the hill—the same place I caught my breath as the lake first appeared below us the day we arrived. There's a black town car waiting in the parking lot, and she directs me toward it.

I put the truck in park, wondering what one says in a situation like this. I'm glad it's nearly dark out.

"I've got it," she says when I start to get out. After retrieving her suitcase, she leans in through the passenger door.

"You're going to be fine, Emily. It's a brave decision to go through something like this."

It doesn't feel brave, to want to forget.

"Read your letter. Trust yourself. But just in

17

case—" She pulls the tao cross over her head and presses it into my hand. "If you ever find yourself in trouble."

Impulsively, I lean across the seat to hug her.

And then she's gone.

Maybe I don't want to waste the trip to town, or maybe I just don't feel like getting the crap scared out of me by the stuffed taxidermy bear in the bedroom that has managed to freak me out every time I try to sleep in there like a normal person. As soon as that black car disappears up the road, I hang the cross from the rearview mirror and decide to pick up some supplies.

But the truth is I'm not ready to read that letter. I don't know what I've left behind—my mind has run the gamut from rape to abusive boyfriends and post-traumatic stress—and part of me is both dying and terrified to hear from that person *before*. Afraid of any indication of the thing that landed me on an island the size of a Dorito in the backwoods of Maine with roots five shades lighter than the rest of my hair.

Inside the Food Mart I distractedly fill a basket with deli cuts, bananas, microwave popcorn, tampons. The grocery is connected to the Trading Post—a camping, fishing, hunting store—making it the type of place you can buy vegetarian nuggets and a rifle, all in one trip. Or, in my case, wool socks and flashlight batteries. I stop in the

18

wine aisle last. It seems fitting to toast my past as I hear from my former self. Who knows, depending on what's in the letter, I may even need to get drunk.

I've just picked a cabernet with a cool label off the sale shelf—because how else do you choose when you don't know one from the other?—when I sense someone staring at me farther down the aisle.

I look up to find a guy in a green Food Mart apron frozen on a knee where he's been stocking a lower shelf. For a minute I wonder if he thinks I'm shoplifting or, more likely, not old enough to buy booze.

I deliberately slide the bottle into my basket. As I start to leave, I hear quick steps behind me.

"Hey. Hey—"

I turn reluctantly. Not only because I already wish I had just gone home but because, now that he's closer, I can see the chin-length hair tucked behind his ear, the blue eyes beneath thoughtful brows. And I'm standing here with bad roots and tampons in my basket.

He grabs something from the shelf. "We just got this in," he says, eyes locked on mine. The couple days' stubble on his cheeks is the color of honey, a shade lighter than his hair.

I glance at the bottle of nonalcoholic cider. "Thanks," I murmur. "I'm good."

"It's organic," he says, not even looking at it.

He's got an accent so slight I can't place it, but it isn't local.

By now I just want to get out of here. The letter sitting on the counter back at the cabin has launched a march of fire ants in my gut. If what's written in that envelope is meant to be reassuring, I need that reassurance now, because I was doing a lot better with my questions before Clare and her level counsel left and I ever knew the letter existed.

I put the wine back and grab a bottle of tequila on my way to the register.

There's no one there. I swing the basket up onto the conveyor belt and look around. A moment later the same guy comes over and starts to ring me up.

"Hi again." He smiles. I look away.

Halfway through checkout, I realize I can't find my debit card. I pull out my keys and dig through my jacket pockets. And then I see it lying on the counter back at the cabin, right next to the list of all the things I just bought.

"I forgot my card," I stammer.

He shrugs. "No problem. I can set these aside or have them delivered if you want. You can pay for them then."

"No," I say quickly, stepping away. "That's okay." By now two more people are waiting in line behind me. "Sorry." I turn on my heel and hurry to the door, leaving the things on the conveyor belt.

Outside, bugs swarm the lone parking lot light. I get to my truck, grab the door handle . . . and then drop my forehead against the window with a curse. My keys are back inside on the little ledge old ladies use to write checks.

I peer through the dark window like the truck is going to come unlocked by sheer force of will. It doesn't. And there's the flashlight with the nearly dead batteries lying between the seats.

"Hey!" The voice comes from the direction of the mart's automatic door. I push away from the truck.

It's the guy, holding up my keys. "You forgot something."

"Yeah. Like my mind."

He hands me my keys and two plastic grocery bags. I look at them, bewildered.

"On me," he says.

"Oh. No, I can't—"

"Already done. Besides, that tequila looked pretty important," he says with a slight smile.

"I'll pay you back."

"It's no problem." He hesitates, and then wishes me a good night.

I pass a whole five cars on my way up Lily Bay and none on the road to the lake. Six houses tucked in the trees along this mile-and-a-half stretch of gravel called Black Point Road share the dock where the boat is tied beneath a motion-sensor light. Modest homes of normal people living lives full of details they might like to forget, but have somehow learned to live with.

The water is black beneath the boat and I'm glad for the cabin's wan kitchen lights, relieved even for its parade of moose above the window, the bear waiting in the bedroom.

Inside, I dump the bags on the counter and sit down on the sofa with the letter, not bothering to take off my boots. After a long moment of staring at my name, I slide my finger under the edge of the envelope and tear it open.

> Emily, it's me. You.
>
> Don't ask about the last two years. If everything went as planned, you've forgotten them along with several other details of your life. Don't try to remember— they tell me it's impossible—and don't go digging.
>
> Start over. Get a job. Fall in love. Live a simple, quiet life. But leave the past where it is. And keep your face off the Web. Your life depends on it. Others' lives depend on it.
>
> By the way, Emily isn't your birth name. You died in an accident. You paid extra for that.

I look up from the letter and take in the tiny, eco-friendly cabin with new eyes. No computer.

No phone. No cable television. I'm twenty minutes from the nearest town, population sixteen hundred, where people are outnumbered by invisible moose.

I didn't come to start over.

I came to hide.

2

I wake the next afternoon beside an empty shot glass. I stumble to the kitchen to find the groceries put away, flashlight waiting by the door, batteries swapped out. There's a notepad on the table with a wobbly spiral scribble where I attempted to get a pen to work. Apparently it never did.

The letter I reread at least fifty times is nowhere to be found. I finally find a piece of it in the ashes of the living room's wood-burning stove. The bear in the bedroom is turned toward the corner.

At least I had the sense to cork and put away the tequila. I find it shoved to the back of a cabinet, only an inch of it gone. Whatever I did in my prior life, heavy drinking was obviously not a part of it.

Even burned to ash, I can recite every word of the letter, picture each determined arch of the script. Whether I ran from the mob (my latest theory, given the almost alarming amount of cash I brought with me to Maine) or stole drug money from that abusive boyfriend, I was resolute by the time I wrote it. And though I remember only unhelpful details—that I grew up in a yellow house and had a high school friend who lost his finger in a tubing accident—I know for sure I was no idiot.

Your life depends on it. Others' lives depend on it.

So this is what it is to be dead: afternoon breakfast of cold cuts and a banana. Maintenance on the composting commode. Boat to shore to take in the trash. Head an hour out of town to purchase three boxes of hair color and cheap shades. Drive back to town to the local fly shop for supplies. Return to cabin, dump everything on kitchen table. Dye roots so the scrubby patch looks far less conspicuous. Eat dinner in front of the first season of *Roswell* because it's the only DVD set in the cabin's library I haven't seen yet.

Work at the table until dawn.

All this time, the letter is running in an endless loop through my head.

Two days later, I am out of cold cuts and sick of bananas. I need to make a run to the Fly Shop and pick up gas for the boat.

I grab my bank card and driver's license and then pause. Who is that girl in the picture? Is she a victim? A criminal? I try to see her in each light. I can't. But what else is there, when you're living a false identity?

I flip the license over. It was issued in Maine, though I know for a fact the Center I woke up in is in Indiana. My identity might be fake, but the license itself is not, despite the suspiciously good photo. I wonder for the fiftieth time if I'm in a witness protection program. And for the forty-ninth time, I hope to God if I am that I'm living far enough away from whatever it was I witnessed.

Trust your decision, Clare said more than once to me. But it was so much easier to find peace in that mantra when she was here.

In town, I drive slowly by the small public library. I tell myself I should see if they have a DVD collection. But I'm really thinking about the computers inside. It'd be an easy enough search to look for a fatal car accident earlier this month.

An easy trace, too.

Don't go digging.

I stop instead at Citgo to fill the Bronco and the boat's plastic gas tank before heading to the Fly Shop.

My case of flies—streamers, mayflies, beetles, and caddies—is light but full. The owner's wife, Madge, who can no longer tie them since her stroke, inspects a full fifteen of them before squinting up at me.

"How long did you say you been tying flies?" she says.

"As long as I can remember."

"Well, you didn't lie when you said you were good. I'll give you that."

No. But I'm pretty sure I lied more than once about how I learned. I don't remember whose hands I watched weave thread and feathers into

26

colorful nymphs and midges, but I never forgot the patterns.

I convince her to lower her commission if only by five percent—it's not like either one of us is going to get rich at any rate—and ten minutes later, I'm out the door with some cash in my pocket. Not that I'm strapped.

The Food Mart is busy in the middle of the day, no fewer than five people waiting in line at the deli counter. I scan the register and then the produce section on my way in, an empty five-gallon water jug in each arm. I drop the jugs in the bin and walk along the ends of several aisles.

"Can I help you find something?"

I whirl around and come face-to-face with a friendly-looking man in his fifties. Tanned face, white bushy brows, sunspots on his forearms.

"Yeah. There's a guy who works here—he helped me with some wine the other night."

"Wine's this way," he says, gesturing for me to follow. "Do you know what you're looking for?"

"Actually, no. He made a recommendation and I forgot what it was. I was wondering if he's working today."

"Was it Dave?"

"I, uh, didn't get his name. About my age . . . brown hair?" Blue eyes.

"Oh, Luka. I'll see if he's gone to lunch yet," he says.

Luka. Definitely not from around here. I loiter

near a display of saltines, canned tomatoes, and chili beans. A moment later a familiar form strides toward me down the aisle. I shove my hands in my pockets and hope my smile is friendly enough to have warranted his kindness the night I was an ass.

"Bronco!" He grins. The stubble on his cheeks is gone. He's got a nice mouth and really great jawline, and with that hair I wonder why he's not teaching ski school in Utah or modeling under-wear or something.

"Yeah." I give a little laugh. "Keyless Bronco girl."

"I hear you're back for that cider."

"No, I just came to get some water and"—I dig three twenties out of my pocket—"pay you back. Thanks, by the way."

I hold the money toward him, but his eyes are searching mine. I slide my fingers up to the hat covering my stubby patch of hair. His gaze follows. I drop my hand. "Here."

"That's too much."

"Actually, it's thirty-eight cents short, but I don't have change."

He frowns. "I never gave you a receipt."

"I remember what everything cost. Take it."

He slowly folds the bills and slides them into his pocket. "You need help with that water?"

Ten minutes later he's following me out of the Food Mart, a jug in each arm. After loading them in the back of the truck, he says, "So, Bronco. I have an idea."

"Oh yeah?"

"You're obviously not from around here—"

"Speak for yourself."

"Okay, yeah." He laughs a little. "You been to the Mad Moose yet?"

"I've been pretty much nowhere."

"I thought I'd go into town and grab a sandwich. Join me."

I had been planning to head back, but it's not like I have a full afternoon planned. And aside from the Fly Shop, Food Mart, and gas station, I've never been anywhere in town.

I shrug. "Sure."

His face lights up, and I decide there must be some woefully slim pickings around here to warrant a smile like that.

He unties his green apron on the way to his Cherokee, then gets the door for me. It's a whole three-quarters of a mile to the restaurant on the public dock where resident feral ducks dart between outdoor tables fighting over the intermittent dropped French fry. It's warm enough that the place is half full. He pulls my chair out for me, and as I sit down I realize this is the most people I've been around since my arrival over a month ago.

"Were you really coming here before I showed up?" I glance at him over my menu.

"Nope."

We order, and he sits back and regards me. He's the kind of ruggedly pretty that makes me wonder if I went for his type before—and if that's what landed me here. I remember exactly one date from my past, if it can even be called that, when some kid's mom dropped us off at the mall with thirty dollars to see a movie in sixth grade. I don't remember the name of the movie— or the kid.

"How do you like Maine?" he says.

"It's quiet. You live in town?"

"I'm renting a studio over Charlie's down the street. It's not bad. I basically hear whoever's playing at the Dropfly on the weekend for free. So, Bronco, do you have a name?"

"Emily. Porter," I add.

"Emily," he says, trying it out. And then he leans forward, hand extended. It's warm, his grip firm. "Luka Novak."

"So what brought you to Greenville?" I ask, fiddling with a straw wrapper.

"The fishing."

"Really?"

"No." He laughs, though it sounds more ironic than anything. His eyes have turned gray as the drifting clouds. "A fresh start, I guess."

My skin actually prickles.

It's then that I begin to notice a few people at the next table over staring in our direction. Mine, specifically. I reach toward my ear, checking that the scrubby patch of hair is covered by my ball cap. It is. I tug the hat a little lower.

"Hey," Luka says quietly. "Everything okay?"

"I feel like people are staring."

"It's because you're pretty," he says.

I stammer something stupid about thinking it has more to do with not looking like I'm from around here.

When our food arrives I busy myself spreading mayo on my burger, glad for something to do.

Luka offers me some of his lobster roll, but I'm suspicious of anything that looks like a scorpion, no matter what it tastes like. He eats with relish, shaking his head with appreciation after each bite. "You don't know what you're missing, Bronco."

I'm just happy to be eating something that isn't made of cold cuts or my cooking. And to be socializing like a normal person, the sun shining on the parts of my face not obscured by my Red Sox cap.

I glance up when I realize he's stopped eating. "What?"

"What are you doing Saturday night?" he says.

"Working, probably."

"On a Saturday?"

"Pretty much every night."

"Doing what?"

"I, um, tie fishing flies."

31

"At night?"

I drag a French fry through some ketchup, flick another onto the ground, and immediately regret it because it incites a stampede of feral ducks— not to mention several more gazes our way. "Yeah. I guess I'm kind of a night owl."

"Come catch a band with me for an hour or two."

"Wow. Groceries, lunch, live music . . ."

"I just got in last month and haven't had a chance to make many friends yet. I'm guessing you haven't, either." He smiles when he says it, though there's a tension in his posture that doesn't match his offhanded shrug. I don't get it. A guy this good-looking and outgoing just can't be that desperate.

The next table over is talking about a bear one of them shot on a hunt the day before, and orders a round of celebratory shots. I was envious of the couples and groups seated around us when we first sat down. Now, as laughter erupts from the table and a few more stares bypass them to turn my way, I feel jittery and more isolated than before. I told myself to live a quiet life, to fall in love, even. Obviously, the former me didn't think this through; I might make friends, might even be attracted to a guy like Luka. But I'll never be able to tell the truth. And what kind of friendship—let alone relationship—is that?

"It's the fall spawn and the weather's good. There won't be much demand once it gets cold."

I'm not exactly desperate for money, but he doesn't need to know that.

"I'll tell you what. I'm going to be at the Dropfly at eight—"

"I thought you could hear them from your place for free."

"I can. But I don't have Guinness on tap."

"Ah . . ."

"So if you can, come by. If not, we'll do it another time."

"Okay."

He asks for the check and I try to pay—he bailed me out the other night, after all. But he waves me off and lays one of the twenties I gave him on the table.

As we return to the Cherokee, I notice a guy in a pair of khakis and a black jacket standing near the small crowd outside the ice cream place, staring in our direction. What *is* it with people here? I glance at Luka, but he's opening my door. When I climb in and look over again, the man is gone.

By the time Luka drops me off at my truck, I'm relieved to head back up the hill. But I keep one eye on the rearview mirror all the way.

3

Sunlight is slanting through the windows of the living room by the time I wake on the sofa. I shield my eyes and squint at the clock in the kitchen. After 4:00 P.M.

That can't be right.

I shove up, clammy beneath the down comforter from the bedroom. But when I twitch it aside and drop my feet to the rug, I pause. My legs are bare. So are my arms. I glance from the clock to my legs with rising confusion.

My name is Emily Porter . . . I am in a cabin on a lake in the north woods of Maine. I stayed up late making—I glance at the table—nymphs and streamers, by the look of it. It's September 25. It was warm yesterday and the day before, when I went into town. Warm days translate into very cool nights this time of year. Hence the comforter, which gets too warm with my sweats. I exhale. No wonder I threw off my clothes.

I drag the comforter off the sofa to carry it back to the bedroom, but my foot tangles and my knee hits the coffee table. I stumble away and gather up the comforter before I trip on it again. That's when I notice something blue sprawled beneath the edge of the table.

34

A faded towel from the bathroom. I lean down and pick it up. It's damp.

I drop the comforter back onto the sofa and take the towel to the bathroom. After hanging it on the rack, I grab my toothbrush and root around for the toothpaste. At the sight of myself in the mirror, I stop. Tilting my head, I slide my fingers into the thick side of my hair. It, too, is damp. And now I'm chilled.

I glance around me, walk into the bedroom, for once ignoring the bear. The floor and bed are empty. I pad out to the kitchen. The table is filled with multicolored bits of feather, glues, thread scraps, and an impressive array of flies. The spool on the bobbin is empty. A half-finished lure is still in the vise.

I don't remember running out of thread. Granted, I've also woken up more than once to find the mustard on the counter after a forgotten predawn sandwich—further proof that my meds are off. But if I showered sometime this morning, where the heck are my clothes?

In the tiny laundry room just off the kitchen I rifle through the basket, peer in the washer and dryer. In the living room again, I shake out the comforter, check beneath the sofa. Hands on hips, I take in the DVD case sitting open on top of the TV, a stack of board games on a listing double shelf just to the right of it, the wooden coasters on the coffee table next to the year-old copy of *Discover Maine* magazine . . .

Clare's tao cross is lying on top of it.

I know I left that hanging in the truck.

I rush to the bedroom, pull on jeans and a T-shirt. Not bothering with shoes, I hurry out the front door. Outside, the sun has dappled the water gold against the pebbly shore. The johnboat is beached, the rope tied to a nearby fir exactly the way I left it. But there—at the end of the floating swim dock: a rumpled pile of clothes.

What was I doing? Swimming in my underwear in broad daylight? It's somewhere in the sixties. Not exactly swimming weather. And I have never once had the urge to jump off that wooden platform.

I walk to the beach and drop a foot ankle-deep in the water. It isn't freezing, but it's cold enough to wake a person up.

Or merit a comforter after getting out.

I spend the next hour trying to retrace my steps. I can't imagine that I drove into town in dripping-wet underwear. What did I do—swim to shore just to retrieve Clare's cross? Why?

But it's impossible to retrace what you can't remember. I begin to wonder if my activity the other evening had nothing to do with tequila.

Back inside, I sit down with the tao cross, turn it between my fingers before looping the string over my head. And then a thought makes my hands go cold. It's not possible that I had company—is it? No. I never told Luka where I was staying, and no one followed me home. Even Madge at the Fly Shop has only my box number at the post office. Still, I clasp the cross so hard that the string digs into my neck—and then goes slack as the pendant slides right off its bail.

I sigh, pull the string over my head, and move to the kitchen table where I grab my bottle of head cement and brush some on the end of the thick wire bail. I'm just about to push it back into the hole at the top of the cross when I pause . . . and reach up to turn my work lamp on.

Tilting the cross this way and that, I see it wasn't a trick of the light; there's something curled within the tiny opening. I pick up my needle and press the tip against the lining, slide it upward until I can grab the edge of it with my tweezers. I pull slowly, turning the cross as I do. The paper comes out in an elongated spiral half the length of the cross.

I spread the tiny scroll open on the table with the tweezers and a fingernail. A series of minuscule numbers is written on the inside.

385911571269

Twelve digits. No sequence I recognize.

This was Clare's cross. Did she know this was here when she gave it to me? I don't recall seeing a number like this associated with anything religious. Was this series, this code—if it's even that—intended for her or someone else before her?

Or for me?

I squint at the numbers. Too many for a phone number. A bank account, then. A tracking number. A ticket number. A bar code. A serial number. Latitude and longitude. I rifle through every series of numbers I can remember—even in reverse order—but I have never seen this sequence before. If I had a computer, I could search for it, but out on the Dorito I don't even have a landline.

I try it as a number with commas. I try adding them together. I try finding the difference between the first two, then the second two, and so on. I add up the occurrence of the digits.

By now the sun has dropped low enough across the water that the cabin is getting dark. I retrieve the notepad from the counter, tear off my latest grocery list, find the roll of tape in the drawer. Spreading the tiny scroll on the top page, I carefully affix it to the pad.

I glance at the clock: 7:43. The library is long closed by now on a Saturday. The Center in Indiana, my only access to Clare, is closed now as well.

A thought itches the back of my mind.

I bolt up and throw a jacket over my smiley-face Nirvana T-shirt, pull on my sneakers. Hurry to the bathroom to brush my teeth and smooth my hair. Three minutes later I'm in the boat with the flashlight, headed toward shore.

I find the Bronco just as I left it—minus Clare's cross—and drive toward Lily Bay Road just slow enough not to die on the off chance I actually encounter a moose.

4

It's a quarter after eight by the time I pass the Fly Shop and turn onto the town's main drag. Pritham Avenue is lined with sandwich, sweet, and ice cream shops interspersed with tourist traps and a handful of restaurants, all centered on the public dock on the south side of the lake. I drive two blocks to the Dropfly, across from the small high school.

Before I even cut the engine I can hear muffled music and people talking outside—a town turned out for the last gasp of Indian summer at the end of tourist season.

The entrance, on the opposite side of the building from where I parked, is crowded with smokers. I duck my way through a carcinogenic cloud to the steps, show my ID to the bouncer on the landing, pay the cover, and shoulder my way inside.

The bodies inside the small pub are packed against the hewn-log bar. Those fortunate enough to have snagged a stool are penned in place by people standing in groups behind them. A band is wedged into the corner of the adjacent dining room, the singer barely two feet from the nearest table. The entire place smells like hot wings, beer, and body odor.

I search the tables and then worm my way toward the middle of the bar, craning to see around a really tall woman in boots and a denim skirt—probably the most dressed up I've seen anybody around here. A few people glance over their shoulders at me, and I check to make sure the stubby patch behind my ear is covered, wondering for the second time this week if there's a stamp on my forehead marked NOT FROM HERE. If I had something in my hand I'd at least feel less awkward.

"You want to order something?" a guy in front of me with a better view of the bar offers.

"Guinness," I say, loud enough for him to hear me. He leans between two stools and calls down to the bartender.

All this time I haven't seen one head of dark honey hair resembling Luka's. Did he take off when I wasn't here right at eight?

A minute later the guy is handing me a beer. I try to give him six bucks, but he waves it off.

"Thanks," I say, glancing around as I take a long pull off the top, wrecking the clover in the foam.

I scan the group near the door. Not a single familiar face. Not that many faces around here are familiar to me. But even though it's packed and some chick to my right is wearing a perfume that knocks the smell of fried food right out of my nostrils and a part of me feels lame for being

41

here by myself, new energy is jittering up from my stomach, making me wonder why I haven't wandered into town—even alone—at night before.

Because you've spent the last month moping around like a depressed, sleepwalking convalescent. And then you learned your life was in danger and faceless others were depending on you.

And maybe I shouldn't be here. As good as it feels to have waded into the human current for a brief swim, maybe sticking out—alone—in a crowd doesn't qualify as the quiet life.

But I also came here for something.

The girl with the perfume is telling some story to a guy, and when she laughs she falls away and almost crashes into me. She grabs my arm to steady herself. Beer sloshes over my hand. "Sorry!" she says, but then she smiles and I think she's more sober than I gave her credit for.

"I'm Keri," she says, leaning toward me so I can hear her, and offers me her hand. I shake it as the guy she was talking to takes me in over the rim of his beer.

"This is Nate, that's Joel," she says, and I spend the next ten minutes making small talk. Which basically amounts to lying when they ask where I'm from and what brought me to town. I say something about taking a semester off from U Mass to write a novel.

"I knew you seemed wicked cool!" she shouts.

She pokes Joel in the chest. "Did you hear that? She's a famous writer!"

I was wrong. She's drunk.

Meanwhile, I'm pretty sure I've been bona fide stood up. I tell myself I shouldn't be surprised; if Luka comes on that strong to everyone with his intense gaze and stormy eyes, he's probably back at his place with some girl he met before I got here. Nor do I care, even if my ego is bruised. But it does throw a wrench in things . . . until my gaze drops to the wristlet dangling from Keri's hand.

"We're going to the Limit after this drink," she announces over the music, looping her arm through mine. "You should come with us."

"I would," I half-yell into her hair, "but my friend was going to meet me here, and I don't have my phone."

Keri hands her beer to Nate, unzips the wristlet, and presents her phone with a flourish. I flash her a grin and signal that I'll be back.

I glance toward the door, but I'm no longer in the mood to run into Luka if he shows. Instead, I weave my way toward the back, where I assume I'll find a bathroom. I find the line first—leading midway down a short hallway toward the kitchen. I slide past the line and the men's room just beyond it, stop outside the kitchen door, and peer through the window. A man in his forties is delivering plates to the pass-through in the bar as a cook mans the grill. There, to the right, is the side door.

I pocket the phone and then lunge into the kitchen, hand over my mouth.

"Hey!" the older man says, pointing. "Get outta here!"

"Sorry," I say. "I feel really sick." My fourth lie in the space of thirty minutes. I am so going to hell at this rate. The man yells at me again, and I shove through the door as though I might spew any instant. Never mind that I've still got a beer in my hand, sloshing over my fingers.

Even with the waft of stale cigarette smoke clinging to the bricks outside the kitchen, the air feels crisp and clean. I kneel behind some trash bins, wait to see if the man comes after me. He doesn't. Apparently I'm not the first person to drunkenly wander through the kitchen.

With my back to the building, I set down the beer and take out the phone. Dim the brightness. Pull up a private browser. Enter the numbers. *3 . . . 8591 . . . 157 . . . 1269.* I can picture each one as I tap it, written in tiny script taped to the pad in the cabin.

Not a single result comes up.

I stare at the screen, wondering how that's even possible. I check the numbers, but they're correct. I try searching tracking numbers—UPS, FedEx, the post office—and then bar codes. Bank routing numbers. Latitude, longitude.

Nothing.

I wipe the history and close the browser, mind churning. But I've been gone too long already.

I grab my beer and head toward the back of the building, from where I can circle around to the entrance on the other side unseen from the sidewalk—or the apartments across the street. I have no intention of staying here or migrating to the Limit. As soon as I give Keri back her phone, I'm out of here.

Just as I round the corner I stop short. Two men stand in hunched conversation less than fifteen feet in front of me, barely illuminated by the lone light on the back of the building. Great. I'm inadvertently within range of a drug deal.

The one facing away from me is talking too low for me to hear. But his gestures are quick and emphatic, the dark jacket stretching with each movement across broad shoulders.

The other is Luka.

So he's not at his place with some chick but scoring weed instead—from a guy he owes money to, by the look of it. I'm tempted to walk right past them, let him know I see what's going on. But the last thing I need is trouble.

Just then Luka's eyes meet mine. What am I supposed to do now? I have no desire to talk to him. But if I stalk off, I'll look like I actually give a crap.

Rather than register surprise, however, his gaze

returns to the guy as though he never saw me. A few seconds later he says something and gestures over his shoulder, then loops an arm around the guy like they're old drinking buddies and walks the other way.

I watch them disappear around the corner.

Meanwhile, I'm standing with a beer in one hand and Keri's phone in the other, trying to figure out how I'm going to get it back to her so I can leave.

I stride around the building to the entrance, past the clot of smokers sociably bumming cigarettes off one another. Just as I reach the short steps to the door, I spot Luka near the sidewalk. He's jerking his thumb toward the street, hand still on the other guy's back. It's like he's trying to *steer* him out of here, and can't do it fast enough.

Fine with me.

I'm just nudging my way up the steps to show my stamp to the bouncer when I see, from the corner of my eye, a stationary figure watching me. What is it with people staring in this town? Fed up, I turn and glare—and then falter.

It's Luka's companion, standing at the curb. And when I see his face, I know it's the same man I saw in front of the ice cream shop yesterday. He's a few years older and a little taller than Luka himself, who is starting to strong-arm him toward the street. A jealous lover, perhaps? My gaydar is usually better than that. But I can't think of any other reason for the look he's giving me now or Luka's hauling him away.

After a moment the guy relents, but not without a backward glance at me.

I am so ready to get out of here.

It takes me five minutes to work my way to Keri, where she is draped around Nate's shoulders.

"There she is!" Keri beams, opening an arm toward me.

"Big line for the bathroom," I say, handing her the phone. And then I give her lie number five: My friend is sick and I need to go check on her. Joel looks a little crestfallen, and Keri insists we swap numbers. I give her the digits to the Fly Shop. And then she's hugging me good-bye and I'm trying to find a place to put the stupid beer that's been glued to my hand this whole time.

By the time I finally push my way out of there, I cannot get to my truck fast enough.

As I'm speeding up Lily Bay Road, my mind returns to the numbers in Clare's cross, and whether I should call the Center, my only contact for her, on Monday.

What had she said when she gave it to me? *In case you find yourself in trouble.* What could possibly help me if I'm in trouble? I don't even know what I'm running from. What propels a person to leave her life, fake her death, and start over in tiny-town Maine? And if it's that bad, why didn't I relocate to Greenland or, better yet, Fiji?

The packet with my driver's license and letter to myself contained nearly eighteen thousand dollars in cash. A person can do a lot of disappearing with money like that.

That number's got to be a bank account.

Then why didn't I put something about it in my letter? How am I supposed to find it if I don't even know where to look?

Or maybe that's not it at all and Clare never knew it was there, and all she meant about trouble was something concerning prayer and God.

I'm so busy cycling through these thoughts that I nearly miss my turn. Luckily the closest car is a quarter mile back when I brake so fast my flashlight flies onto the floor.

I drive a mile past three mailboxes belonging to houses deep enough in the trees that I can barely make out their lights. Within a few weeks only one of them may be occupied as the other residents leave for warmer climates. I don't look forward to winter, when it gets so cold that Madge says logging rigs drive right across the frozen lak . When I'll be forced to drive to the Dorito or, much more likely, hole up until a thaw.

Maybe that's what I had in mind all along.

The moon's full, sending a streak of serrated light across the lake when I park near the end of the point. I unhook the seat belt and fish for the flashlight on the passenger side floor, the edge of the console digging into my ribs.

I hear the vehicle before I see it, the crunch of tires on gravel road driving far too fast. When I straighten, my rearview mirror nearly blinds me as headlights barrel down the drive.

There is only one person I know aggressive or desperate enough to have followed me here—presumably to explain himself under the misguided assumption that I care.

A familiar vehicle skids to a stop, barely missing my back fender. And now I am pissed.

I shove out of my truck before he can even cut the engine, and storm to the driver's side door as it opens.

"You have ten seconds to leave before I call the cops!" I yell. I don't own a cell phone, but he doesn't need to know that.

That's when I realize—too late—that the SUV I mistook in the darkness for a Cherokee is actually a Pathfinder. And when I shine my flashlight right in his face, it isn't Luka who emerges from the vehicle. It's the man I saw with him.

Two thoughts slice through my mind at once: That there was indeed a drug deal and he now knows I saw it. Or that he really is Luka's jealous boyfriend and has followed me home to accuse me.

Either way, this isn't going to be good.

"You need to leave," I say, backing several steps.

He raises his hands as though confronting a wild animal. He's taller than I thought, with a

49

military build and short hair to match. "I'm not going to hurt you."

Yeah, because that's exactly what people say when they aren't thinking about it.

"You're trespassing. Get back in your car and go." My hands are shaking, the beam of my flashlight jagging around his head.

"You're in danger. You need to come with me. Now."

The instant he moves toward me, I drop the flashlight and bolt for the Bronco. He's too fast. Before I can yank the door open he grabs me by the arm, spinning me back. My fist connects with his nose.

He staggers and I run, but I haven't stopped him. I hear the crunch of his steps behind me, gaining speed. I veer for the trees, toward the lights of the closest house, shouting for help.

When he tackles me, I go down hard. He rolls, pulling me around to stare at the sky, but even as I claw at him my lungs have turned to iron. My vision prickles over.

"Breathe," he says. I can't. I kick my heels into his shins, slam my head back. I connect, but not nearly hard enough. He's got at least sixty pounds and half a foot on me, and at this point, I genuinely believe I'm on the verge of getting kidnapped or worse.

"Listen to me," he hisses when I'm finally sucking air.

I can't fight him, so I go limp. If he's going to get up and try to get me to the car, he's going to have 125 pounds of deadweight on his hands until I can find a tree to grab, some leverage—anything—to get away.

"Luka isn't who you think he is!"

"I don't even know him!"

"No. But you did."

I go completely still, heart banging against my ribs.

"I know what you've done," he says, urgently, near my ear. He's got an accent heavier than Luka', European, but different. "Your memory's gone and now you don't even know who to trust! Don't you wonder why he's here? Or why he was in such a hurry to leave before I saw you at the bar?"

He's not making sense. Nothing he's saying makes sense.

"He knew you were in the area. Why do you think he's working at the grocery? Because he knew you'd show up there eventually!" He shakes me a little with each statement. "Why do you think he's trying so hard to draw you out, get you alone?"

"I don't know!" I shout. But his last words strike something inside me. The offer to deliver my groceries. Paying for them, knowing any decent person would come back to reimburse him. The spontaneous lunch and weekend invite, each interaction assuring another. I took them for come-ons—aggressive, sure, a little desperate maybe . . . but only marginally creepy.

Faintly, from up the road: tires on gravel. The man tenses against me.

"We have to go. Now." His hold loosens. I instantly roll, but before I can get my feet under me he grabs me and shouts in my face.

"He's going to kill you, Audra!"

I blink at him in the darkness.

Audra?

"You really don't know who you are, do you?" he says with an incredulous exhale.

"No!" I lash out, as much from fear as anger. "I don't know anything you're talking about!"

A car is speeding down the gravel drive, skids around the last turn to the point. He grabs my wrists.

"Your real name isn't Emily Porter," he says, inches from my face. "It's Audra Ellison. You didn't die in a car crash. But if you stay here, you'll be dead by morning."

5

There's the shock of hearing my real name—if indeed that's it. The eerie way his words collide with the letter to myself.

But the thing that gets me up and running for his car as the Cherokee speeds down the point, gravel flying from its wheels, is this: Even if he's lying, he also knows the truth.

Which means he knows more than I do. Even if I manage to skip town now, I won't know who's really after me. And I definitely won't get answers if I end up dead.

There's no way this counts as digging. My past, after all, found me.

I collide with the passenger side door, yank it open, and barely get inside before he throws the Pathfinder into reverse. Without even bothering to turn around—there's no time and no space, nose-to-nose with the back fender of the Bronco— he slams the gas and backs full speed up the drive, right past Luka. As the Cherokee blasts past us I see his face flash in my window. Staring in a tight-lipped grimace, right at me.

"Turn!" I yell as we hit the bend. My savior/ captor/whoever he is jerks the wheel, sending us sliding, and for a moment I think I'm going to die here after all, thrown into a tree. And then we're blowing backward onto a mile of gravel, with me shouting directions as Luka's headlights fill the windshield.

We get to the edge of Lily Bay Road and I think for sure Luka's going to ram us right into oncoming traffic. In the end it doesn't matter because the guy with me doesn't even stop, hitting the pavement with a sharp back turn that throws me into the console. The dead stop is terrifying; Luka's headlights are two seconds from drilling us straight into the ditch, and for that split instant I wonder if my faked car-accident death is a self-fulfilling prophecy.

The guy throws the Pathfinder into gear. Tires squeal on pavement, and then we're speeding north up the road.

"You okay?" he says.

I'm shaking, but I nod and then realize he can't see me. "Yeah." It takes me three tries to lock my seat belt.

His gaze snaps between the rearview mirror and the road in front of us, which is only mostly straight. The needle inches toward 90 as we pass two cars, and I pray to God there are no moose out tonight.

"Where'd you learn to punch like that?"

I don't answer. I don't know.

"Who are you?" I demand.

"Rolan. Vasilescu," he says, eyes on the road.

"There's a turn coming up. There—" I say. It's

followed seconds later by a far sharper left. We go another mile in tense silence, pass two more cars, one of which honks loudly as we whiz by. Luka's headlights never leave the rearview mirror. He's alternating between speeding closer and dropping back, but only by a matter of feet.

Twenty minutes ago I was actually looking forward to a night of frozen pizza and the last two episodes of *Roswell*, season one. Debating whether or not to attempt to sleep in the bedroom like a normal person. I'd even considered leaving a coating of flour by the front door just so I'd know by morning whether I wandered out in the middle of the night. Now I'm in a car with a complete stranger who knows more about my past than I do, fleeing a murderer I ate lunch with two days ago. I glance at Rolan. His expression is grim.

"Once we get to Kokadjo, we run out of pavement," I say. I know because Clare and I once drove to the northern outpost, where the trees thin around the open expanse of river that runs through a hunting and fishing hub so small the population is listed as "not many" on the sign.

With one hand on the wheel, he reaches into his jacket, and for a second I wonder if he's going to pull out a gun. He produces a phone instead, unlocks it with his thumb, and flips it at me.

"Pull up the map. Look for the next good bend."

I do my best, but the map twitches and zooms

beneath the involuntary tremor of my fingers, refusing to refresh, the signal lost.

"Hurry."

I close my eyes, retrace the drive that day with Clare. "Another mile—maybe two," I say.

"One mile or two?" he snaps.

"Two. The road goes left, south of Kokadjo at a fork. A dirt road goes right along the south edge of the pond."

I open my eyes and he glances at me, but he doesn't question me, either.

Lily Bay Road has by now turned into generic Main Street, briefly straightening out before us. Rolan guns it. The speedometer hovers around 97. The headlights in the rearview mirror fade around the last bend as we come up on a car, ride its bumper, unable to see oncoming traffic.

Rolan flashes his lights, but the driver ahead gives a distinct bird high against his rearview mirror, refusing to pull to the side and let us pass.

The sign for First Roach Pond rushes at us, the fork ahead divided by a tiny grass island with an electrical pole smack in the middle, a gravel outlook over the valley to the right.

The car hugs the line. The instant I realize Rolan means to break right—sending us careening into the pole or skidding off the outlook into the valley—I catch sight of a row of mailboxes along the main road, the hint of a drive in the trees ten yards beyond. "There!" I shout, pointing ahead.

He follows the car and breaks hard, killing the lights as we pull into the trees.

Not two seconds later, the Cherokee flashes around the bend in pursuit of the taillights in front of it. I close my eyes, and listen for the angry screech of tires, the stillness like torture. 1 . . . 2 . . . 3 . . .

Rolan throws the car into reverse, backs onto the road, and then accelerates south.

"Find us a road," he says. "He'll be on us in thirty seconds."

We go two miles before I get the signal back. "Nothing east through the mountains. West we're in the lake. This is it."

We pass three cars in silence. Nothing in the rearview mirror.

"You know you can't go back," he says.

"There's a police station in Greenville—"

"No." He shakes his head.

"If he's trying to kill me, we have to go to the cops!"

He tears his eyes from the road long enough to look at me as though I've lost my mind. "Cops? The cops can't help you!"

"What do you mean? Of course they can!"

"Do you think you would've gone to the lengths you did if the police could help? You don't get it, Audra. He won't stop! He'll never stop until he kills you. If not today or this week, then next month, next year. One day when your guard is down, he'll find you. Like he has now, like he did before. And next time, he'll kill you." He pounds the steering wheel and shouts, *"Why'd you do it?"*

"Do what?" I shout back.

"Go in and—" He gestures to his head. "Erase everything!"

"I don't know," I say. Except that I had a reason. It's all I know and trust in this world. "I don't know," I say again, quietly. "So you better start talking."

He shakes his head a little, and a few seconds later he chuckles. And then he's laughing. I don't know what's more alarming: this man, this complete and utter stranger, telling me someone wants me dead . . . the fact that I have no idea what's going on except that we nearly just died on a two-lane road . . . or the fact that he apparently finds this hysterical.

"You've always been smart—smarter than you know." He shakes his head again, eyes on the road. But the lines are deeper across his forehead than before. "And you've always had moxie."

"I'm sorry, do I know you?" I hiss, less sharply than I mean to. Now that the only cars following us are those traveling well within the speed limit, drifting back farther and farther each time we pass one of them, I can feel the fingers of panic at last. With the initial shock wearing thin,

I am terrified in a way I have not been in the month since I arrived.

I am also far more alive. Speeding down the road past Beaver Cove, I swear I can smell the pine wafting from the shore of the lake. Can see by the moonlight more sharply than before.

And don't you know it—there's a moose standing in the trees off the corner of Scammon Ridge Road.

"I'm sorry," Rolan says a moment later. We're nearing town. "Navigate us out of here. And then I'll tell you everything."

6

Highway 2 is winding and unlit, flanked by trees and telephone lines, the occasional New England farmhouse. We've deliberately gone west, away from Bangor and Interstate 95, which would have taken us to Portland and south along the coast, opting for New Hampshire instead.

We stop in Skowhegan just long enough to fill the tank, grab water, coffee for Rolan. And then we're back in the car with nothing but road and an unknown destination in front of us.

"Where are we going?" I ask.

"That depends on you."

Great. I had one safe haven in this world, and it's sixty miles behind us.

I fiddle with the cap of the water bottle, stare out at the sky. It's starry, the moon sharp as mottled silver. That is to say, far too normal and therefore deceptive.

I take a swig of the water. "So tell me," I say. The last hour of driving the limit, even in the dark, feels painfully slow. Between that and the questions swarming through my mind—questions I'm not even sure I want answers to—I am ready to claw my skin off.

He offers me his coffee. I shake my head.

60

"It'll calm you."

He obviously isn't aware how caffeine works.

Rolan is silent for a minute. "This isn't a story I'm used to telling," he says at last.

"I only need you to tell it once."

"How are you at history?"

"I suck at history." My own, especially.

He lets out a slow breath. "You . . . are not a normal person."

"I think I have that figured out."

"No. You're *very* different. Your mother was, too."

Hearing the word *mother* sets off an inexplicable ache in me. Try as I might to summon a face, there is nothing. "Do you know her?"

"I knew of her, your birth mother."

Birth mother.

"She's gone, Audra," he says.

I stare out at the dark line of trees. I've studied Rolan intermittently for the last hour, searching for anything in the lines of his face or set of his jaw that might tell me what I'm doing leaving the state with a stranger in the middle of the night 4ewith nothing but the clothes on my back and the cash in my pocket. But suddenly I can't look at him.

He lets out a slow, audible breath. "You, your mother, your grandmother, her mother before her, for four hundred years . . . You're all descended from a Hungarian noble named

Elizabeth Bathory. The Blood Countess. The most prolific female serial killer of all time."

I slowly turn to look at him.

"And you've all been hunted by people like Luka."

Serial killer. Hunted. "I don't understand. Blood . . . Countess?"

"According to legend, she tortured and killed over six hundred servant girls in her lifetime. She bit, whipped, and starved young female servants before killing them. Poured water on naked girls in the winter until they froze. Burned them, stuck them with needles, ate their flesh . . ."

I lift my hand. "Okay, wait a minute . . ."

"After her husband died she continued to move between her estates. Bodies showed up wherever she went. Outside city walls, in gardens, even under beds."

"I said stop!"

"You want to know? I'm telling you!" he says. "The servant girls were peasants. Their families had no recourse. But when Elizabeth started an etiquette school and several young noble-women disappeared, the Hungarian king opened an investigation. After more than three hundred testimonies, Elizabeth's accomplices were burned at the stake. Elizabeth, though, was the widow of a national war hero, niece to the former king of Poland, cousin to the prince of Transylvania, and richer than the crown, which owed her money.

She never faced trial. Instead, she was walled up in a room in one of her castles, where she lived three years until she died, in 1614. The name Bathory has been a curse ever since. That is the short version."

I stare at him, realizing I have placed my life in the hands of a raving lunatic.

He glances at me. "I'm not telling you anything you can't look up on your own."

"Okay . . . but even if that's true, so what? It's the twenty-first century. This has nothing to do with me."

"It has *everything* to do with you."

"How?" I demand.

"The crown's debt was canceled and the king confiscated her remaining land when he banished her descendants from Hungary. But the peasant families of her victims received nothing—justice least of all. And so the Scions of the Dispossessed was founded nearly thirty years later, as her descendants began to return from Poland. And they have carried out retribution against her progeny ever since, hunting and killing without mercy."

"You're insinuating a whole family has been systematically murdered for four hundred years."

"I'm not just insinuating."

"I don't believe in"—I gesture wildly—"vampires or monsters."

"Vampires don't exist. But monsters most certainly do."

"Then why hasn't anyone stopped them? And how is there anyone left to kill?"

"They don't get caught, Audra," he says quietly. "They've become powerful through the centuries. No one's going to convict them. And there *are* descendants left to kill." He looks pointedly at me.

This time it's my turn to laugh. It's a brittle sound, tightly exhaled with an incredulous gaze at the ceiling. "I don't believe this."

"Whether you believe it or not doesn't change the fact that it's true."

"And this . . . is why I did what I did? Because I'm being *hunted* by a *guy from the Food Mart?*"

But even as I say it I recall the way Luka stared. The weird desperation to see me again. The accent. Eastern European.

"Why have I never heard about this League of Medieval Justice? Why haven't I read about it somewhere?"

"You probably have and didn't know it," Rolan says. "A man dies in a car accident on a deserted highway. A woman jumps off a bridge. They're ruled suicides, accidents, random acts of violence. They're not. Their hunters are precise, highly secretive, and they don't get caught—or if they do, they admit no affiliation. Each of them receives orders from a source known only as the Historian. Because of that, one hunter wouldn't know another if he passed him or her on the street."

"Oh, come on. That many accidents and suicides

in the same family have to get suspicious after a while."

He shakes his head. "Progeny are rarely raised by their birth parents—at least those aware of who and what they are. For that reason, the Scions might go decades without a kill. But they are nothing if not devoted to their cause. Few Progeny survive beyond the age of thirty."

"So you're saying Luka killed my mother."

"No. I'm saying someone like him did. Luka himself is singly and wholly dedicated to one murder. Yours."

I can't help it; the hair rises on my arms.

This is so not the mob involvement I was expecting.

"If I'm adopted, how did he find me?"

"Two years ago you went looking for your birth mother."

"You're not saying . . . that I was the reason she—"

"No," he says quietly. "She was already gone by then. And it isn't as hard as you'd think to find others like you. Anyone wanting to know where they come from can get a DNA kit, upload the results to a genealogy site. The Scions have fingers in all of them. Most Progeny who know what they are stay away from computers, are careful to leave no digital imprint. Those who don't end up dead. I'm assuming you don't even own a computer or a cell phone."

Keep your face off the Web.

"No," I say, as the indifferent landscape slides by. But now my mind is roiling. "So what you're saying about Luka . . ."

Rolan picks up his phone, unlocks it. With one hand on the wheel, he begins to scroll through his photos.

"This was taken last year." He turns it toward me.

It's a picture of me. I'm in a café somewhere, talking on a phone.

Sitting three tables away is Luka.

"Where is this?" I whisper.

"Trieste, Italy."

He takes the phone from me and thumbs to another photo, holds it out. Also me, crossing a street. I scan the pixelated image. Farther down, standing near a street vendor, is Luka.

"He's probably been hunting you for years."

My throat is dry.

"Then why am I not dead? And why would I erase my memory if I knew I was being followed?" I can't bring myself to say the word *hunted*. "If I needed to know that *to stay alive?*"

He clicks the phone off, shifts in the driver's seat. "When I said you were different, I meant that there are things that set you apart. Things you can do that normal people can't."

This is not news to me. I've always seen the world differently, in snapshots and shapes and symbols. Shuffling them, repeating them in my mind like an obsessive counting steps. Despite the procedure, this has not gone away. I've noted the curve of Rolan's ear no fewer than eleven times in the last forty-five minutes, overlaying it with the image of a conch shell I collected once at some beach, and then each of the eggs in the refrigerator of the cabin, one by one, until I found the one that matched most closely. I've always been weird.

"Hunters are different, too," he says. "Namely in their ability to retrieve key aspects of a Progeny's memory in the moment of his or her death—assuming they're close enough to touch their victims and haven't blown the brain to bits."

"That's impossible."

"No, it's not. Hunters are sensitive to the last burst of activity in a dying Progeny brain, which has tremendous capability to project thought. Hence your ability to plant suggestions in the minds of others or demand their attention without speaking."

"What?"

But even as he says it, I picture the faces turned toward me at the Mad Moose and the Dropfly. I had assumed something about me screamed "outsider" at the end of tourist season. Now I see the distracted interest in their eyes. But lots of people wonder about strangers, where they came from, what they do. Right?

"Something came down through the ages with you. Call it the sins of the father—or mother, in this case—a curse, or Bathory's last gift to her descendants. It's really just epigenetics. On steroids, maybe."

"I don't know what that is. The epigenetics, not the steroids."

"It means external factors have changed how your cells read your genes. The genes haven't changed. Just the way they're expressed. They said Bathory bathed in the blood of her victims to stay young and beautiful—a legend to explain the fact that she was striking. They called her "witch" because she was extremely persuasive and highly intelligent. Those same qualities are in you in unusual quantity. The next time you're in a crowd or really want something from someone, notice what happens."

I feel like people are staring.

It's because you're pretty.

But I have never been a "pretty girl." And I have never been mistaken for beautiful. Strange, perhaps. Different, always. From my fractured attention span to my horrible grades despite being labeled "gifted" at a young age.

I prop my elbow against the window, trying to process, not having ruled out the raving lunatic theory.

The sky has clouded over, a thin layer of gauze blurring the stars. A few minutes later it starts to rain, tiny droplets lighting up the windshield like dull glitter.

"This doesn't make sense. How can an assassin kill any of us if we have mind control?"

"It isn't control. It's suggestion. Except for the powerful and passive moment of your death, they are immune to active persuasion—endowed with 'righteous armor' against the wiles of your bloodline," he says wryly.

"A veritable tinfoil hat."

"More or less."

I may sound glib, but my hands are cold. I help myself to his coffee. Take a long slug, nearly emptying it.

"This doesn't explain why I did it. Wiped my memory."

We slow through the tiny town of Rumford, and he's quiet for a minute before he says, "I know why. I don't agree with it and I can't begin to understand your logic, but I know."

"Then tell me!"

"Because you're protecting something or someone—or some *ones*—you know. Because at some point you realized you were being hunted and thought you might end up dead. And the only way to keep that knowledge from passing, ultimately, to the Historian was to have it deleted from your memory altogether."

Your life depends on it. Others' lives depend on it.

Rolan's crazy must be contagious.

"Who are you in all of this, anyway? One of them—us? Please don't tell me you're my uncle Rolan."

"There are those of us committed to protecting the lives of Bathory's direct descendants. Since the day four centuries ago we concealed the whereabouts of her illegitimate first child, taken away in secret before she married. We are an old order who watch and intervene only when we must."

I almost take comfort, hearing that. But something's bothering me.

"I *saw* you. Talking to Luka behind the Dropfly."

"I was. I told him everything."

"What?"

"He followed you to Maine. He obviously knows you're living under an assumed name. So I told him I was your stepbrother, that I'd been looking for you, had seen the two of you together at lunch. That you went through some unknown trauma back at home you refused to talk about, erased part of your memory, and faked your own death."

"Why would you tell him that?"

"I needed him to know killing you now would get him no information. I told him I was the only family member who knew you were alive, and that I was worried about your mental state. He acted upset, made up some story about how often you seemed forgetful since you started dating, and said he wanted to talk."

"We weren't dating."

"I told him to let me talk to you first. That I'd bring you by his place tomorrow so we could stage an intervention or some such thing. But he was suspicious. And then I saw him following me on the way to your place and knew you were out of time."

"Why didn't he kill me in Europe? Because you were there?"

"A hunter will follow, even toy with a mark for years. Insinuate himself into her life if necessary, give her time to discover who she is, to find others like her—all to gain as much information as possible on her death."

I lean back and cover my eyes. I feel sick. Fifty questions are careening through my skull, but one takes precedence over them all.

"Who am I trying to protect?"

"It doesn't matter. *You're* my priority."

"It matters to me!"

He sighs. "Friends. Other Progeny you met in Europe, your adoptive parents . . ." I glance at him sharply, and he hesitates before saying, "It isn't unheard of for a hunter to threaten a non-Progeny family member to gain what he wants."

Family. The parents who took me in and raised me as their own. And now I don't even know who or where they are.

"How long have you been following me?" I ask suddenly.

"Almost a year."

"Then you know where they are." I grab his phone. "Tell me where they are!"

"Audra." He shakes his head, lays a hand on the phone. "You returned less than two months ago from Europe. I've never seen you go home."

The air leaves my lungs.

What have I done?

"My last name. Ellison . . ." But even I know that by the time I search the slew of Ellisons in the United States, they could be dead. If they're not already.

As though reading my train of thought, he glances at me. "If you were trying to protect them, maybe you have."

And maybe I haven't.

"Why didn't you stop me?" I say angrily.

"It isn't up to me to intervene except to save your life. The decision was yours. That, and you disappeared several months beforehand. We lost track of you until you showed up in an obscure headline, dead. Except the Audra I knew was too smart to die."

"How did you find me?"

"By tracing Luka. He abruptly disappeared from Europe five weeks ago."

My heart won't stop pounding.

I tilt my head back, press my palms to my eyes,

sifting through the remnant of my memory. There are pieces, like the shards of a cherished, broken thing: the garnet ring given me by my mother, an afternoon fishing with my father, my first, clumsily tied fly. Hugs, stories about Mickey Mouse. But their faces, like their first names, are gone. And you can't remember what is no longer there.

"I can get you to a safe house," Rolan says. "But unless you have something more to go on, there's nothing we can do for them."

I may not remember names or faces. But I am the same person I was. Dealing with the consequences of my own actions is one thing. Putting faceless, even forgotten others in danger is something else.

I grab the phone, begin to map a route. "I know where we need to go."

7

Interstate 65 through Lebanon, Indiana, is an unremarkable, even homely, stretch of road surrounded by brown cornfields on impossibly flat earth. But I have never seen a more comforting sight than those six divided lanes.

It is 3:30 on Monday afternoon, and I am at the wheel. After two days of catching a couple hours' sleep at a time in a Walmart or motel parking lot, eating whatever we can grab at the usual cluster of fast-food restaurants just off the exits, and otherwise driving nearly nonstop, I should be exhausted. And I am. But less than an hour away from Lafayette, Indiana, adrenaline has electrified my veins and brought me to wired life.

Rolan, not so much. He drowses against the window, having done the majority of the driving with only brief breaks from the wheel and none at all from my incessant questions.

"Can you tell a Progeny by looking at them?" I had asked him that first night, thinking I sounded insane to even my own ears.

"No, though when we do find out that an actress, model, or rock star is Progeny, it makes a lot of sense."

"Rock stars . . . Do the ones who are Progeny know what they are?"

"Often not until it's too late. Those that do may go into hiding to avoid dying in a plane or car crash, of a drug overdose, so-called suicide, a gunshot . . ."

"Can a hunter take a normal person's memory?"

"No."

"Can a Progeny *persuade* another Progeny?"

"No. But they can sense them, when they're near enough."

"How?"

"You'll know it when it happens."

After a while I said, "What are you called?"

He hesitated then. "You can call us Watchers."

I was strangely disappointed at that, thinking they really needed some better branding in the name department. As though following my line of thought, he quietly recited, " 'I saw in the visions of my head . . . and behold, a Watcher, a Holy One, came down from heaven.' The Book of Daniel."

"Like an angel."

"Perhaps."

"Your accent . . ."

"Romanian."

It was a while before I finally worked up the courage to say: "Tell me about my birth mother."

"Her name was Amerie Szabo. Though she lived under the name Barbara Bocz."

Amerie. I said her name to myself again and again. It seemed exotic and beautiful. And though I never knew her, I thought it fit. I tried to imagine what she looked like. Did she have my eyes, was her hair the same color as mine? The pout of my lower lip—was that hers, or my nameless father's? Did she know who had adopted me, where I had been living all these years? Had she ever come looking for me?

"She was killed three years ago," Rolan said. "Which is probably how the Historian first knew to search for you, if not how to find you. Your mother would not have allowed herself to learn that, knowing her memory was at risk of harvest."

Harvest. Such a clinical word for the rape of a memory. And though I understood, it hurt. How many years had I been allowed to believe I was simply unwanted?

After a stretch of silence, I finally asked: "How was she killed?"

He raised a brow at that. "Are you sure you want to know?"

"Yes," I said quietly, not sure at all. And then: "I want to know."

"Her body was found in the Danube near Csepel Island, south of Budapest. It was ruled an accidental drowning."

"It wasn't accidental."

His sidelong look was his only answer.

I watched mile markers glide by through a blur of unshed tears. Sometime later, I said, "My father?"

Rolan hesitated as though choosing his words carefully. "Your mother . . . was rumored to have several lovers."

"You don't know who he is." I wondered if she did.

"No. But it's possible you have siblings. And that you even found one of them."

I had feigned sleep for most of the drive from Ohio to Indiana, just for the privacy of the dark behind my eyelids. I hoped my mother hadn't suffered. But of course she had; she died. I wondered if I had found a sibling in Europe. If it was for him or her, along with my parents, that I laid down my memory. I was pretty sure I never had siblings growing up; I faintly remembered creating an imaginary big sister for myself when I was four or five. A strange concept, choosing to forget the one person in life you've always wanted there. And now, for all I knew, my actions had exposed her. Him. How long would it be before I learned that person had washed up on the shores of the Danube or died in some freak accident God knows where?

In Indianapolis we got caught in rush-hour traffic before we could skirt the city.

"Look out the window," Rolan commanded.

I didn't want to. The last thing I needed was to be seen by anyone packed into the lanes around us. But I did, afraid the entire time I'd find a homicidal Luka gazing back. What I saw was almost worse: the eyes of men, women, children glued in my direction as we inched past.

"I don't get it," I said, sinking lower in my seat and wishing for the sunglasses I had bought last week. What could they possibly be staring at?

"You probably began to notice it a few years ago. It happens around eighteen. One day you're invisible. The next, a few people notice you. And then a few more. Some Progeny thrive on it. Others go into hiding. A few go crazy."

The minute he said it, I had a flash recollection of two memories. Of a kid I'd crushed on all through junior high asking me to prom out of nowhere. Telling me, weirdly, when I got mono and couldn't go, that he loved me. Of studying a year later in a college library—a soaring, vaulted cathedral to the gods of higher learning. Not at one of the many long tables in the open reading room, but in a cubicle in some obscure wing. Of crossing campus early before class or hours after dark, eating sandwiches covertly behind the stacks. I assumed, when the image had come to me in the weeks since my procedure, that I was a loner by choice, an introvert by wiring.

I realized now I was hiding.

"What they're seeing isn't me," I murmured.

"It *is* you, reflecting whatever it is that enthralls them most. Beauty. Power. Mystery. Seduction. Intelligence."

I flipped down the sun visor and looked in the

mirror. The same face that met me every morning as I brushed my teeth stared back, bags under her eyes.

"You can't see it," he said. "But it's there." I didn't ask him what he saw. I didn't really want to know.

At least there had been no sign of Luka. Since we'd left Maine my pulse had quickened every time I saw anything resembling a Jeep Cherokee. But wherever he was, we had left him long behind. And for that, at least, I could be grateful.

I accelerate as we leave Lebanon. For two days we've consciously driven the speed limit in order to avoid notice, but now I'm antsy, ready to get on with this. Scared to death, too. And I only know one thing to do when I'm close to petrified: keep moving.

When I exit I-65 into Lafayette, I feel as though I've both come home and returned to some alien way station. The small houses, strip malls, and red-brick buildings of the university are familiar and aberrant. The kind of place that should not have progressive science nestled within its small-town Americana, weekend pep rallies, and burger joints.

"Rolan," I say, my heart accelerating as I slow to a pained thirty-five miles per hour. He jerks instantly awake.

Five minutes later I turn off Creasy Lane into

the parking lot of a small, nondescript medical building well away from the St. Elizabeth campus.

I come to a stop, turn off the engine. And find myself staring at the glass doors of the St. Francis Center for Memory Research.

For several seconds, I can't move.

The last time I saw this building, I was leaving it in a wheelchair under a name that is not mine— mere hours after having known exactly who I was and everything I was running from or trying to hide.

Now here I am with a stranger who's rescued me from an enemy I don't remember. But he cannot save the people I've forgotten.

Only I can do that.

My name is Audra Ellison. I am twenty-one years old. And I am prepared, once again, to protect those I love . . .

Whoever they are.

8

The reception area is modern and clinically white, lit by a giant fluorescent disk on the ceiling. A man in a navy suit sits behind the high desk. He's broad-shouldered and his beard is meticulously trimmed, and though he smiles politely when I approach, I can't help but feel he is more security guard than medical center staff. The entrance to the rest of the clinic is armed with a security pad behind him. I assume the waiting area is past that metal door. And somewhere beyond even that is the room where I left the details of my life.

The man does not wear a name tag, nor does he ask if he can help me. I hesitate before speaking, wondering if he recognizes me. An awkward moment ensues as we look at one another expectantly, but the only thing in his eyes is polite forbearance. Finally, he says, "I'm sorry, our trial is closed."

"I was just here a month ago. As a patient," I say, fingertips resting on the edge of the desk. "I'm here for a copy of my medical records. Is there some form I need to fill out?"

The man doesn't move. "We require twenty-four hours' notice and a written request from your power of attorney," he says, and though I appreciate the fact that he doesn't just hand my records over, a small surge of alarm turns my stomach.

"I—I don't know who that is."

"It should have been in your packet."

But the only items in the packet I received were my driver's license, meds, and a stack of cash.

"It wasn't. There isn't . . . anyone."

"I'm afraid I can't help you without it."

"Look. I just drove a thousand miles to get here. This is an emergency." I grab at the only thing that comes to mind, because it also happens to be true. "I've been experiencing blackouts. I lose time. I do things I don't remember doing. My caretaker told me to contact the Center in case of any complications. So I'm here. Please help me."

He glances away, and I think it's toward the door behind him until I notice the camera in the corner. "The name of your referring physician?" he says, pulling a keyboard toward him.

"I don't know. My procedure was . . . extensive." I look around me, but I'm back in Maine, mental gaze scanning the coffee table, and then the pill bottle on top of it.

"Peterson. Dr. Julie Peterson."

He types into the keyboard.

"I'm sorry. There's no record with a referring physician of that name. Do you have ID?"

I dig in my pocket, find my driver's license, and slide it across the desk. He glances at it and taps at the keyboard for far longer than it takes to enter my name and driver's license number—or to type a small thesis.

When he finally looks up, he gestures to the screen in front of him. "I'm sorry, but there's no record of you having been a patient at this clinic."

What?

"It might not be under that name. It probably isn't. I changed my name during my procedure."

"And your former name?"

I glance up at the camera and lean forward on my elbow as though studying something on his desk with confusion, fingers curling over my mouth. "Audra Ellison."

"Do you have ID under that name?"

"No. Only the new one. They should be linked."

His fingers return to the keyboard, but a moment later he shakes his head.

"I'm sorry. There's no record of that name."

"It has to be under one or the other," I say, hearing the panic in my own voice. "Please look again. Emily Porter. P-O-R-T-E-R. Audra Ellison." I spell it out as well, not caring about the camera anymore.

A few seconds later, he shakes his head. "There's no record of anyone by either name ever having visited this Center."

"I didn't visit. I was a patient!"

He lifts his gaze to me. "There is no record of you entering the clinic in *any* capacity."

I look at the lettering on the wall behind him.

St. Francis Center for Memory Research. This has to be it. This *is* it. In fact, I finally figured out why Clare wore a Franciscan tao cross. But how do you convince the watchdog at the front desk that you know—remember, even—that this is the place you had your memory selectively erased?

"Clare Thomas," I say swiftly. "My caretaker was Clare Thomas. Look it up under her name. She left here with me the day of my procedure, traveled and stayed with me for four weeks."

He types again, but he's already shaking his head.

"We have no log of a Clare Thomas visiting the Center."

"She wasn't a visitor! She was my caretaker, on staff here! If you would just page her—"

"That isn't possible."

"Yes, it is. She finished her term with me a week ago, so she's back."

"You don't understand." He levels his gaze at me. "There *is* no Clare Thomas on staff at this Center."

The white-tiled floor tilts beneath my feet.

"Could you just . . . try one more thing," I say. "Could you look it up by record number? Please."

"I can try," he says.

"Three . . . eight . . . five . . ." I give him the number from Clare's cross.

I stare at him for a suspended moment, willing him to find it.

"I'm sorry. There's no record with that number."

I clasp my hands together on the desk to hide my agitation. "Do you have a supervisor, some-one I could speak with? Please. It's important."

"Not at this hour. You're welcome to come by again tomorrow morning."

But whoever I'm protecting may not have that long to wait. I glance past him to the metal door, wonder how hard it would be to get this man's access card and a log-in to the patient system.

He slides back slightly in his chair. Just enough for me to see the gun at his hip.

After a moment's silent standoff, I turn and push my way out the door, brain firing, grasping for straws.

9

Rolan's on his phone when I emerge from the Center. Seeing me, he abruptly ends his call and gets out of the car—then stops, staring at my empty hands.

"Something isn't right. They have no record of me. Under any name. Told me I could come back tomorrow," I say, walking past him to the passenger side. I try to breathe, but once I'm in the car I'm this close to what I imagine a panic attack must feel like. I remotely register Rolan getting in, shutting the door.

He rubs his face, fingers audibly scraping over two days' worth of stubble. "You sure this is the place? We passed a hospital campus a few blocks back."

"Yes."

He stares intently at the Center, and for a moment I actually wonder if he's thinking of going inside. And then I follow his line of vision to the camera at the corner of the building.

He's *casing* the place.

My eyes narrow. "Why are you helping me do this?" I say. "Why search for them? You said your only priority is me."

"It is," he says. "Which is why the last thing we can afford is you flying off the handle and doing something equally insane again. When you said we should come here, look up the emergency contact and address in your file, I thought, fine. We'd get your family to a safe house. Because I know you're not going to let it rest. You may not know me, but I've spent months watching you, Audra."

"I'll try to make sure I don't die and lose you your Christmas bonus," I say sarcastically.

My mind runs ahead, to tomorrow. But I may not have until tomorrow. Tonight, then. I don't need to look to remember the cant of the security camera over the entrance. The glass doors.

"Whatever we do, we can't stay here," he says, starting the car.

Rolan checks us in to a hotel off the highway, one of those inns with suites, complete with fireplace and kitchen. I note that his credit card has a different name on it.

As soon as I'm staring blankly out the window of the room, he leaves to park the Pathfinder around back, pick up a few things from the mini-mart downstairs.

By the time he returns with sodas, sandwiches, and bottled water, I've already called the four hospitals listed in the hotel's guest services binder. None of them has a Clare Thomas on staff.

"You followed me for nearly a year," I say, the tuna sandwich untouched where it sits on a plate beside the hotel binder. "There has to be a hostel or hotel or someplace you remember me staying. Someplace I can call, say I need a copy of my bill—anything that might have the address from my old passport, a credit card . . ."

He shakes his head. "You stayed with people you knew. I never once saw you check in to a hotel."

"Then give me an address! A street name. Anything." While he appears to have recovered his cool, my adrenaline level has ratcheted so far up that nothing short of a five-mile run is going to calm me down.

"If they were Progeny, they've moved since the news of your death, if not before."

"You don't know that!"

"It's what they *do,* Audra. Hide in plain sight in large cities or as far off the grid as they can get. Assuming they know who and what they are, they never stay in one place for long."

How long had I planned to stay in Maine? I hadn't specified anything about moving after a certain amount of time. I told myself to live a quiet life—to even fall in love. Nothing about moving. Had I thought I would be safe enough, unplugged in the north woods of Maine, to stay indefinitely?

But I wasn't always aware of what I was. I went to school like a normal kid—college, even, at least for a while, though I don't know where.

"E-mail," I say suddenly. I had it at some point. How hard could it be to come up with an address based on my name from a popular service? "Can I see your phone?"

"No." He shakes his head. "Any search for your old name will flag the Scions."

I ball my fists and get to my feet, drop my hands on top of my head.

Even if I had an old e-mail address, how would I get the password? I've effectively deleted the details with which I would have encrypted my life; I wouldn't know my adopted mother's maiden name any more than I know the street I grew up on, or the city in which I was born.

"So much for superpowers," I say sourly. "I couldn't even get him to find my record."

Rolan goes still. "You *persuaded* him . . . and it didn't work?"

I throw up my arms. "I don't know. I thought I was persuasive."

Do I imagine it, or do his shoulders relax? "Not the same thing."

"Then I guess I don't know how."

"You don't *remember* how."

"Whatever!"

Maybe it's because I'm tired. Maybe it's because my head is swimming, I'm hungry but can't eat, amped on adrenaline. I can't focus. I miss my meds. For too many waking hours in a row I have fervently held to the idea that today I will learn enough to ensure this wasn't for nothing. That I will rediscover the face or faces behind my choice of anonymity over my own life. But right now I am completely stymied. More than that, I am afraid.

Think, Emily. Audra—whoever you are. But nothing so far has made sense—from my missing records to the numbers in Clare's cross. I must have known it might come to this. Must have left a fail-safe somewhere . . .

I pause, glance from the Formica cupboards of the kitchenette to the Keurig coffeemaker plugged into the crooked outlet. But what if Rolan's right? If I was willing to publicly die to protect myself and others . . . if the situation was indeed so deadly . . . could I have given specific instructions not to share my records—even with myself? A veritable "Do not resuscitate" on my memory?

"What are you thinking?" Rolan says.

"That I'm too tired to think. I just keep going in circles."

"Is it possible you ever had a criminal record?" he says. He is surprisingly focused despite his own lack of sleep.

"Somehow I doubt it."

I should eat, though my stomach's in knots. I pick up the tuna sandwich from the coffee table with a glance at the open three-ring binder of the hotel guide, then pause, the sandwich halfway to my mouth, as my gaze travels the tabs.

CHECK IN/OUT . . . TV STATIONS . . . AREA DINING . . . BUSINESS CENTER . . .

INTERNATIONAL CALLS . . .

I drop the sandwich back on the plate and grab the hotel guide as Rolan sighs and pushes up, paces several feet away. I flip to the International Calls tab. It's a page of instructions for dialing out of the country, with a complete list of country codes.

"Rolan."

He doesn't answer at first.

"What countries did I spend the most time in, in Europe?"

"Uh. Maybe Hungary or Croatia."

My gaze slides down the page, which has been unceremoniously colored in crayon by a previous guest's child.

Hungary.

36.

I scan up the list.

Croatia.

385. A three-digit country code.

My heart begins to pound. I pick up Rolan's phone, tap in 0-1-1, and slowly begin to dial.

3-8-5-9-1-1-5-7-1-2-6-9

Rolan turns, starts to say something, and stops.

"What are you doing?" he says, striding toward me.

A phone on the other end rings.

I lift my eyes to Rolan, who is on the cusp of tearing the receiver from my hand. The ringing stops.

A pause. And then:

"Audra? Is that you?"

10

I spin away from Rolan.

At first, I can't speak. After several seconds of silence, the accented voice—a man's—says, "If you can hear me but can't talk, cough."

"Who is this?" I say at last.

"Audra!" Relief mixed with wonder. "I heard you died! I held on to this phone just in case—"

"Who is this?" I ask again.

A pause. "Audra. Are you all right?"

"Yes. Please tell me who you are."

A slow, audible exhale on the other end. "My God. You did it, didn't you?"

"Please, who is this!" I can barely hear through the hammering in my temples.

"It's Ivan. Not that it will mean anything to you now. You did the right thing calling me."

The name conjures no image. Triggers no memory.

"How do we know one another?" I ask. "Do you know where my family is? My adoptive parents? Any siblings? I need you to tell me how to find them! All of them." My voice falters. I feel strangely fragile. Far too vulnerable.

"Audra, are you sure you're safe? I can't tell you anything unless you're safe."

I glance at Rolan, who slowly sits, gaze fastened on me.

"Yes. I'm with a Watcher."

"A Watcher."

"Yes."

"You're with someone claiming to be a Watcher."

"I need to warn my family. He can send someone to get them to a safe house. But I don't know how to contact them or where they are. I don't remember their names. And I can't remember who I knew there, in Europe, but if they're like me they're in danger. Please."

The voice on the other end is speaking, but something else has snared my attention: Rolan's jacket, gaping open as he leans forward on the sofa. The butt of a gun peers from his side.

"Audra?"

I quickly look away. "Yes."

The voice says, very low, "Is there someone with you? Clear your throat for yes."

I quietly clear my throat.

A soft curse from the other end. "Listen to me very carefully. There is no such thing as a Watcher. Your adoptive parents died a few years ago. Anyone close to you knows that. Whoever you're with, he's testing you. Get out of there, Audra! If he thinks for a second that you know or remember anything of value, he'll kill you for it."

I feel the color drain from my face, abruptly pace to the window, back to Rolan.

"I see," I say, my voice unsteady.

"Say whatever you have to to get away and call me back at this number. I'll hold on to it as long as I can."

The line clicks off.

I stand with the phone to my ear a moment longer, try to collect myself.

"Yes," I say to the dead line. "Please ask him to call me. No, at this number. I'm sorry to bother you. Okay. Thank you."

I tap the phone off and exhale a shaky breath before turning around.

Rolan looks expectantly at me. "Well?"

"Well, he definitely thinks I'm off my nut," I say.

"Who?"

I give a little shrug, mind racing. "This guy named Marko. He recognized my voice, though I guess he only knows me through his brother. He didn't seem to know what I was talking about."

"What's his brother's name?" He's staring intently at me now, eyes that should be fatigued crystal sharp.

"He didn't say. He just said his brother was at work and that he'd have him call me back at this number."

"Did he know anything about your parents?"

"No. He barely knew me. Like I said, he probably thinks I'm crazy." I hand him back his phone and hug my arms around myself.

He hands me a glass of Diet Pepsi. "Where'd you get that number, anyway?"

I take a sip and then a long pull, just now realizing how dry my mouth has gone.

"I found it a few days ago. I couldn't figure out what it was, so I memorized it. I thought it was too long to be an international number, but Croatia's country code has three digits instead of two . . ." I gesture toward the guest services binder.

I'm trying to act normal, but I feel like he's seeing right through me. If he is, though, he's a better actor than I am.

"You always were sharp," he says, a faint smile turning the corner of his mouth. For the first time since leaving Maine, I do not find it reassuring. In fact, I find it unnerving—the smile and the way he talks about me as though he's known me for years. "So we'll wait for him to call back. Unless you can think of something else?" His brows lift slightly.

But all I know is I must call that number back.

I shake my head. "I can't. I can't even think straight." I turn away, down half the Diet Pepsi.

"You should get some sleep. I'll wake you if he calls."

"Yeah. Okay," I say, before looking around me as though lost and then wandering into the bedroom and quietly locking the door behind me.

Inside, I set the glass on the desk, look around frantically.

So he's not a Watcher. Watchers don't exist. Or was the mysterious Ivan lying? Clare gave me his number. If there was ever a question of whether that number came to me by mistake, it's gone now.

I walk into the bathroom, lock the door, and turn on the faucet full blast.

Think. Think! Two men, both trying to appear helpful. Rolan, whom Ivan says is a liar. Ivan, whom Rolan would call a liar. One *is* a liar. Which means one must be telling the truth. And Ivan . . . Why did Clare leave me his number? What did she say? *In case you find yourself in trouble.*

One thing I know for sure: Both Clare and Rolan are not who they claim to be.

I lean down to the sink, rinse out my mouth. My stomach is knotted so tight I actually think I could puke.

I turn off the water, grab a towel. According to Rolan, Luka's out to kill me. According to Ivan, Rolan is poised to kill me.

If he thinks for a second that you know or remember anything of value, he'll kill you for it. This, about the man who claimed his only priority was my safety—and then spent two days driving me to Indiana to retrieve my past. I think back to the night I saw Rolan behind the Dropfly—was it only two nights ago?—arguing with Luka. Luka, who saw me, but hid it from Rolan before chasing us halfway to Kokadjo. In an effort to do what? Get me away from Rolan so he could kill me?

And then I see them again, walking away, Luka's arm draped over Rolan's shoulders as if they were old fraternity brothers.

Only then does it occur to me that they could have been working in tandem, that the chase up Lily Bay Road was all for show. If the endgame was to get me to return to the Center, it worked. And if what Ivan says is true and Rolan is a killer, I don't dare return to the Center tonight. I don't have that long either way; if Rolan's phone doesn't ring in a matter of hours, he'll know something's wrong.

I tentatively open the bathroom door, half-expecting to find Rolan standing there, gun drawn. But the room is quiet and dark, the sun having long set so that the only light comes from under the door to the sitting room. I pause near the nightstand, fingers on the phone. But it's one of those types with the light that comes on if a handset is lifted.

I need to talk to Ivan. He's the only one I seem to have placed as a contingency in my post-procedure life . . . which means he's the only one I trust.

I cross to the door, press an ear against it. Nothing but the faint sound of the television.

I unlock the door and quietly push it open. Rolan is not only *not* dozing as I had hoped but sitting forward on the sofa, talking in low tones on his phone in a language I assume to be Romanian.

I've hardly made a sound, but he glances up the moment I crack the door open and ends the call.

He's also shed his jacket. It lies folded on the coffee table, the pistol atop it. His eyes follow my gaze and return languidly to me. "Everything all right?" he says, laying the phone aside.

"Yeah," I say, as though I regularly see guns sitting on coffee tables. My heart is thudding in my ears, and for a crazy moment I wonder what it feels like to be shot—if I will know for myself within minutes. "I mean, no. Nothing is all right. I've got a guy trying to kill me, and find out I'm this *thing* from some ancient history. So, no. Everything is not all right." I rub my forehead as though I'm seriously on the brink of a breakdown, which I might be.

"I'm sorry," he says, elbows resting on his knees.

"I keep thinking, what if Marko's brother doesn't know anything? What if I can't find any-thing to help—my parents, my siblings, friends . . . whoever they are?"

His brow wrinkles slightly. "Then we wait. You said he'd call."

I drop my hands to my sides. "I appreciate you doing this for me. I know it's not your prime directive, or whatever. So thank you."

He shrugs a shoulder, his black, long-sleeved shirt clinging to muscles that make me certain he's some kind of ex-military. I studied him covertly all the way here, but now I'm looking at him anew. Is this the face of a man who wants to kill me? Because apparently I'm a bad judge of that.

"It's the only way I know you'll let it be and keep from doing something dangerous."

I nod and then fold my arms around myself. They feel heavy. "Too bad this place doesn't have one of those minibars." I smile slightly. But I'm thinking very, very hard about how much he should offer to go down to the little shop near reception and pick up one of those miniature bottles of wine. If what he says about me is true, I can compel—persuade, whatever—him to do this. "I could use a drink."

"Yeah." He rubs his face. "Though alcohol doesn't sit well with your kind. There's coffee."

"I hate that stuff," I say, glancing at the Keurig. "Though I'd go for a latte. You didn't see a coffee shop nearby, did you?" *Starbucks. Go get it, Rolan.* I know for a fact we passed one less than a mile away.

"Better to stay out of sight," he says. "There's creamer, if that helps. Or more soda."

So much for Jedi mind tricks. I glance around, as though looking for options. But I'm thinking as hard as I can that he needs to get up, walk out the door, and drive down the street. When I look back at him, he's reaching toward the table, where the gun is. My heart trips, but then he picks up my neglected sandwich. "Get something in your stomach," he says, holding it out. "You'll feel better."

I move toward him and take it, my spine prickling as I return to the bedroom. He's just picking up the remote as I close the door behind me.

So now I know that I have no idea how these supposed powers of mind suggestion work, that Rolan made it up completely . . . or that he's immune.

Which makes him a hunter. And means Ivan was right.

I force myself to sit on the edge of the bed facing the door, sandwich on the floral bedspread beside me. I glance at the clock: 8:45 P.M.

I sigh and lie back to stare up at the ceiling in the dark. I'm exhausted, my limbs heavy as though the earth just doubled in mass.

I mean to wait in silence for the better part of three hours. To give the impression that I have finally given in to exhaustion.

Which means, of course, that I do the one thing I have no intention of doing.

I fall asleep.

I rouse just enough with the first violent twitch, the kind your body does when it refuses to go gently. I shove up from the bed in a panic, limbs like tar, and grab the edge of the bedspread to keep from falling in slow motion onto the floor.

What's wrong with me? My legs are stupid, and I end up dragging the bedspread halfway off

100

the bed. Something soft topples to the carpet with a crinkle of plastic. The sandwich.

I stagger back against the desk and almost knock over the glass of soda.

The one Rolan poured when I wasn't looking.

My tongue feels too thick to even curse. I didn't drink it all—on that count, the proverbial glass is half full. But the fact that Rolan wants me out is enough for me to realize it's time to go.

I glance at the clock: 9:13.

I force my eyes to widen, myself to straighten. Shake my arms as though they're wet. Take inventory. One door, leading to the sitting room, where Rolan is no doubt still awake. One window, looking down from the second story onto the bushes below.

One option.

I unlock the latches at the top of the window with clumsy fingers. With one last glance at the door, I push the inside pane up a tentative inch. It squeals against the sill. With a quick breath, I shove it loudly all the way up at once.

Commotion in the front room, pounding on my door. Time's up.

I climb awkwardly over, fighting for purchase, and dangle just long enough to see a pair of headlights illuminate the bushes—and a length of concealed pipe—before I drop.

11

When I open my eyes to intermittent darkness, I know I have failed. Gone, the ugly floral bedspread. The leather beneath my cheek is clammy. I'm staring at a partial wall—no, the back of a seat in a moving vehicle I do not recognize. My wrists are tied with what looks like part of a torn-up T-shirt.

My name is Audra Ellison. I am twenty-one, and I am in deep trouble.

The acceleration of the engine sounds like a freight train, the occasional bump in what I assume to be highway jars my throbbing head to the base of my skull.

At least I'm alive. I might not have escaped Rolan, but I'm not done working on that part. I tug on the ties around my wrists with my teeth. They're knotted tight.

I slide my feet off the edge of the seat in the darkness until my knee finds the hump in the middle of the floor.

With a quick breath, I shove up from the seat and throw my arms around Rolan's head. The car swerves, sending us skidding onto the shoulder and almost into the ditch. Even better. If I'm going to die without answers—or a seat belt—I am not going alone.

I throw my weight back, bonds cutting into my

wrists. He brakes, and my cheek crashes into the headrest. He's gotten his fingers within the circle of my arms, and I'm positive one of my hands is about to pop off.

"Audra!"

I falter, hearing my real name. In that split second, he grabs me by the right elbow, hits the brakes again, and hauls me to the front, my body twisting onto the console. My left arm, caught on the headrest, feels like it's ripping from its socket.

I look up then, and see him.

Luka.

With no more leverage against his throat, I drive my head forward. He's buckled in and jerks away just in time. I catch his shoulder instead, lip splitting over my teeth.

"I'm not going to hurt you!" he shouts.

I spit blood. Behind the headrest, I can no longer feel my hands.

"Right, because that's why you have me tied up!"

I struggle to pull my arms over the top of the seat, but he yanks them back down. A car whizzes by, horn blaring.

"I tied you up because I knew this would happen when you came to! You took a hard fall from that window."

"Let me go!" I shout. But I am freaked out. There's no way he could have followed us this far without our noticing, which means that he knew about the Center from the start.

I shove up, trying to free my hands, and he grabs me by the shoulders. "Audra, whatever that guy told you, none of it's true."

"He told me what you *are*," I hiss. "Showed me pictures of you following me last year!"

Luka presses his lips together.

"You should've done it then. You should've killed me. Because guess what? *I don't remember anything*. Whatever I had is gone! So when this is all over and you trot back to your Historian master with nothing to show for—what? A year's worth of work? Two?—what's he going to do to you? What's the punishment, Luka, for returning empty-handed? Because I may be new at this, but even I know that you *suck* as a hunter."

During all this time, he hasn't moved. And just as I'm contemplating whether I can get one good jab in before he stabs or shoots me or whatever he plans to do—because I'm sure I've got it coming now—I realize he's staring at me. Two and then three seconds tick by, but there is no rage, no hint of homicide in his expression.

And then he lets go of my arms.

I exhale a short laugh. "You won't even deny that you're supposed to kill me."

"No," he says quietly, and I wonder what he's waiting for. "Now ask me if I'm going to." A car whisks by, and then a rumbling truck, air shuddering around the car.

"Don't you think we're past that?"

"No."

"No what?"

"No, I'm not going to kill you."

For a moment, neither one of us moves. His gaze is stony, and I wonder if I'm looking into the eyes of a murderer.

"The Audra *before* knew that. She also knew I was going to follow her to Maine. That I would be waiting. To protect her."

I laugh in his face, but I'm trying to keep my arms from shaking. Adrenaline has long since obliterated whatever Rolan put in my glass, and now it's all I can do to keep my teeth from chattering with it.

"I knew your address before you even got there. Little island two hundred feet from shore."

"I get it. You're creepy."

"You gave it to me so I could find you!"

He reaches up and lifts my arms over the rest. My wrists scream, my shoulders have all but seized up.

For the first time I actually take in our situation: cockeyed on the shoulder of some two-lane highway surrounded by cornfields. "Just let me go. Let me out here."

"No way. He'll kill you."

"Well, that's really interesting. Because that's the same thing Rolan told me about you!"

Luka grabs me by the wrists, sending a shock of pain through them. "He'll find you within an hour. Think, Audra! The fact that you erased your memory means you knew something extremely valuable to the Historian. That guy—Rolan?—he will not stop. He'll take you back to the Center. He'll force his way in. Possibly kill someone— maybe even you. And you'll both die for nothing, because *you have no records there*."

In the near distance, the tread of tires speeds toward us, slows.

I stare at him, about to ask how he knows that, but his eyes have gone to the mirror.

"Get down!"

My head hits the steering wheel as the back window shatters. Luka's bent low over my neck one second, and the next he's shoving me headfirst into the passenger seat as tires squeal against pavement beneath us.

"What was that?" I roll hard against the car door as we veer into traffic.

I can't see a thing, head dangling into the footwell, nor can I get turned around. And all I can think is that I'm going to die after all, neck broken against the glove compartment, an ignominious bullet in my butt.

"Rolan," he growls over the engine accelerating in my ear.

He swerves into the next lane, and I brace myself against the dash before being thrown back into the passenger door. I've just climbed up enough to get my back against the dash when I see Rolan's Pathfinder through the driver's side window—too close. I scream on impact. The car careens toward the shoulder and then jerks violently back.

"Stay down!" Luka shouts. The passenger side window splinters. I turn my head toward the console, eyes squeezed shut, fists over my face.

Luka brakes suddenly, jamming me into the floor mat. My feet fly toward the ceiling. He grabs me by the waist of my jeans and hits the gas. We accelerate hard for a weightless instant— and then smash into a vehicle. Rolan's.

I hear the impact as we speed away, the collision of the Pathfinder with the ditch—and then the embankment.

"Are you all right?" Luka shouts. "Are you hurt?"

He slows to what feels like a crawl, glancing back in the rearview mirror.

"I'm okay," I say shakily.

I clutch his arm, and he hauls me up, my vision prickling. Shards of glass trickle to the floor.

Behind us, the Pathfinder has shrunk in the distance, a shadow against a pale crop of corn in the moonlight. I imagine a waft of steam rising up toward the sky.

"Do you believe me now?" Luka says, his mouth a grim line.

I refuse to answer, then do one better and black out.

12

Wake up in the back seat, take two: this time there's a hunter-murderer leaning over me, blocking out the dome light.

"Audra. Audra!" He's smoothing the hair from my eyes, searching my face with a frantic gaze.

"Get off me." I plant my foot against his groin. He backs out the door, hands up, and then extends one toward me. After a moment, I take it and slowly sit up. A wave of nausea rolls over me.

"Remind me not to let you drive anymore," I say.

We're in the parking lot of some office complex off the highway. The sky to the east is still dark. Cars whiz by in the distance, crickets twitch in nearby fields. And somehow the world seems far too quiet.

"You banged your head pretty hard in that fall," he says.

"Where are we?"

"Just over an hour from Chicago." He leans into the front passenger side. With a wary glance at me, he starts to brush glass off the seat with what I recognize as the torn shirt he tied me up with.

I look back the way we came and instantly regret it; my neck is not going to be my friend tomorrow.

"You okay?" he says.

My head is killing me. I've been chased, drugged, fallen from a window, almost crashed upside down, passed out, and haven't slept more than two hours at a time in days.

"Yeah." Because despite all that, I'm alive.

"Is he dead?" I ask.

"I doubt it," Luka mutters.

"How'd you get here from Maine?"

"Caught a flight."

Hence the car I don't recognize, which I assume to be a rental.

"My records," I say, feeling the back of my head. "If they aren't at the Center, where are they?"

"I don't know. You didn't tell me."

"So I didn't trust you."

He pauses, not looking at me. He's wearing the same outfit I last saw him in at the pub on Saturday. But then, so am I, stupid Nirvana T-shirt and all. But neither one of us resembles the people who ate lunch on the lake four days ago.

"We decided it was best neither one of us know."

"We?" I chuff. "Good try. I saw you talking to Rolan at the Dropfly."

"I know."

"So you were trying to get him away," I say slowly. "How'd you know he was there?"

Luka assesses me through the seats. "Did you forget that I live across the street? I was watching for you and saw him. Same guy I'd seen around town for days. When you showed up and he followed you in, it was pretty obvious."

"You asked me out . . . so you could see if he followed me there?"

"It worked."

I'm not sure how I feel about being my own bait.

"Wait a minute. He didn't tell you I had my memory erased," I say with realization. "*You* told *him*."

Which means Luka knows—knew then—what Rolan was. Is.

"I had to or you never would've made it back up the road alive. I also said I thought you were dead until just a few days before. Which is a lie, so if you want to call me a liar, now's your chance."

I don't, and he starts picking glass off the floor.

"Then it's true. You're both . . . hunters." I wrap an arm around myself, suddenly chilled.

"He is. I . . . was."

"So he replaced you."

Luka doesn't answer as he throws out a piece of glass. It hits the pavement with a musical tink.

"How do I know you're not working together?"

"Hunters don't work together."

I think of what Rolan said about hunters toying with marks for years. "How do I know you're not playing me?"

110

"Seriously?" Luka stops to stare at me. "Did you notice I saved your life back there?"

"He might have been shooting at you."

Luka leans over the seat and studies me, hair hanging in his eyes. "Believe me, I've had many chances to kill you. Many. At close range." His brows lift meaningfully.

"You're an ass."

He goes back to cleaning.

"So now what?"

"I don't know, Audra!" He slams his hands down on the seat. "This hasn't gone the way it was supposed to. None of it!"

"How was it supposed to go?"

He sighs and pushes out of the passenger seat, paces several steps away, kicks a piece of glass. "This was supposed to be behind us both! No more Progeny. No more hunters. A normal life. Whatever that is. That's how it was supposed to go. But of course God, fate, whatever couldn't let that happen." He turns back, laces his hands together on top of his head. "So here we are. You can't go back to Maine. I'm not trying to scare you, but anywhere you start over, they're going to be looking for you. Now, more than ever. They won't stop. So where we go from here . . . your guess is as good as mine."

"Who am I protecting?"

"Audra, are you listening to me? Right now you need to worry about yourself."

111

"Tell me who!"

He lifts his hands. "Progeny like you. People who help them. You didn't tell me names! It wasn't safe. And trust me, you didn't want me knowing and I didn't want to know."

"I didn't want you knowing because you were supposed to *murder* me. Then you decided to protect me? And here you are still following me around. What are you, my personal stalker?"

"Something like that," he says, lifting his chin. He looks angry. "Yeah. Your personal stalker. That's great." He walks away, and for a minute I think he's going to actually take off.

I watch as he picks up something in the parking lot, chucks it at a light post. A moment later he comes striding back.

"You know your story sounds a lot like the one Rolan told me," I say.

"Listen." He drops his head, shakes it, as though second-guessing what he's about to say. "Rolan. Was lying. Because he wants what you knew. Very badly. Acting like your buddy was the only chance he had of getting it. By the way? I don't know what story he told you, but no Progeny would knowingly keep a photo of another Progeny on their phone. Not in a million years." He shakes his head. "And right now, the more I tell you, the more dangerous it is for you—and *everyone* you know."

I don't tell Luka that Rolan never claimed to be a Progeny. Somehow I have a feeling he'll tell me the same thing Ivan did: There's no such thing as Watchers.

"I don't know anyone," I say and realize just how true that is. As unsavory as they might be, the introduction of Luka and Rolan in the last few days has increased the grand sum of my dubious social circle to two. Four, if you count the nonexistent Clare and Madge at the Fly Shop, though it doesn't look like we'll be socializing much anymore. And I realize now there is no one I trust.

I wonder if I have ever felt so alone.

"You did," he says, biting out the words. "You did know people. You had access to a lot of information from your mother."

"What do you know about my mother?"

"She was a radical. Infamous in Progeny and Scion circles alike. She was determined to find a way to end it. Which made her dangerous. To everyone."

My eyes narrow. "You said you didn't know anything."

"I said I didn't know names. But anyone remotely plugged in knew hers."

"What do you mean?"

"She was at the front of a movement among Progeny who'd rather die than live in secrecy one more generation."

"That's why they're after me?"

"They're after you because you're *alive*. But even more because of who you are and what you used to know. Your mom prepared for the day a hunter caught up to her—and protected a lot of people and information in the process. Information you acquired."

"You're full of crap."

"Am I? Weren't you doing the same thing when you had your memory erased? Creating a fail-safe in case that day came? That's exactly what you did! But you did it better."

"On what planet is this better?" I demand. "Whatever she knew, the hunters have it now! So what was the point?"

"Whatever you learned from her, you found more. You went further. Even before we were friends, you—"

"We were *friends?*" And I know I've just screwed up my face like I ate something disgusting.

He leans in through the back door, his eyes dangerous. "Oh yes. Because I got involved in your life, remember?" he hisses. "Yeah, I was *that* hunter—intent on bringing the big haul back. And you had it. Enough to fill in a slew of blanks. To set me up for life when I turned it all in. And you had no idea how close you were to dying. The daughter of Amerie Szabo. You were the mother lode."

Gone, the man who called me Bronco and tried to sell me nonalcoholic cider at the grocery. His expression is feral.

"Until the day I realized I couldn't do this. I didn't want you dead. More than that, I wanted to keep you alive. So the joke's on me. The ambitious one who got too close instead of just getting it over with and taking whatever you had in that mind of yours. Now that's gone and you don't know who you are anymore. Well, neither do I! So here we are. The Historian will know soon—if he doesn't by now—that you're alive and I'm a traitor. So who knows. Maybe Rolan was shooting at me after all."

"For all I know, I erased my memory to keep it from *you*."

"I'm not the enemy here. Not anymore. Not for a long time."

"How am I supposed to believe that?"

Luka straightens and practically shouts: "Because it's true! You might not know me anymore, but I still know you, Audra!"

"I'm so sick of hearing people say that!"

"Yeah, but I'm the one *not lying* to you. Did it occur to you that if I wanted to kill you I would have done it before you erased your memory? You trusted me. You still do. Listen to your intuition," he says, and for a moment it seems like he's actually pleading with me.

I shrug. "Sorry. I got nothing. I wish there was

some way to prove it." And a part of me really does mean it.

He drops his head and walks away, hands on his hips. A minute later, he turns back. "I *can* prove it. I know things about you you don't share with others."

I wait expectantly.

"You hate math and don't know how to cook."

I roll my eyes. "You just described three-fourths of the population."

"The first guy you had a crush on was some kid in seventh grade."

"Every girl has a crush on some kid in seventh grade."

His blue gaze fastens on me. "Your parents died in a freak boating accident four years ago. Your dad was an avid fisherman. You studied art for a year and a half at the University of Chicago. You used to take meds for ADHD, which you don't have. You have a photographic memory. You superimpose shapes on things in your mind when you're thinking. You never forget a face. Well, I guess you have now, huh?"

I go very still. For a moment there's only the occasional whir of a car on the highway.

He nods toward my arm. "You have a scar on your right elbow where you crashed riding your bicycle. You were fourteen. You call it your salami scar, because you skidded on the pavement and it looked like salami. Still does, a little."

I don't move, except for my eyes, which turn toward my sleeve.

"There's another scar on your right shin that looks like a dent, where the bike landed on you, pedal first. You haven't ridden a bike since. You took martial arts as a kid. Swam in high school. Love eighties music—Devo especially, because you're basically a nerd. You don't like makeup. Hate black coffee . . ."

"Stop," I whisper.

"You touch your hair when you're nervous, used to have a dog named Attila. Your litmus test of a true history geek is whether or not they know Attila the Hun died of a nosebleed. You love mulligatawny but won't eat soup unless it's hot enough to scald—"

"I said stop it!"

My hands are shaking. But even as I tell myself I could have shared any of these things under the guise of friendship and that he's conning me, I can't help the fact that I am desperately clinging to a shard of hope that he's not. Four days ago, I was considering that I could never be honest with anyone, that no one would ever really know me. That sense of despair only got worse as I listened to Rolan's entire story about where I came from, what I am. Now there's a person in front of me who knows it all, better than I do. Or claims to, at least.

"You said yourself you acted like my friend to

find out what I knew. Any so-called friend would know things like that."

"I said I got too close and *became* your friend."

"Same thing."

"It isn't to me."

"Then prove you're no longer hunting me. Let me go, and leave."

He crouches down in the open door in front of me. "I can't do that. I promised I'd be here afterward. We made this decision together, remember?"

"No, I don't remember!"

"Maine was a new start for me, too—you're not the only one who lost that. So if you take off without me, I'll just follow you. Because I made a promise. And because that's what stalkers do, I guess."

I stare at him for a long moment before glancing down at the leg of my jeans. Without a word I lift up the right hem. And there it is: the scar like a little dent, nestled against my shin.

Even as my pulse trips, I tell myself anyone could have seen it and made up some story. I remind myself I never said anything in my letter about Luka. But I never did about Clare or Ivan, either.

Ivan.

I look around, and then at Luka. "Do you have a phone?"

"Yeah . . ." he says cautiously.

"Give it to me."

He hesitates, then pulls the phone from his pocket, unlocks it, and holds it out.

I dial in the numbers.

"What are you doing?" he says.

"You want me to trust you? Trust me for a minute."

Ivan picks up on the first ring. "Did you get away?"

I slide from the back seat, walk out of earshot. "Yeah."

An audible exhale on the other end. "Did he get anything?"

"Please, how do I know you?" I say.

"Did you give him anything?" the voice insists.

Luka storms over and reaches for the phone. I spin away.

"No. Because I don't *know* anything! I went back to the Center and my records are gone."

"What are you doing?" Luka hisses.

"Who's with you?" Ivan says.

"A friend." I stumble on the word, shoot Luka a warning. He's glaring, looks ready to rip the phone from my hand.

"The fact that you're alive is enough," Ivan says. "They know you're hiding something important or you'd never have done this."

"*They* who? The Scions?"

And then, a faint exhale: "It isn't . . . it isn't possible you found it?"

"Found what?"

"Where are you now?" he says quickly.

"Near Chicago," I say, glancing toward the highway. "Please. Whoever I did this for—I think they're in trouble. You have to tell them. You have to warn—"

"Audra, they're not just after your life."

My parents—all of them, ostensibly—are gone. "I know. They're after the Progeny I knew."

"No. No, something much more important."

"Than a life? What else is there?"

"If you found what I think you did, you and anyone close to you is in far worse danger."

"Found—what?" Luka is staring at me.

"You have to get here. We can hide you. If nothing else, at least you'll be safe for a while."

"I can't come to Croatia! I'll go to a battered women's shelter, or—"

"Audra, get out of the States. Now."

"I don't even have a passport!"

"You're Progeny. Get one. I have to get rid of this phone. I'll leave you a new contact in the next five hours."

The line clicks off before I can say anything else.

I stare at the space between Luka and me for a stunned moment, and then, belatedly, at the phone in my hand.

Without a word I pull up a browser, type in "University of Chicago" and "library." Tap on a list of images.

The Harper Memorial Library comes up.

And there it is: the cathedral of learning, with its vaulted ceiling and rows of long tables I remember.

There is an actual place with real records of my existence. If I had an ID with my old name on it, if I weren't supposedly dead, I would be able to walk in and get my student record, find something about my former life.

I realize Luka's watching me. He looks pale.

"Okay," I say, more to myself than to him.

"What was he saying about rediscovering something?" Luka says. He looks ill.

"He wouldn't say. Something he thought I found."

Luka's gaze is locked on mine. An instant later he walks to the driver's side and gets in.

"He's right," he says. "We have to get you out of the country."

13

"I can't just go to Croatia!"

Back on the two-lane highway in flat Farmville, USA, we might as well be talking about one of Pluto's moons. I hug my arms around myself against the cold, touch my tongue to the inside of my lip where it got cut.

"He's right. You'll be safe. No one knows how to hide like the Progeny," Luka says, eyes on the road.

"There have got to be Progeny here somewhere."

"Not like there. If the Historian knows you're alive, that you faked your death and erased your memory to protect something . . . something important enough that he sent Rolan to get you to rediscover it . . ."

"So he could kill me and then harvest my memory and give everything to the Historian—I get it."

Luka's jaw twitches, the set of his mouth flat.

"What does he think I found?"

Luka's quiet for a moment before he says, "The diary."

"Diary?"

"That has to be what he meant," he murmurs. He passes his hand over his face and then pounds the rim of the steering wheel with a curse.

"This wasn't supposed to happen. This isn't what we planned!"

"What diary?" I demand.

"Bathory's. People have been searching for it for centuries. I knew Rolan would let you live long enough to find something you remember, but if they're talking about the diary . . ." He looks shaken, even in the dark. "You're lucky to be alive."

"So I hear. About this diary?"

He lets out a slow breath. "It's the Progeny holy grail. They think it contains proof she was set up so the king and her sons-in-law could take possession of her land. That finding it will end the hunt once and for all. But the Scions believe it's a detailed account of the girls she tortured and killed. Proof of their reason for being."

"So which is it?"

"Who knows? No one's ever found it, if it even exists. Years after Bathory's death, her son Pál believed if he could find his mother's diary and prove her innocence, the king would be forced to return the property the crown had taken and clear the family name. It was illegal by then to speak Elizabeth Bathory's name in public. But Pál never found it. The king—by then the Holy Roman Emperor—accused him and his siblings of treason, confiscated the rest of their land . . ."

"And banished them from Hungary."

He nods. "Bathory's descendants have been

searching for the diary ever since. As have the Scions of the Dispossessed."

"Could that really end it?"

"It's a myth, Audra. Or was until rumor started circulating that your mother was close to finding it. The Historian wants it so badly, he's put a ten-million-euro bounty on it."

"Which is why you didn't just kill me outright," I say quietly.

Luka doesn't answer.

"And Ivan thinks I found this diary."

"I don't know. No one could have gotten closer. You have no idea what your mother was to the Progeny. What you were to them before you died."

"What was I?"

"Hope. That the generational curse would be broken. That Progeny could live in the open for the first time in centuries, have families. Die a natural death."

I blink into the wind streaming through the broken window.

"So did I find it or not?"

"If you had found it, there's no way you'd have gone in for the procedure. You would've ended this if you could. Unless . . ."

I glance at him as his expression changes, along with his tone. "Unless you found it and it didn't prove her innocence."

"If we were as close as you say, how could you *not* know whether I found it?"

"You knew what was at stake. It superseded everything. And I knew that. When I finally told you who I was, you withdrew from the underground to protect them. From me, too, of course. You were spooked, imagining how close you came to having their blood on your hands just because you knew me. You had nightmares about it for months."

"How do you know?"

"You told me. Later, when you decided to trust me again, before you went in for the procedure."

"To protect the underground."

"Not just that. Can you imagine two years of this? Always looking over your shoulder? Going more and more into hiding? I watched the change in you. Toward the end, before you returned to the States, anything having to do with the Scions, the diary, the Progeny was the last thing you wanted to talk about. You were tired of the underground, the hiding. Even of your own gifts— the persuasion, charisma. You would have gotten rid of them if you could, if you didn't need them to survive. By the time you made up your mind, persuaded your way into the trial at the Center, there was no point in talking about any of it at all. It was going to go away. It was like watching someone prepare to die. When all you do are the most normal things you can. Eat a meal. Watch the sun set . . ."

I look at him sidelong, his profile illuminated by

the gauges on the dash. And even in the darkness, I think he looks haunted.

"Why *did* I decide to trust you again?"

He's silent for a moment before he says, "You said you missed me. You were tired of being suspicious all the time, with everyone. You wanted one person who really knew you that you could trust, and barring that . . . you didn't want to do it anymore."

"Do what?"

"Live."

Luka's eyes are hollow. I turn my face toward the shattered windows, welcome the blast. Close my eyes.

After a few miles, I say, "Why didn't I leave the information with you, if you were in on the decision and I trusted you as much as you say?" Even as I say it, I see any hope I might have had of a normal life—a life without centuries-old myths and killers and people with strange powers— slipping away from me. Quiet backwoods Maine must have seemed like paradise to me before I gave up my memory. It still does.

"Who do you think is the first person the Historian would turn to if it came out you weren't dead as I reported? I took the credit for your accident. You couldn't leave anything with me. Besides, apparently you did leave something for yourself."

"Ivan's number."

"Names would defeat the whole purpose. And any locations you knew are useless because the Progeny move. A single lifeline, though, would be enough, assuming Ivan could stay alive to hold on to it. You knew what you were doing."

I hear Clare's voice again. *Trust your decision.*

But it's hard to trust anyone you don't know. Especially when that person is you.

We stop at a twenty-four-hour convenience store near Hammond, pick up a prepaid phone, a couple of prepaid credit cards, some Advil, and a baseball cap for me. Luka's concerned about my apparent concussion. But that's the last thing I'm worried about.

By now it's very late, and adrenaline and neck pain have given way to mind-numbing exhaustion. Luka tells me to sleep, but he isn't willing to stop. And though I'm moving through a fog, there's no way I can attempt sleep with him sitting two feet away in the driver's seat.

We drive until the city lights are within sight and my ear is practically deaf from the cold wind.

On the outskirts of Chicago he pulls into an all-night diner with free Internet and slides the cap carefully onto my head, pulling the bill down low. "Come on."

It's the kind of place a diner should be: greasy-looking, chrome on the counter stools, squiggly lines on the laminate tabletops with red pleather booths. I ask the waitress for a vat of coffee when she comes to drop off the menus. Luka, meanwhile, is tapping away at his phone.

"Let me see that driver's license," he says. I slide it over to him and he just stares at it for a moment.

"What are you doing?" I ask, as he returns his attention to the phone.

"Booking us tickets to Croatia."

"Us?"

Suspicion and relief collide somewhere inside me.

"I'm going with you."

"This isn't your problem."

His brows draw together. "Actually, it kind of is. Rolan knows you're with me, which means the Historian sent him. They know I'm a traitor, and there's probably a price on my head. And I told you I'd protect you."

"Look, if you're trying to make up for something, I'd say the fact you haven't killed me yet makes us even. I release you. Okay?"

He lifts his gaze, eyes locked on mine. "You don't get it," he says. "There is no 'yet.' There will never be a 'yet.' I will *never* hurt you." He looks for a moment as though he's about to say more, but then seems to remember the phone in his hands.

Why this loyalty from him? Some need for absolution? To make amends? Was his mission to kill me such a great part of his life that he can't function without a replacement cause?

My other theory is too uncomfortable to consider with him sitting across the table from me.

"Great. So we're two targets instead of one," I murmur.

He says nothing, ferociously tapping at the screen.

"By the way, I don't know if you heard, but I don't have a passport."

"We're going to fix that."

"How? By heisting the passport agency on the way to the airport?"

I pour several ice cubes, two sugars, and half the tiny pitcher of cream into my coffee and drink it down. A minute later, Luka slides my license back and sets the phone aside.

"When she comes back for our orders," he says, "ask her for a recommendation."

I shrug. "I'm pretty sure waitstaff hate that, but okay."

"But the entire time you're talking, I want you to *see* her serving you a cheeseburger."

"This is a breakfast menu," I say, waving it.

"Doesn't matter. If she suggests anything that isn't a cheeseburger, compliment her and ask again," he says, giving me a pointed look as the waitress comes back with an expectant smile, pad in hand.

"All set, hon?" I'm not a fan of endearments,

but there's something about the *hon* that makes her seem friendly enough to not spit in my coffee for my doing what Luka asked.

"What do you recommend?" I say cheerfully.

"Our stuffed French toast is *really* good."

"Wow, you have a great smile," I say, peering at her.

"Well thank you!" She laughs. "You just made my day."

"So what do you recommend?"

And I realize as I'm asking it, that I am starving. And that the thought of French toast—or pretty much anything—is literally making my mouth water.

"Stuffed French toast for sure." She beams.

"Well then . . . stuffed French toast it is," I say, smiling not at her but Luka.

Luka mumbles something about the same, and she leaves.

"You have to be able to do this," he hisses.

"Listen, Yoda—"

"You can do this."

"See, that's the problem. I can't."

"Look—" He points. "See that guy yawning? Over there?"

I glance over and feel my own mouth stretch open in response.

"Exactly," he says, leaning across the table. "He yawns, and then so do you. It's the same thing."

"Yawns are contagious. And I haven't slept in days."

"Thoughts are contagious. What happens when you see a pizza commercial? What are you hungry for the rest of the day?"

"Sushi."

"Thick, cheesy pizza. Normal people do this all the time. You just do it better. Whether it's pizza or hot donuts. Or a greasy burger."

I drop my hands on the table. "We're talking about getting people to *do* things. Not eat them. I don't need a burger. I need a passport, and right now I can't get anything but breakfast food!"

"Listen to me, Audra." He points toward the counter. "Unless that waitress is a hunter who secretly knows how to strangle someone with their own shirt, it *will* work."

I feel the blood leave my face.

He leans back. "Sorry."

"Can you really do that? Strangle someone with their own shirt?"

"I don't know."

"No, really. Can you?"

"I guess. If I had to."

"Have you ever 'had to'?"

"Audra—"

"Have you? How many people did you kill before I came along? What about my mother?" Something is boiling up in me that I didn't see coming, but suddenly my hands are shaking. "Is

131

that what happened before she ended up in the Danube?"

"No," he says. "No! One hunter. One mark. You were mine."

The waitress passes our table, and I stop her. "You know, I'm sorry. I'm not sure I'm in the mood for French toast . . . anything else that might be good?"

I tip well, and I want the biggest cheeseburger you've got.

"Well," she says conspiratorially. "We're on breakfast, but we do have the best cheeseburgers outside the metro. I think I could talk Matt into firing one for you," she says with a wink.

"That would be great," I say tightly. "With everything, please."

The moment she leaves, I suppress a shudder. The release of adrenaline that relieves my shaking hands is immediate, and real.

When I slide my gaze back to Luka, he's nodding. "There's the Audra I know," he whispers.

By the time we leave, I'm full and so tired I'm swaying on my feet. Luka finally finds a residential neighborhood off the expressway, parks behind a little church.

"You should try to get some sleep," he says.

I pull my sleeves down over my hands, tuck them under my arms. But despite my exhaustion,

132

sleep feels like the last thing I'll ever be capable of again.

"Who did you tell me you were when I met you? Before, I mean," I say. Somewhere a transit train rolls in the distance.

"I said I was taking time off from university to work for my father," he says into the darkness. "Making some money so I could transfer to a school in the States. Which was true."

"How did you end up involved in this in the first place? How does someone even become a *hunter?*"

"It runs in families," he says.

"Christmas must be fun at your house."

"It isn't exactly something people discuss. The call may skip a generation. Maybe two. There's never more than one hunter in any generation from the same family. Out of two siblings, one might get the call and the other will never have any idea that such a thing—any of this—even exists." His accent, normally light, is thicker when he's fatigued.

"Or that his or her brother is a murderer."

Do I imagine his flinch?

"What will happen to your family?"

"I don't know," he says quietly. But somehow I think he has a pretty grim idea.

"This 'call' . . . how does it happen?"

"It was after mass," he says with a soft, bitter laugh. "I was thirteen when the new deacon invited

133

me to join a secret group of 'up-and-coming young people' that my grandfather had been a member of. A kind of fraternity that supports the—what do they call it . . . 'mutual advancement' of its members."

"What, like Skull and Bones?"

"What's that?"

"Old boys' club at Yale."

"All I knew was he was the youngest deacon I'd seen. My grandfather had bought the bank he worked for at twenty-five; he passed it on to my father, who became very successful. I felt a lot of pressure, even then. I was called in a year later. Told I was special, given a mission. A single thing I had to do, when the time came, that would set me, my family up for life, and right an age-old wrong."

"Then you can identify them!"

"I never saw their faces. And I never saw the rest of the fraternity again. By the time I was seventeen, I was working for a startup. It landed a major contract the same week I was accepted to Eötvös Loránd University."

"So, did everyone in the fraternity go on to become a—"

"No. I suspect the Scions keep many charitable organizations as grooming grounds for positions in their members' enterprises. The hunters are a small and very specialized part of what the Scions do as a whole. I actually don't like talking about it. I was . . . completely brainwashed. I hate thinking about it, actually."

"So what changed your mind?"

"You."

I'm quiet for a long moment.

"What did you tell them you got from my memory?" I say finally.

"I said I botched it. That you were too badly burned for me to retrieve anything."

I swallow. "And what did you get for my death?"

"I told my contact I didn't want anything. That I wanted to travel and just be left alone. I dropped out of university, quit my job. I didn't want anything to do with them. Forty thousand euros showed up in my account the next day."

"That's *it?* The going rate on a *life?*"

"Audra, I failed."

"You *killed* me as far as they knew."

"But I retrieved nothing. Based on who you are—what you possibly knew—I failed. They probably should have killed me but paid me instead. Leave with your life and a little bit of money—it's enough to keep anyone indebted and paranoid. That's how they work."

"You could have reported it as an error, refused to keep it, so they couldn't have anything on you—"

"How do you think we paid for this new life?"

I let out a breath, recall the stack of cash in my packet upon arriving in Maine.

135

He's gazing at me in the darkness as though there are fifty things he'd say, given the courage to voice them all.

"You could still go back," I say. "To save your family. Say I faked my death and you've been tracking me ever since—"

"I lied to you at lunch," he says abruptly. "The other day. I said you were pretty. You're not. You're beautiful."

I stop, and then give a short laugh. "Okay, you must be—"

"Really tired. That's what you were going to say, isn't it?"

I hesitate. Actually, it was. "How'd you know that? Hunter prowess?"

"It's what you always say."

I open my mouth, but before I can say anything else his phone chimes, startling us both. Luka holds it up, shows me the text.

Café Abbazia, Opatija. 16:00 Wednesday.

I don't recognize the number except for the first digits of the country code. Croatia.

Ivan.

When Luka puts down the phone and takes my hand, there is no word for how disconcerted I feel.

No, I know how I feel. And I know what I feel like doing right this minute. And even though in all this time I haven't once tried to match his ear to an egg or overanalyze the angle of his nose

(106 degrees), some rational part of my brain is yelling at me that I also chose to trust Rolan—to jump in a car and drive all the way to Indiana with him—and look how that panned out.

I study Luka in the darkness, see his face again in the Greenville grocery, eyes locked on mine. Is that the gaze of someone searching for an ancient diary and ten million euros . . . or the recognition he once saw in my eyes?

Girls like me don't get European guys who look like they should be dating models named Gisele. There is nothing desirable about me. I am not rich, I am smart. A nerd who watched *Firefly*'s lone season three times with friends whose names have been erased from my memory. But he and I? Unless I managed to glamour him with my Progeny supercharisma, I don't see it. And I wonder if he's working the plain-girl-lack-of-self-esteem angle on me. Because I agree it's the best play—and far preferable to getting strangled with my shirt.

"So, obviously . . . you and I . . ."

He looks down.

"And you were okay with me forgetting you."

"No." He looks up, gaze intense. "I was not okay with that. But I was less okay with you being hunted by whoever stepped in after me."

"Luka, I don't know what—"

"I don't expect anything," he says and lets me go.

"I was going to say I don't know where you're from," I lie.

"Oh." He laughs softly. "Slovakia."

"Nice to meet you. I'm Audra Ellison," I say with a lame smile.

"From Sioux City, Iowa," he adds.

"You're kidding."

"Nope."

We sit in awkward silence until he says something about getting an hour's sleep and I agree. But my mind is racing.

How many conversations have we shared, he and I? Were we . . . *involved* involved . . . or just kind of involved? I've studied his face in my mind more times in the last hour than I care to admit. The curve of his lower lip, the hair teasing his jawline. And, okay, his ears. Once.

What was it like with him—with us? How did I ever manage any kind of relationship, let alone one with a hunter while chasing my mother across Europe—and how did he? I strain to remember anything about him, but he is gone. Like so many faces and details of a life that had no doubt once been full, a shell now in the absence of those who filled it.

Eventually, I must have slept, because the next thing I know Luka is gently shaking my shoulder.

"Audra, wake up." I open my eyes as he retrieves an envelope from the glove compartment. "Time to go."

14

"What about the car?" I say, glancing back at it. Even in the forgiving light of dawn it looks like junk.

"We leave it," he says, shoving the envelope in his pocket.

It's nearly half a mile to the closest Walgreens. My hands are freezing, and my mouth tastes gross. My head feels worse. The hour's sleep I got wasn't nearly enough, and my new passport photo shows it. Luka prints our itineraries while I buy toiletries, and puts in a call to the passport agency for an appointment. And then we're out the door and hurrying to the Red Line station. Luka dismantles his phone as he goes, breaking the SIM card in two. He tosses half into a sewer, the other half in an open cup of stale soda sitting in a trash bin. He hurls the phone itself into the back of a beeping garbage truck.

We take the Red Line of the L into the city, get off at Jackson station. By the time we wait an hour for the passport agency to open, my hands are shaking from the chill as much as from nerves.

Luka takes them between his own and rubs them. His fingers are warm. He's been talking in low tones the last five minutes, though I couldn't repeat a word of what he just said. I hate to say it, but I miss my meds.

"Just focus," he says, low near my ear. I close my eyes. "It's a Progeny thing, the jitters. You always had to work them off somehow—running, swimming, working some poor souvenir guy over for a deal. Just to get it out."

"I feel like I'm going to climb out of my skin."

"That's good."

"No. It's not."

He bows his head against mine. "You can do this. You have to. Or you'll never get out of the country. You don't have any contacts here, and the underground here is an inch deep. You'll die if you stay. We both will."

"You're not helping," I say. All I can think is that I'm going to be picked up for having an identity that doesn't exist. Maybe, at least, I'll be safe in jail.

The very nice man on the eighteenth floor takes my appointment confirmation, which isn't for two weeks yet, and issues me a number. When it's finally called, I pass my application and driver's license beneath the agent's window. She smiles at my story about our elopement to Amsterdam as Luka beams and puts his arm around me.

"And your birth certificate?" she says. I look at Luka. He slides me a page from the envelope. It's a folded map of Greenville, Maine. I look blankly from the map to him. He shoves it into my hand.

"Here," I say, not even attempting to smile as I hand it to the woman, fingers tapping a nervous SOS against the countertop.

My name is Emily Porter and I was born wherever you were, lady.

She takes the map, stares at it for a long moment, looks up at me. My heart stops.

"Well, what a coincidence! I'm from Ogallala, Nebraska, too!"

Luka and I make inane comments about fate, love, the size of the world.

"I'm just . . . trying to find your date of birth," she says, finger scanning the map.

I point to Mooseless Lake but fumble for a date. I search desperately and then see the digital display behind her.

"Well, happy birthday!" she exhales with a laugh.

"Yup. Happy birthday to me." I smile stupidly. "I've got my honey and my birthday cake, all together."

Luka gives me a weird look as the lady returns my "documents" and tells us to come back at one o'clock.

We have enough time to buy a change of clothes, backpacks, sandwiches. We check in to a nearby motel long enough to take turns in the shower and change. The spray of hot water in that chipped and scuff-marked bathroom is the most luxurious thing I can remember. And I will never take brushing my teeth for granted again. I even have time for a half-hour nap, the experience at the passport agency having drained the last of my reserves. When I wake, Luka's gotten me some ice for my lip, which is still a little swollen but already beginning to heal.

By the time we return at one, I wonder if there'll be police waiting to detain me. Instead, I'm handed a spanking new passport.

Less than an hour later, we're back on the L to O'Hare. And for the first time since we left Lafayette, Luka, in a new black sweater, face half-obscured by a hat, looks nervous.

"Keep your head down and phone on," he says as we arrive, and then strides out of the train ahead of me.

I make my way to ticketing, through security, and catch a glimpse of him only once before reaching the gate. I sequester myself near the window and keep an eye out. Ten minutes before boarding I start to panic.

Despite my suggestion that he should have taken his shot at freedom while he had it, and the knowledge—if not the memory—that I have taken this trip before, I am afraid. Not of abandonment, or even of being alone. But at the prospect that the one tie I have to who I was has disappeared.

It occurs to me in that moment that, regardless of what she was to others, a part of me hates my faceless mother. Despises her for not going into hiding or doing whatever she had to in order to keep me. For leaving me with the inheritance of a cause that superseded her daughter, took my mother from me . . . and may, at any moment, end my life as well. Yes, I'm thinking only of myself, it's selfish and I don't care.

A sound chimes from behind me and I realize it's the phone ringing in my backpack.

"I'm standing across the concourse, near the McDonald's," Luka says. I glance up, just under the brim of my cap, and find him facing the other direction, phone held to his ear.

"I see you," I say, feeling instantly, stupidly better.

A pause, the sense that he might say more.

"See you in Amsterdam," he says at last.

I nod, though I know he can't see me, and line up to board.

Midway through the flight I head to the bathroom and spot him near the back of the darkened cabin, hat pulled low on his head. Asleep like the other passengers around him.

I emerge from the lavatory to an empty galley, having *suggested* to the two attendants on duty that it's time for drink refills in coach. Meanwhile, I've started the slow climb out of my skin again. I'm just pouring myself an unsteady cup of coffee with a full inch of cream when the curtain parts.

I glance over my shoulder.

Luka says nothing as he steps behind me. His fingers cover mine on the cup. He takes the coffeepot from my other hand. His breath is warm on the curl of my ear as he pours, steam risin in the too-dry air. I close my eyes, the cup weightless in my hand. A bead of sweat slips down my sternum.

A passenger comes through the curtain and Luka moves away. But electric verve has fired my veins, and the moment he moves I gulp the coffee, burning my tongue.

I'm aware of him as I return to my seat. Glance back once. Know he sees me.

I tell myself I can't sleep after that. Try to watch a movie—

And I am gone.

I wake just before landing, a crimp in my neck. Rub my eyes and grab the napkin off my drink tray.

The guy next to me has apparently finished the entire Steven James novel he started before takeoff. There's an in-flight magazine on the tray in front of me, open to the crossword in the back, a pen resting in the fold. But what catches my eye is not the magazine itself, but the smattering of *T*s scattered across the page.

No, not *T*s, with their thin middles and thicker ends. Tao crosses.

That, and a drawing of some kind of dog—a German shepherd, maybe—inside a circle.

I slide the magazine closer. What the heck?

"Excuse me," I say to the man beside me, offering him the pen. "Is this yours?"

"Yes, thank you." He slips it in his pocket. I wait several minutes and then tear out the page, wad it up, and drop it in the melted ice of my drink just in time to hand it to the flight attendant upon landing.

On the other side of customs, I make my way through Amsterdam's airy Schiphol airport, past duty-free stores, open eateries, the casino. It's early morning, the terminal bustling with the promise of a new day. But I'm not taking in the neat little sandwiches in the café cases, the tulips with their easy-carry boxes, the stores selling postcards of the famous Red-Light District. I'm looking for the hat obscuring that honey-dark hair, coffee on the brain.

My phone rings, and I glance around, full panorama.

"Hi," he says.

A half hour into the next flight, I make my way back to the empty galley. This time he's waiting for me. He pulls me toward the window, arms winding around my waist, mouth already on mine.

By the time we lay over in Munich, pass through the chaos that is Rome's Leonardo da Vinci airport, and land in the seaport of Trieste, I am exhausted, strangely elated, and thoroughly distracted.

Outside the Trieste airport, which seems downright tiny compared to the ant farms of Amsterdam and Rome, Luka catches me by the hand.

"Quickly," he says, hailing a cab ahead of the line. I slide across the seat as Luka leans forward to say something to the driver. All I catch is "autobus" and what I assume to be something like "hurry." He passes the man a fifty-dollar bill, and the car takes off with a screech.

Luka glances back. I follow his gaze to the broad terminal doors in time to see someone rush through a clot of passengers, knocking the luggage from several hands.

Luka talks to the driver, who nods abruptly several times, and eventually—after some lengthier explanation from Luka—gives in to a chuckle.

When Luka sits back and winds his fingers around mine, I say, "What was that all about?"

"I was watching you through the airport. Or rather, watching someone watch you." He pinches the bridge of his nose, and I wonder if he slept on the last flight at all. "I might be wrong. I can't tell."

"Why was the driver laughing?"

"I told him we were running away together, and that I'd pay him double to help us get away from your husband."

"You speak Italian," I say belatedly, realizing

146

that he's back on his home continent—something he doesn't look particularly pleased about at the moment.

"A little," he says.

"More than I do."

"You know what they say," he says.

"No, what?"

"If you speak three languages, you're trilingual. Two, you're bilingual. One . . . you're American."

"Sad but true."

We ride in silence, looking out at Trieste's crowded streets filled with eateries, shops, banks, and offices with modern signs set in limestone buildings that look no less than hundreds of years old. We catch glimpses of the Adriatic. In another life, I'd want to walk, go down to the beach, take in the medieval charm of this place, along with some pizza.

For all I know, I've done that.

But more than that, I am aware of the gravity of him, of the air, heavy between us, filled with images of the flight before. The way he pulled back and touched my mouth where it was swollen yesterday, before kissing me again more slowly as my fingers tangled in his hair. This, from the man once charged with killing me. I am haunted, heady, at odds with the surreal fabric that has become my life.

We arrive at the bus station and Luka pays the driver—this time in euros.

"Where'd you get the euros?" I say, berating myself for not having thought of exchanging money.

"Left over from when we were here," he says, getting out and reaching back for me.

And just like that I am revisited by the echo of a past I no longer own.

At the station he buys two tickets for the Auto-trans bus just beginning to board, and we hurry down the stairs of the terminal. I climb on first and slide into one side of a bus only half full, next to the window. To my surprise, Luka sits beside me.

We say little as we travel east along the coast. When I start to droop against him, Luka draws me into his shoulder. The steady heart rate I enjoyed for the last leg of our trip spikes and never quite settles. Now that we're here, the danger of my life *before* seems far more immediate and real.

"Luka . . ." I whisper.

"Hmm?"

"Do you know anything about my father?"

He tilts his head toward me. "Only that he was like you. Your mother was said to keep to her own kind."

"Rolan basically called her a whore."

"If that's true, it's news to me," Luka says, and somehow I'm genuinely happy to hear that. Not that I'm into slut shaming, but all this time I was picturing some Sarah Connor *Terminator* fanatic sleeping with whoever would put her up or help her out.

"Take anything you hear about your mother with—how do you say it—"

"Grave offense?"

"A grain of salt," he says wryly. "There was a lot said about her, but from what I've heard, she moved in a very tight circle."

"Are any of them still alive?"

"I don't know. I was only given information pertaining to you." I practically hear him grimace as he says it. "Another Progeny could get on this bus right now and I wouldn't even know it, let alone anything about them."

"Did you know Rolan before this?"

He shakes his head. "I've never known another hunter, other than my grandfather, who's dead. Makes it impossible to implicate anyone but ourselves if we're caught. Even if one of us tried to talk, what would we say? We'd be written off as conspiracy theorists at best, delusional murderers at worst." He hesitates. "Audra . . ."

"What?"

"You can't tell anyone like you what I am. Was. If they guess, for even a minute, they may or may not kill me, but one thing is sure: They won't trust you. And you need them right now."

We look out at the blue waters of the sea

practically below us. The view is gorgeous, and I think if I'm going to die without family, at least I'll do it in a beautiful place.

Assuming, of course, that Luka, with his heady gaze, doesn't do the job himself.

His story's been perfect so far. And I'm tired of triple- and quadruple-thinking everything. He's telling either a very intricate lie, or the simple truth.

The problem is I don't know which. And right now I need him.

15

Café Abbazia is a hole in the wall, boasting no more than eight tables in its dim interior. I take a seat near the back and apologetically explain that I don't speak Croatian when a man I assume to be the owner comes to greet me. Even with the door propped open to let in the fall air and Luka watching the café from somewhere across the street, I feel both cornered and exposed in this cavelike place.

That's not all I feel. There's a strange buzz here—not from the speaker over the bar, which is silent, or from the floor, which vibrates with the jackhammer at work in the street outside . . . but from something in the air.

"Vino?" the man says, which still isn't English, but is at least something I understand.

"Coffee," I say, though I really want a glass of wine—something Luka warned me against. "Alcohol jacks your persuasion," he said before he exited the bus ahead of me. "Better to be nervous and amped in case you need it."

No worries there. My heart is drumming so hard I actually felt dizzy the minute I stepped inside.

My gaze lingers on a couple seated near the front window, their hands twined atop the table. They're all European chic—he, in skinny black

151

pants and a fedora, she with her thin sweater dress, sunglasses perched on her head. There's an older man sitting at a table against the wall, a paper folded in front of him. He taps away at a phone, glasses low across his nose. They're the only guests other than myself.

I glance at my phone. Three minutes past. I try not to bounce my knee or drum my fingers on the table. I'd shoved my hat in my backpack after I sat down, so I settle for obsessively smoothing the hair over my scrubby patch until the owner comes back with an espresso-size cup of coffee. He sets it in front of me with a small glass of water. I drink the water right away, shot-style, my mouth drier than I thought possible.

The fact is, I'm not just nervous to meet this person I don't remember. I'm desperate to lay eyes on someone else like me. To hear, firsthand, what it means to be what I am. To get some answers.

Just as I start to doctor up the coffee, I find myself glancing at the open door as though a horn has just sounded from that direction. But there was no horn. A couple of teenagers pass by the café door, one laughing and jabbing the other in the shoulder. A dog barks somewhere outside. And then I feel the café itself fade into my periphery and fall away. There is only the door and the street beyond.

An instant later a lanky form fills the frame,

blocking out the afternoon light. He steps into the café and unwinds a scarf from his neck, the end of which was draped over his head as though he has come in not from the September sun but from the desert. He's scraggly from the hair on his head to his beard, wearing work pants and a long-sleeved shirt, messenger bag slung across his chest. I am hyperaware of him, as though he exists more than the rest of the patrons combined.

He walks directly to my table as the owner greets him with a barely perceptible nod. Taking me by the arm, he says, "Come, hurry." And I know by his voice this is Ivan. Behind him, the couple rise from their seats, move toward us in his wake. They are no longer holding hands.

I grab my backpack as Ivan leads me past a curtain to the rear of the restaurant, through the kitchen and a grungy back door. Despite my nerves, I note, if slightly hysterically, that I've done this trick before.

We move down the crooked alley behind the café. It's narrow and who knows how old, open windows overhead gossip length apart, the occa-sional clothesline bridging the gap between them. I glance back to see that the woman has put on her sunglasses, that the pair follow wordlessly as we turn past a grotto chapel. We stop at a wooden door, a crest of some kind carved into the stone above it. Ivan pulls a key from his pocket, glances past us as he unlocks and then holds the door open just enough for the couple to usher me inside.

The minute he locks the door behind him, the dizziness is back, and this time I know it isn't my overloaded adrenal glands but *them*. Ivan in particular. I feel his presence like a wave—not the kind of surge that knocks you over but the eddy that buoys and surrounds.

I put out my arm to steady myself, and the guy in the fedora catches me by the shoulder. We are standing in a side room lit through a lattice by what looks like construction work lights. Some kind of restoration has been halted on the other side, and I realize as I take in a stack of hymnals that this is an annex to the chapel.

The woman removes her glasses and studies me coolly as Ivan moves to peer through the lattice. Seeming satisfied that we are alone, he finally turns to me.

"Audra. It's really you," he says, as though he had not fully believed it until now. He is not in his forties, as I first thought, but younger, grizzled less by age than by weather or choice. He is not striking, though who knows what a haircut and shave might do for him. Nor is he tall, though the instant he stepped into the doorway of the café, I would have sworn he was over six feet. And while I find some of this weirdly disappointing, he has an energy that makes me dizzy, as though I had had that glass of wine.

The woman is silent, looks me up and down. She's like one of those pouty models from a magazine. The kind of person you instantly don't like on meeting, but stare at anyway just because you're jealous.

"Returned from the dead," Ivan whispers, eyeing me as though I were some kind of living apparition. His brows lift. "You changed your hair."

"Yeah," I say. It's weird feeling like your own impostor. Before I can reach up to touch the scrubby patch behind my ear, he tugs me into a tight embrace.

"A daring move, Audra. From the bravest woman I know," he murmurs in my ear.

"Thanks," I say, stupidly.

He holds me away to look at me, and then lets go with a shake of his head. "I never knew what happened after you disappeared."

"Well, I guess you know now," I say with a levity I don't really feel.

"I mean the first time."

I hesitate. "The first time?"

"Six months ago. It was March. We were in Zagreb. One night, you simply vanished. Gone, the clumsy American who left her traces everywhere." He lifts his palms. "You became a ghost. And then, just weeks ago, I received an alert that you had died in the U.S." He's looking right at me, and it's awkward feeling like you're being asked a question no one expects an answer to. Though it doesn't seem he's waiting for an apology, either.

I glance at the woman, who has crossed her arms.

"Ah, forgive me," Ivan says. "This is Claudia, and her sibling, Piotrek."

"It is an honor," Piotrek says, in an accent different from Ivan's as he sweeps in to buss me on both cheeks. Claudia, who has not moved, says something to him in another language and he ignores her. When he moves away, his eyes sparkle with the kind of look that isn't shy about liking what he sees.

"I *felt* you when I walked into the café," I say, and then look at Ivan. "And you, before I even saw you."

"Naturally," Claudia says. Her accent, I note, is different from her brother's.

"My parents were both of the blood," Ivan says. "Unlike Claudia and Piotrek, whose mothers were, but fathers were not. The legacy is passed through the women." He lays his hand over his chest. "But I have become something of a hermit. The charisma weakens when the Utod are seen by so few, as it does with age. But you, you always could tell." Is that admiration in his eyes?

"The Utod . . . ?"

"Hungarian," he says. "It means Progeny."

Piotrek studies me as though I am the most fascinating creature on earth. "You really *don't* remember anything, do you?"

"No," I say. "Which is why I was hoping you could give me some answers. Like why I did this."

"You're asking us?" Claudia snaps.

"The answer is simple," Ivan says, ignoring her. "You were protecting something of great value."

It's nearly the same thing Rolan said.

"Like what?"

Ivan takes a seat on a column of stacked hymnals, folds his hands between his knees. "Something too important for you to say. Or for me to ask. That is the way it is for us. To speak is to put your life and that of any other Utod you know in the hands of another's fate. It is a great show of faith that Claudia and Piotrek have come here with me today."

Faith is the last thing Claudia looks like she has in me. "I notice I had no choice in the matter," I say.

"Thanks to your so-called Watcher friend, the Scions already know of your resurrection," he says. "Rest assured, the risk is solely ours. If you are killed, they will harvest your memory. They will know where you saw us. What we look like. Anything we told you. If *we* are killed, they will learn only that you are here, and that you remember nothing."

"You say you don't know why I disappeared. But when we spoke you knew what I had done."

He shakes his grizzled head. "Not at first, though it became obvious. You had talked once, in theory I thought, about doing such a thing. There was some new unsanctioned clinical trial in the U.S. that you had heard of. You wondered out loud about the benefit of such a procedure to any Progeny who knew too much. You called it a last, life-saving defense. I didn't believe you would actually do it! Then you vanished. I left Zagreb two weeks later. Many did, spooked by your disappearance. The same thing happened after your mother went missing. And so imagine my surprise when I heard your voice again, especially after the news that you were dead."

I unsling my backpack and set it down. "I take it you didn't know about the dying part."

"You couldn't have told me. Had something happened to me, the knowledge of your plan would have been harvested from my memory." He shrugs a shoulder. "You knew this."

"So you're saying you have no idea why I did it? That doesn't make sense. The only thing I left myself was a single link to you!" I try to tamp down the rising wave of panic, but it's not working.

"I said I did not ask and you could not tell me," he says, far too calmly. "I never said I had no idea."

I feel myself squinting in the pattern of light thrown across the room, yellow diamonds strewn against the walls. "Is this about the diary?"

Claudia makes a sharp gesture. "Do not speak of that here!"

Ivan stays her with a mild murmur. "Reason dictates that if you were close to finding it, you would not have stopped until you ended this all," he says. "You would not have buried it and abandoned the legacy simply to stay alive. And the Audra I knew did *nothing* without reason. And many things seemingly *contrary* to reason. *That* was her genius."

I note that he hasn't answered my question.

Then I realize: *He doesn't want to talk in front of the others.*

"Well, I don't know what that reason was anymore," I say.

"You see?" Claudia says. "She knows nothing. Why should we risk any more lives for her?"

I am so over this chick.

"You told me to come," I say to Ivan, steadfastly ignoring her. "That I would be safe here. Well, here I am. Now what?"

"Yes," Claudia says succinctly. "Safe. At great cost to ourselves! By now the Scions know you were desperate to keep something from them by any means, which makes them want it even more. Make no mistake: The killings will accelerate, if only because they know you are

159

alive. Your return is more of a danger to us than if you had truly died!"

I actually blink at the blunt force of her words.

"You have forgotten who you are," Ivan says gently. "But I have not. I told you to return for your sake, but for ours as well. Your 'resurrection' will send a surge through the underground court. It will give them hope. Some who left will return. In that way, Claudia is right. You cannot come back after disappearing if you are unwilling to give them that. Better that you never returned at all."

"What are you saying?" All this time I had pictured spending my foreseeable future in some underground safe house. Not posing as the Progeny poster child! What can I possibly offer them? Hope? Resurgence? I can't even summon those things in myself.

"I am saying you are the daughter of Amerie Szabo. By virtue of that fact alone, anything you knew was of interest to the Historian. But this thing that was so great a liability that you had it removed from your memory, it is of interest to us as well."

"So let me get this straight. I *faked my death* and *erased my memory* to keep something from falling into the Historian's hands. Now that he knows what I did, he'll let me live long enough to rediscover it—before killing me and harvesting my memory to get it."

"Or perhaps not even that long, depending on what they think it is," Piotrek says.

"Noted. Meanwhile, you want it, because if the Historian wants it that badly, it might be useful to you."

"To *us,*" Ivan says quietly. "You . . . are one of us."

"But every minute I'm with you puts you in danger. Which is why you won't help me unless I'm willing to *undo everything* I did. Why? Because you don't trust my reasons?"

"No," Ivan says. "Because the stakes are far higher. Had you stayed dead, we would have mourned you, and you would have achieved your goal. But now, as Utod and Scion alike learn you are alive, everything has changed. The Historian will not rest until he discovers what you were so intent on keeping from him. Which is why *we* must find it first."

I don't know how to tell him that I couldn't retrace my steps even if I wanted to. They, along with every pertinent detail of my life, are gone. To make matters worse, the only person I remotely trust other than Ivan is the man who was supposed to kill me for it all. And right now Luka and I both need their help.

But Ivan isn't done.

"The fact that you contacted me is proof you prepared for this possibility. As you yourself said, the sole thing you left yourself was a link to me.

And, as it turns out, I do indeed have something for you."

My gaze snaps to him. "What is it?"

Ivan gets up. "We have been here too long." He looks at Claudia. "Are you satisfied?"

Claudia gives a curt nod that is mirrored by her brother. But she looks disconcerted by this last statement of Ivan's.

"Come, Audra. You will stay at my house tonight."

"The friend I mentioned," I say abruptly, "is waiting near the café."

Ivan shakes his head. "I'm sorry, but your friend cannot come with us."

Ivan's quick refusal shifts me into panic.

If Luka is lying, I need to be able to control what he thinks he knows.

But if there's any truth to Luka's story, I won't leave him to the hunters as payment for saving my life. I may not know who I was, but I know at least that much about who I am.

"I need him," I say. "He remembers things I don't."

"Not possible," Ivan says, moving toward the door.

"Then the underground will have to get their hope somewhere else."

Ivan slowly turns.

"Do you really know whom you can trust?" he

says. "I wonder: How did he find you, anyway, the so-called Watcher you escaped?" I understand instantly what he's insinuating.

"I wonder the same myself," I say, looking at each of them in turn.

It's weird having a Mexican standoff in the middle of Croatia.

"There is an old saying among the Utod," Ivan says, at last. " 'Better to die blindly than having seen too much.' But I say: Better to live. If you have any question in your mind at all, then you must leave your friend behind. Particularly if you care for him."

"He's not a threat," I say, and pray that I'm not lying.

16

Booths line the street advertising boat tours and deep-sea fishing trips. The beach beyond is filled with pedestrians eating gelato, couples walking with strollers, kids running ahead of their parents.

I've just reached the main thoroughfare when Luka falls into step beside me.

"So what now?" he says.

Along the horizon, the Adriatic Sea is a sapphire beneath the setting sun, far too beautiful and serene to exist in the same dimension as my fractured existence.

"The last ferry for Cres island leaves at eight thirty. We need to be on it," I say. I don't mention Ivan's parting words as he wound his scarf over his head:

"Be wary, Audra. Your return is a great gift to the Utod. Be careful of those you surround yourself with, and most careful for yourself. For your own sake, I wish you had never been found."

When I asked what he meant, he kissed me on both cheeks. "Tonight we will talk. I will tell you things you want to know, and many others it would be best you did not." Despite the way his statement unsettled me—as it was designed to do—it contained the reassurance, at least, of answers to come. That, I could live with. For the moment.

Luka pauses. " 'We'?"

"I told them I had someone with me. A friend."

He stops cold.

"Ivan's taken the earlier ferry," I continue. "He'll meet us on the island dock."

"Audra, I told you—"

"What was I supposed to do? You're here, by your own insistence."

"That's my problem, not yours!"

I realize the irony. A hunter going into hiding with his mark. But I need him off-kilter, under more experienced scrutiny than mine. Just in case. After all, I trusted Rolan, too.

The possibility has never left my mind that Luka might be after the exact same information Rolan was. That he might have lied about having had the opportunity to kill me before I removed every trace of it from my brain. That I am still his mark. But as the logical side of my brain continues its waning code orange, it also sees the value of bringing him along. Talk about keeping your enemies closer.

"If it's any consolation, they didn't want to let you come," I say.

"They shouldn't have agreed. It wasn't smart." I can practically hear the wheels turning in his head.

"You promised to protect me. Kind of hard to do

165

if you're not with me. Besides, if we were as close as you say, I would've thought you'd be happy."

"I would have followed, kept close on my own."

"And you think they wouldn't have noticed?"

"I did it for years! Audra, I don't think you understand the kind of scrutiny you're going to be under," he says, though he might as well be talking about himself.

I shrug. "If anyone asks, just say you're my boyfriend. It'll make sense to anyone who saw you with me earlier this year, right?"

"What am I supposed to say if I get questioned by your friends?" He seems genuinely at a loss.

"That you know as much as I do. Listen. We met while I was leading my double life in Europe. We fell in love, I told you what I was. As far as you know, the trauma of being constantly on the run and hunted was more than I could take. That's why I got the procedure. You agreed because it was the only way to save my life from the threat of some nameless, faceless hunter you were inept to protect me against—"

"Thanks."

"It was an out, an opportunity for us to start over and be together. It's very romantic," I say drily.

He looks sharply at me. I smile. "Hey, look at it this way: If we were a thing, it's not even lying."

He pulls me into a doorway then, penning me

166

in the shadows. He's not smiling. "One problem: The Progeny don't share who they are," he hisses.

"You don't know that."

"I do, and they've killed their own for less."

"Bullcrap, Luka. I just met two people whose mother was Utod and father was not."

"I guarantee you the father had no idea." His expression has darkened. "And if he did, there'd be serious consequences."

"As serious as me hooking up with my own hunter? Would that be more believable?" I shoot back.

For a moment, he actually looks rattled, a quick succession of emotions playing across his face.

"Listen. You're the golden child of Amerie Szabo. Don't lose that card. You need them on your side." He searches my eyes, says more softly, "Please."

Is that the look of someone urging—no, practically begging—for my sake, or for his?

"Fine. You're the friend I met over here during my time off from college. You came back to the States with me. You said yourself you were working for your dad to earn money to go to school in the U.S. When we got back I told you my abusive ex-boyfriend was stalking and going to kill me. I got the procedure, faked my death to get away. You came to Maine to look out for me because that's the kind of stand-up guy you are, and yeah, okay, you're into me. Everything was fine until my ex found me and started harassing me again, taking me all the way to the Center to try to get my memory back. As far as you know, we're here meeting up with my old friends to get me away from him. Good enough for you?"

He turns his head slowly, eyes on me. "It's scary, how fast you came up with that."

I lean closer.

"You want scary? Try this: If, for any reason, I find out you've been lying to me all this time, I will out you to them all. I'm pretty sure that would have 'serious consequences.' "

He steps away, and I brush past him.

Five minutes later we're heading down the street after a quick stop at the tourist agency to book ferry passes. We grab sandwiches at an outdoor café—cheese and tomato baguettes that would be considered understuffed by American standards—and take them down to the water to eat. A breeze is blowing in from the ocean, and though it isn't cold, it's bracing enough to remind me that I'm alive. Right now, for this moment. And I'm ravenous. Impossibly, I eat the entire thing, wash it down with a bottle of Fanta.

"Cres island, you said?" Luka asks. I nod. "That doesn't make sense. The Progeny don't usually hide in underpopulated areas."

"He called himself a hermit, but he's Progeny. I could feel him coming a block away."

Luka frowns as we walk up the road past several

small boutiques toward some larger hotels. It feels good to move, to lengthen my stride and walk—fast. Despite the fatigue and drain of the last several days, I suddenly feel like I could run.

"You need to burn," Luka says, his long legs keeping up easily with mine.

"What?"

"Some energy. You're amped. But we don't have time or gear to swim." He looks around.

"Is that what I used to do?" I say. My mind is instantly back in Maine the morning I woke with damp hair. Is that what I was doing? The reason I swam to retrieve the cross from the truck instead of taking the johnboat?

"Anytime you could."

We near the driveway of a boutique hotel. From the sidewalk I can see the swimming pool with the broad dining deck looking right out over the ocean.

"There," Luka says, pointing to a taxi preparing to pull in.

"What?"

"The doorman called that cab for a guest. Get him to take us instead."

A minute later we're in the back of the cab and the edge is off. We ride the twenty minutes to Rijeka past magnificent homes facing the water with gates of climbing vines, window boxes full of flowers.

I think back again to the way Ivan and the

others looked at me, as though I were the ghost of my mother. Recall what Ivan said about forgetting who I am and wonder how I'm ever supposed to remember in the shadow of her dubious celebrity.

And I can't stop hearing Claudia's statement that it might be better if I had truly died.

The ferry landing in the port city of Rijeka is a curving stretch of road. By the time we arrive, it is filled with cars lined all the way up the hill so far that we can't even see the ferry itself. Farther down, several people have gotten out of their vehicles.

The driver is saying something, lifting the hand that was dangling over the wheel a moment ago to gesture in the direction of the bay.

"There is some problem," he says and then clucks his tongue at the rearview mirror as the lane fills with more cars behind us.

"Stay here," Luka says, getting out. I watch him walk twenty yards down the road to get a good look at the dock.

The driver is becoming impatient, sighing and gesturing to the meter.

"Don't worry about that," I say, not sure if he understands me. *This is the only place you need to be.* A moment later, he turns off the engine and steps out of the cab for a smoke as a few cars farther down negotiate tight turns and begin to move back up the road.

170

I lose sight of Luka a few minutes later and find myself staring out the window, drumming my fingers against my knee. At last I can sit still no longer and get out of the cab, start walking down the road.

When I reach the bend, the scene opens below me: white police vans blocking the landing, blue lights flickering in the early evening. I hurry several steps, trying to see what's happening. There are people in front of the dock craning to see around the police blockade.

A hand on my shoulder. Luka.

"We need to go," he says.

"What's going on?" I say, eyes glued to the growing crowd. The police don't seem to be breaking up a fight or arresting anyone. Just a few officers keeping the passengers back while others talk to what look like the captain and some ferry workers. And one lone car in the gaping hull of the ferry itself.

Luka pulls me by the elbow. I yank my arm away.

"This is the last ferry. We have to get to—"

"There's been a murder. We have to get you out of here. Now."

Just then a murmur passes through a group of people standing ten feet away from us. I turn back in time to see a covered stretcher emerge from the hull, two uniformed men wheeling it toward the back of a van.

The tremor, when it starts, begins in my knees. Luka seizes me by the arm and walks me swiftly toward the cab. He spots the driver, who has wandered down to get a look for himself, and says something to him, gesturing to the car.

Back at the cab, Luka climbs into the back seat after me.

"You don't think that—" I can't get the words out.

"The police were waiting when the ferry got back. Someone with a car never got off on the island."

The 7:30 ferry. The same one Ivan was taking back to Cres.

My mind races as I try to remember if I knew anything about Ivan having a car in Opatija. Well, there's one good way to find out for sure whether Ivan's safe. I look for my pack and, as I do, realize Luka is frantically searching around us.

The backpacks are gone.

"Have you seen our bags? Our things?" he says to the driver.

The driver shakes his head, answering in Croatian, and gestures to where he was standing outside.

"I got out last," I say, stunned. "I got out after he did. I left them in here."

Luka curses, shoves out of the car to look in the trunk and then along the road. A moment later he's talking to the people in the car in front of us, gesturing in our direction.

I was out of the cab for what—ten minutes? Fifteen? How long did I stare at the body being wheeled into the van?

"Please," I say to the driver urgently. He's backed to the very edge of the shoulder and is cranking the steering wheel. "Can I use your phone?"

My hands are starting to shake. I have to redial the number twice.

This time it is not picked up on the first ring, or even the second or third. By the fifth ring, I feel sick.

It is answered on the sixth.

"Hello?" I say. "Ivan? Are you there? Are you all right?"

Silence.

And then: "Hallo, Audra."

It isn't Ivan.

17

"Who is this?" I demand, heart pounding against my ribs. "Who are you?"

The call clicks off.

The cab door opens and Luka gets back in. "They're gone," he says grimly. "No one's seen them." And then he notices the phone tremoring in my hand. "Did you reach him?"

"Someone else answered," I say.

The driver has finally managed to get us pointed across the road and is about to pull forward into the other lanewhen a light shines through the back window, right in my face. I shield my eyes. The light disappears. Someone pounds on the window.

Luka lunges across me to lock the door, tells the driver to go.

"Wait!" I say, unlocking the door. Hands from the outside pull it open.

"What are you doing?" Luka shouts, and I practically feel him prepare to launch through the door at the figure outside. At the sight of Claudia, he pulls up short.

"Hurry!" she says, grabbing my arm.

"What are you doing here?"

The driver shouts; Claudia snaps back and then launches into a diatribe that culminates with her

174

throwing several kuna at him. A moment later he seems to apologize. Too profusely. And I sense she's worked her Progeny ways on him, though I have no idea what she's just said.

"He cheated your meter," she says as we move away. A lie—for Luka's sake, I assume.

We trek up the hill after Claudia as one car after another pulls from the line below us.

"Have you heard from Ivan?" I say.

"I did." Her eyes dart to Luka.

"Where is he? Is he okay?"

"Come," she says, and though her tone is brisk, her face is pale.

She leads us farther up the hill to a car idling on the side of the road. Piotrek's behind the wheel. We get in, and Claudia turns around in the front seat. She looks younger in the dark without her black sunglasses, and far more human.

"So this is the friend," she says, as Piotrek pulls ahead of the traffic.

"Luka," I say.

"Well, Luka, I'm sorry to say you have come at a very bad time." She slides a meaningful look to me.

"Any idea what happened?" Luka asks tightly, well aware, I know, that he isn't supposed to know anything about this.

"I am afraid for the worst. Ivan has a history of bad company. It appears the past may have caught up to him tonight."

"You mean like the mafia?"

"Well, he was from Serbia."

"How did you know to come for us?" I ask.

"We were headed to Karlovac when Ivan called to say he thought he was being followed and to get you away. We came as quickly as we could." She glances at Luka. "Ivan's old associates have a habit of going after their victims' friends." She turns forward, and I can hear her exhale an unsteady breath.

"I tried his phone," I say. "Someone else answered."

Luka says, "If someone killed him on the ferry, they did it on the way over. They'd still be on the island."

"You know your way around," Piotrek says, silent until now. "But your accent is Slovakian."

"I studied in Croatia—it's where we met." He takes my hand. "Before the mess of Audra's ex showing up, of course, and everything since."

For a moment there's nothing but the sound of the car whizzing down the road. And then I realize we are headed not back toward Opatija but east.

"Where are we going?" I say.

"We go to Karlovac and then Zagreb," Piotrek says, glancing at me in the rearview mirror.

"No. We can't! Ivan had something to give me. Something from my mother, maybe. I need it."

"It isn't safe," Claudia says.

"You don't understand—"

"No, *you* don't understand. Ivan lived in Lubenice. There are only two old ladies and hardly any tourists this time of year. You will stand out. And we cannot stay in Rijeka."

"Actually, I would think they'd expect us to be running as far from Rijeka as possible," Luka says slowly. And I suppose he should know, being a hunter himself.

"Whoever answered Ivan's phone knew it was me," I say. "They said my name." I don't need to tell her that Ivan's killer by now knows everything Ivan himself did—including the fact that we had planned to meet him in Cres tonight. The thought makes my skin prickle, because it means they now know everything he did about me.

Piotrek exchanges a glance with Claudia. He says something in another language, which I expect Claudia to snap at. But she murmurs instead and covers her mouth. And I realize that, for as steely as she appeared earlier, she, too, has been badly shaken by tonight.

A minute later she makes a call. After a few brief exchanges I can't make out, she nods to Piotrek. The car slows and pulls off onto a side street. Moments later, we're headed back to Rijeka and Claudia has pulled the chip from her phone.

In the darkness, Luka has not let go of my hand. And I realize that whoever killed Ivan now knows that I'm traveling with someone, even if

177

they don't know his name. And I'm not certain if that is a good or a bad thing.

"I didn't tell you that I met Claudia and Piotrek earlier," I say to Luka. "They came with Ivan."

"Yes," Claudia says. "I promised our friends in Zagreb that I would confirm that she is alive before they go to the trouble of planning a celebration."

"Ivan could have told you that," I say. "I think you wanted to see me yourself . . . because you know me."

Her head turns, her perfect profile illuminated by the headlights of passing cars. "So clever, always," she murmurs. "Even with no memory you are hard to fool. Welcome back, Audra."

18

"I called Ivan a liar when he told me you were alive," Claudia says, turned sideways in the front seat. "But I admit I hoped he was right. Piotrek would not agree to come, said anywhere within a hundred kilometers of Ivan was too dangerous." I know she really means within a hundred kilometers of *me*, though of course she can't say so in front of Luka. I'm a little surprised; somehow I thought it was Claudia, not Piotrek, who called the shots.

"In the end, I had to see for myself," she says.

I think back to the phone conversation that just took place. She was checking in with someone in Zagreb. She might have wanted to see me, but she was indeed confirming I was alive to someone else.

"I'm sorry, but how did we know one another?" I say.

"We were friends," she says coolly.

"You'll have to tell me all about that."

"In the meantime, we have a small problem," Luka says. "Our backpacks were stolen from the cab. Our money, passports, phones are gone."

"We'll get you new ones," Piotrek says. "Under different names. It's better under the circumstances, yes?"

"That seems a little shady. Shouldn't we go to

179

the embassy?" Luka frowns, though I know that's the last thing he would advise.

"Not if you don't want to be taken in for questioning. Audra has ties to Ivan. Better that we call friends."

Piotrek and Claudia are in fast conversation by the time Piotrek parks in front of a ship anchored in the harbor. Some kind of maritime hostel, judging by the sign.

I'm confused. "You don't know anyone we could stay with? I mean, we just had everything stolen." Where's the so-called underground?

Claudia's look is droll. "We're far less likely to be noticed here than in a neighborhood. Besides. We're not exactly checking in at the front desk. Wait here." They get out of the car and head toward the entrance ramp.

The minute they're out of sight I cover my face with my hands. I'm shaking. Luka slides closer, lays an arm around me.

Don't go digging. Others' lives depend on it.

I was right. And Piotrek is right; no one around me is safe.

"He's dead because of me," I say, breath ragged.

Luka pulls me against him. "He knew the risks. He chose to come."

"He was going to tell me everything." My words catch in my throat. I feel like I'm having some kind of breakdown. "He said he had something—something for me."

180

And now, whatever it is, *they* have it. Whatever he knew and meant to tell me has been harvested. They know it now.

"I wonder if I was right, saying we should come back here," Luka murmurs.

"How'd they find Ivan? He was experienced—older. He was smart."

"I don't know. This whole thing feels off."

I glance up at a movement in the parking lot. Claudia. I drag a sleeve across my eyes.

A moment later the car door opens. "Rooms, on the house," Claudia says. "You're 205."

"Wow. How'd you manage that?" Luka says, if only for her benefit.

"A very helpful housekeeper."

We get out of the car and she hands us a key card and a couple of disposable toothbrushes. "Wait a few minutes and then let yourself in. We'll come get you in the morning."

Apparently the bad blood between Claudia and me runs deep enough that she doesn't want to bunk with us. And literally, there are four bunk beds in our IKEA-inspired room in primary yellow and white.

I slump into the metal desk chair, aware of Luka standing at the window, staring out at the water. He's purposefully kept the room light off, cracking the bathroom door just enough that I can see his silhouette against the moonlit harbor.

"We shouldn't have come. This is my fault," he says.

"Do you think Ivan knew his hunter?"

"I don't know."

"What do you get? For making a kill, I mean. A non-botched one."

He shrugs. "An executive position somewhere. A hefty lottery win. Who knows?"

"How do you know you won't just end up with a bullet in the back for your effort?"

"You don't," he says hollowly. "But it doesn't matter. Because you believe in it so much . . . you'd do it even without the reward."

I lean over, cover my face. Steps sound across the floor. And then he's kneeling beside the chair and clasping me tightly by the hands.

"You were supposed to be safe here. As soon as we figure out the passport thing, we leave."

"To go where?"

"The Australian bush. The Maldives." He brushes my hair from my forehead. "I'll build a hut. You'll dive for oysters. Or a rain forest in South Africa. Where the biggest thing we'll worry about is getting worms under our skin."

"That's so gross."

He laughs softly.

I look at him. "And they wouldn't find us there? In the jungle?"

He's quiet.

"Does it even matter where we go?"

"We'll move around. But right now, we just need to get you to the underground or wherever Claudia and Piotrek can keep you out of sight until we get those passports."

"Us, you mean."

"They may not trust me. They probably won't. And they'll be able to protect you right now better than I can. Much as I hate to admit it."

"You're a very convincing liar," I whisper.

"Because I'm telling you the truth."

My gaze settles on his lips. "I want to know something."

He looks up at me.

Courage fails. "Can I have the first shower?"

I lock myself in the bathroom. By the time the spray hits my hair, my face has already crumpled. I slump against the fiberglass wall.

My name is Audra Ellison. I am in a country I do not remember, with a man I barely know and who, by all accounts, I should not trust. My only tie to real answers has just died because of me. Does that make me an accomplice to murder? Am I naïve for wanting to believe Luka—not because he says he'll protect me but because having no one to trust is worse than the thought of dying? I thought yesterday I had never felt so alone. But now, in this tightening knot of pretenses, I feel more alone than before.

No wonder I wanted to forget it all. Given the choice, I'd go back and forget these last five days and wake up in a hut on some beach, none the wiser.

But despite the fact that I can't imagine another day like this—let alone a year or an entire life . . . I also can't imagine dying without answers.

Or living with this much fear.

Today I spoke with a man in the last hours of his life. Tomorrow that could be me.

The TV is on when I emerge from the bathroom. I haven't allowed myself to consider the thing I nearly asked Luka before I locked myself in there. But I am painfully aware that life is far too short.

I find him slumped in the chair. I think he looks nearly as lost as I felt sitting there.

"Before I went into the Center," I say, finding it much easier without him looking at me, "what were we—"

"Audra," he says, sitting up, gaze riveted to the image on the wall. "Is that him?"

I glance at the television and have to stare to reconcile the picture with the grizzled man I met. The man in the corner of the screen is clean-shaven with hair neatly cut. More hot college professor than hermit.

Go, Ivan.

"Yes."

Though I can't read Croatian, the name beneath the photo is plain enough: Imre Tomić. I glance at Luka, puzzled.

So I'm not the only one living under an alias. 'Course, Ivan's not exactly living anymore.

The image shrinks as the telecast shifts to earlier footage of the ferry: a lone, white Peugeot in the hull, paramedics packing up. Luka slides to the edge of his seat.

There's a woman being interviewed as blue police lights flash in the background. Though I'm weirdly picking up a few words—a remnant from my time in Croatia before?—I can't make it all out. "What's she saying?"

"A man tried to revive Ivan—Imre." He pauses a moment and then translates: "And when he failed to resuscitate him, stayed to comfort him as he died. She doesn't know who it was, he left as police arrived. She's calling him an angel."

The video shifts to a still shot taken from a security camera. A man in the act of fleeing, only part of his face captured on camera.

But I know the angles of that face. Recognize the curve of that ear.

Rolan.

Luka gets to his feet, paces away with a curse.

"I knew this was off," he says. "One hunter, one mark. Rolan was hunting *you*. But if he's just killed Ivan . . ."

"Then someone else is hunting me."

Either that, or there is no need for a replacement. I slide a glance to Luka.

"Something's wrong. Something changed," he

185

says. He's agitated, head bowed, knuckles pressed against his lips.

"The woman they interviewed," I say slowly. "Why would she think that, about Rolan being an angel?" I recall the way he recited from the Book of Daniel, the way I equated Watchers with angels.

"You have to hold the head in your hands," he murmurs. "That's why it looked like he was comforting him."

An angel of death, then.

This is on me. It's all on me. *I* called Ivan from Rolan's phone—and then came straight to Croatia to meet him. I've seen no trace of Rolan since we ran him off the road, but all that tells me is that he isn't acting alone.

Why, why did Ivan arrange to meet me? Luka was right: He knew the dangers better than anyone, especially where I was concerned. Why would he risk his life?

I'm sorry, I whisper, if only in my mind, not knowing if he can hear me.

I'm already beneath the covers of the top bunk when Luka emerges from his shower. I watch him pad to the door, check the lock, and then wedge the desk chair beneath the handle. Does he do this every night before he sleeps?

"Luka," I say as he reaches for the bathroom light. He glances up.

"Am I safe with you?"

"With me, or from me, you mean?" He sounds worn.

"Either."

He looks away. "Yes."

I turn onto my side facing the wall, pillow already damp beneath my hair.

"Wake me up if you can't sleep," he says and turns out the light.

He undresses in the dark. The frame of the bunk shudders briefly as he slides into bed. I listen to him sigh. Imagine, even, that he has folded his arms behind his head to stare up at the bottom of my mattress. And I wonder if I'll ever be free from fear again.

19

Breath cools my ear in gentle waves. I am instantly awake, staring wide-eyed in the darkness. Aware of the arm beneath my head, the one curled over the coverlet around me. Smell of skin.

My name is Audra Ellison. I am in a marine hostel in Rijeka, Croatia . . . and I am not in bed alone.

If I close my eyes, I can almost pretend that these arms are as safe as they feel. And I do, for all of three seconds. Any longer and I will stay.

I inch up with supreme slowness, glance back with only my eyes, not daring to turn my head. Slide out from under arm and coverlet both. Reach a foot for the ladder, find the floor instead. I'm on the bottom bunk.

But I'm clothed, at least—having gone to bed fully dressed beneath the covers.

Luka's breath is slow and even. I ease up from the edge of the bed, swipe my sneakers from the floor nearby. Glance at the clock.

6:11 A.M.

There's a light blinking silently on the phone—a message I don't dare check. I pad to the door, feel for the chair. Lift it out from beneath the handle and set it carefully aside. Grab my hat off the desk, pull it onto my head. Turn the lock with

188

painful slowness and a soft, alarming *snick* before depressing the handle.

I slip out the door and catch it until it quietly clicks. The moment it does, I turn down the hallway—

And run right into Claudia.

She's leaning there, shoulder against the wall. Her arms are crossed. Gone, the sweater dress, replaced by a pair of jeans rolled around the ankles and a simple shirt I recognize as Piotrek's. All of it is. His fedora dangles from her fingertips.

"Good morning, Audra," she says and smiles. Her hair is wet. "I take it you're not just slipping out for coffee."

I purse my lips.

She lifts her chin, glances at me sidelong, and then sets the fedora on her head. "We'd better hurry if we're going to make the first ferry," she says and starts off down the hall.

After a stunned beat, I tug my shoes on and start after her, noting that her butt looks better in her brother's jeans than most women's do in yoga pants.

There's a cab waiting at the bottom of the ramp. A moment later, we're headed down the road.

"So . . . was Piotrek planning to cross-dress today?"

"It will keep him put until we get back. There's a message waiting for Luka when he wakes up. Maybe it will stop them both from running off and doing something almost as stupid as we are."

"How'd you manage to shower without waking Piotrek?" I ask.

"I didn't." When I look pointedly at her wet hair, she smiles. "I enjoy a bracing swim before dawn. Don't you?"

My adrenaline is running high by the time we arrive at the ferry. The line is shorter this time, the ferry itself—industrial white with Korean lettering on its side—open for business as though it had never stopped for the night. The driver takes the cab directly into the hull as more cars file in behind us.

We climb the metal stairs to the main deck. I glance below just once, picturing an old white Peugeot sitting alone in that metal cavern, a body slumped at the wheel. I can see the spot from here.

The ride to Cres isn't half as magical for us as it seems to be for the couple snapping photos from the railing. The island, obscured by haze, creeps closer until it becomes a hulking coastline of stone and shrub.

Claudia's phone rings. Standing three feet away, I can hear the irate enunciation of every word on the other end. Piotrek.

Claudia's tone is strangely conciliatory—even as what sounds like a chair crashes in the background.

"How mad is he?" I say when she hangs up.

"He'll let Luka know you're with me. And he's very mad. Rightfully so. On top of everything, I took his phone since I got rid of mine. We'll have to get rid of this one now that he's called it from the hostel."

"He's your brother. He has to forgive you," I say. "He's probably more mad about having to wear a dress."

She turns to face me against the rail. "You don't know anything, do you? His job is to protect me. With his life, if necessary. And I've just thrown that in his face. For you."

"I didn't ask you to come!"

"Yes, but now that Ivan's dead you need me."

"He's your brother, not your warden."

"He's my sibling. Not my brother."

"What's the difference?"

"I have no brother. He's my sibling by choice."

"I don't get it."

"The hunters target females because the legacy passes through them."

"How can you say that? They just killed Ivan."

"Yes, for what he knows! You really don't remember anything, do you?"

"No, I don't," I snap.

"A male line dies on its own—any children he has with a normal woman are not Utod. His only value to the hunters is what he may know. They will always target a female first to halt the legacy—the gifts she passes to her children. So she adopts a sibling if she doesn't have one to protect her. And that bond will be deeper than if they had come from the same womb."

"Do they ever get . . . involved? I mean if they're not really related?"

"Sometimes, of course. But it becomes complicated. And makes both parties vulnerable." There's something like reproach in her gaze. I haven't forgotten her statement that I wasn't worth risking more lives.

I decide to just come right out with the question. "How did we know one another, Claudia?"

She studies me for a moment.

"We met in the Budapest court—"

"Court . . ." I recall Ivan using that term as well.

"The Utod underground."

"Which is in Budapest."

"In many cities. But Budapest, naturally. And Zagreb. The Prince of Zagreb himself sent me to Opatija to see for him if it is true that you are alive," she says with a tilt of her chin.

I lift my brows slightly. "Why would he care?"

"Really, Audra, why did you do this?" She truly seems troubled. "No. You don't know," she answers for herself and shakes her head.

"No," I say quietly. "I don't. So we met in Budapest."

"Through a woman named Katia, yes. Piotrek was her biological brother. Her twin."

"Then why is he with you?"

"Because she's dead."

"I'm sorry."

Claudia leans her forearms on the rail, lifts her face to the breeze. "I had just run away from home. I was sixteen. Katia found me digging in trash cans for food. She felt me in that alley, knew what I was. I remember that night, so perfectly. She had just come from court, and I thought she was the most glamorous and exciting girl I had ever seen. She taught me how to survive. I loved Katia. But you were important to her in ways I never understood. I looked to her. She looked to you. I could tell there were secrets between you I never knew." Claudia glances over her shoulder at me.

"What happened?"

"You were the last person to see her the night her hunter found her. You came and took me into hiding with you. Three weeks later, you were gone. But you brought Piotrek to me first, and for that, I suppose I should thank you."

I hear her words, yet somehow I feel like "you're welcome" might get me slapped.

"You don't approve of Luka."

"I saw him with you once, before you disappeared," she says.

"You did?"

"It was obvious you were lovers."

I don't move. I barely breathe.

193

"It's amazing what you learn living as an adopted stray, always looking in from the outside. I had seen Luka with you. I thought he was your hunter. I even warned you."

"Why? Why not wait to see if you were right?"

Her head swivels toward me. "I'm not a murderer, Audra. I only wanted you to leave. And after Katia was killed, you did leave. Two more Utod died—friends of Katia's—three months later. And then Andre, Katia's lover, disappeared. I thought he was dead until we heard this summer he committed suicide before his memory could be stripped and served to the Historian like meat." Her lips curl. "A month ago, everything in Zagreb fell apart. And I realized it wasn't because Katia or Andre was dead, but because *you were*."

Her gray eyes are as chilly as the sea. And I can't tell if she's wounded or if she hates me.

"What happened?"

"Piotrek and I stayed on in Zagreb. After the underground broke, it became the safest place to be. I was angry at you. I didn't understand how you could throw it—us—all away. Not when you had access to what you did."

"Access to what? I don't even know why I did it, Claudia."

Her laugh is brittle as glass. "No one does. But what Ivan said is true. He died for you, Audra!"

"Don't say that."

194

"It's true! Many people have died for you. And because of you. The underground court has just returned to Zagreb, and you have much to make right."

I turn and look out over the water. I don't blame her. I don't like her much, but I feel for her.

I also can't help her.

"There are a lot of rumors," she says, leaning closer. "That you had information from your mother. Maybe even the diary itself. A lot of people feel betrayed. For every person who talks about you as the daughter of Amerie Szabo, there's one that calls you a traitor. But Ivan had *unshakable* faith in you. Enough to risk his life. And now Ivan is dead. So here I am. I'm going to help you." There are actually tears in her eyes, but her jaw is like steel. "And you will prove that his faith, at least, wasn't misplaced."

I don't know how to tell her that I can't prove anything to anyone. That I'm only here because I don't know how to go back to—or move forward with—my life like this. This isn't about some Progeny agenda or righting some centuries-old wrong. It's about staying alive.

She pushes away from the rail. "I'm going to get us some coffee."

I watch her go to the snack bar inside. And for a moment, I really do wish I could be what she and Ivan hoped I was, once.

But that girl is gone.

• • •

The brightly colored buildings of Cres go right to the quay, their walls rising from the water to red-tiled roofs. Boats are docked everywhere. Rolan would have had no problem returning to Rijeka, or anywhere along the coast, in the middle of the night. Might even now be in Zagreb. In that regard, Luka was right.

Claudia has *suggested* the cabdriver spend a few hours wandering the outdoor market, taking breakfast at one of the seaside cafés. And he actually looks quite content as we drive off in his car.

Claudia takes us through the center of town past restaurants, produce and fish markets. And then we're headed south toward the western ridge of the island as I navigate the map on her phone.

It rings as I'm peering at the screen. I glance at Claudia, who takes it from me. Her answer is abrupt.

"Yes. She's fine," she says. "We'll call you soon. Good-bye." She hangs up just as the voice on the other end demands to speak with me.

Luka. No doubt going out of his gourd. Which I feel bad about—unless, of course, he's been lying to me.

"Well, that was rude."

"Slovaks."

I don't say that I meant her.

"How well did you know Ivan?" I ask.

196

"Not as well as you," she says, the reproach back in her voice. She adds, a beat later, "But enough to mourn for him."

We pass sheep grazing by the roadside, a few men in woolen coats who look about as old as the stony soil itself. The road is more than winding; it is a labyrinth ascending higher and higher until the ocean has all but dropped away beneath us.

When we finally arrive at Lubenice, I am slightly queasy from the drive, but awed by the view. The sun has begun to burn off the haze and as I stand at the very edge of the ancient fort town, I think one could practically paraglide from here back to the mainland in an emergency.

A tiny whitewashed chapel stands near the edge of the settlement, which doesn't even qualify as a town; only a few houses look like they're actually in use. Everything seems to be made of the same white stone as the island itself, the rock that once supported an eastern gate having long since tumbled back down the hill. Shrubs grow in crannies in walls, grapevines and bougainvillea beautifully threatening to reduce anything still standing to rubble in coming years. A lone tree stands in the town center, which is nothing more than a cobbled courtyard between buildings.

"Now where?" I say, glancing at her.

Claudia sets her jaw and looks up, gaze lighting on an old woman setting a pillow to air in the window above us.

"*Dobro jutro*!" she calls up to the woman in a voice more cordial than I've ever heard from her.

The woman echoes her greeting. Claudia asks her a question, and the woman gestures with a rambling and increasingly agitated answer. After several minutes the older woman abruptly stops, wipes her eyes, and disappears.

"What just happened?" I say.

"She's upset—she heard the news about Ivan this morning. She says he moved in earlier this month to the room above the wool museum back there."

"Wool museum?"

"It's open only during the summer. Ivan's been renovating a wall on the edge of the cliff and made some repairs for the two old ladies living here. They liked him very much."

I follow her between buildings toward the edge of the hill.

"She said two men were here last night," Claudia says. "She heard them drive in and assumed one of them was Ivan, that he was up late drinking with a friend. Obviously, she has no idea we don't drink."

"We don't?"

"It dulls the senses."

"Which is why most people do it," I say, droll.

"It dulls *persuasion*. And we can't afford to be without our gifts," she says pointedly. "The old woman said she went to check on Ivan this morning when he didn't arrive for breakfast at her house. The latch was broken on his door."

We come to the small building near the far gate. Claudia steps to the threshold, pauses to listen, and then swings the door wide.

What little furniture there is looks in order, samples of brightly colored wool crafts and some kids' artwork hung neatly on the wall. I glance up at the open staircase and start toward it. Claudia catches me by the wrist, listens for a moment, and moves up the stairs ahead of me.

We emerge into a sparse apartment with a desk and a single rumpled cot. A dresser stands with its top drawer open, but nothing looks openly ransacked. I search the desk, find pens, a ferry schedule, a calendar with nothing written on it. In the dresser, nothing but a few pieces of clothing that look like they came from a secondhand shop. I rifle through pockets, feel along hems, check the linings. Finally I pull out the drawers, upend them one by one before descending on the cot. Empty-handed, I turn out the small cabinet in the bathroom.

Sweat dampening my nape, I retrace my steps across the floor. None of the boards are loose. With a last look around me, I hurry down the stairs to flip over the rug, overturn a chair, even stick my fingers in a pair of green woolen slippers on the wall—all the while knowing that anything Ivan would have hidden has long since been found.

I can't breathe; the air in the old building is stifling. I lurch out the front door into the unforgiving sun.

"Audra," Claudia says, following me outside. A breeze blows up the hillside smelling faintly of sage as bees buzz around a patch of purple flowers near the gate.

"Ivan was smart. I didn't know him, but I could tell. He would've known his memory was at risk . . . found a way—"

"Audra!"

"What?"

"You're right. Which is why we aren't looking for anything hidden, but for what seems to be missing."

"How was he supposed to give me anything?" I demand. "It would have to be something or somewhere he himself couldn't have known! How could he say he was going to tell me everything? How could he?"

"Audra." She lays her hand on my arm. "Ivan was very good. Very experienced. He was nearing the end of his age."

"What do you mean?" He couldn't have been more than thirty-five.

She tilts her head. "The Utod lose their gifts in their thirties."

I blink. "You mean they can no longer—"

"Yes. Don't speak of it here." She gestures

200

toward the apartment. "Whatever Ivan had for you wasn't taken from here as far as I can tell. Which means it's waiting somewhere else."

"How do we know whoever killed him hasn't gotten to it first? They have his memory!"

"There are ways. Even with computers, though it's risky. But Ivan was old-fashioned. Which is far safer when it comes to information, if not to those involved."

"What does *that* mean?"

"It means if we cannot find anything on our own, we must wait for it to find us."

But I don't know how long I can wait.

I had thought the crumbling buildings with their vines and shrubs growing out of every cranny hauntingly quaint when we arrived. Now they look as abandoned as Ivan's apartment, as forgotten by the ages as the stones themselves.

The old woman calls down as we return through the courtyard.

"*Da?*" Claudia says. After a brief exchange, Claudia glances at me sidelong.

"What?" I ask.

"Come. We pray for Ivan."

A little late for that, I think, but follow her anyway.

The chapel, though tiny, has enough wooden pews to cram nearly forty into its rustic space. Two figurines sit on minor altars on either side of the rounded apse: the blue-and-white-robed

Virgin Mary and a man holding the baby Jesus in his right arm, lilies in his left.

I wait, awkwardly, as Claudia genuflects, and I wonder if I should leave her alone. But instead of sliding into a pew, she moves toward the second altar and considers the figure draped in wooden rosaries on top of it.

"The woman said to me, 'At least the last time I saw him, he had just come from mass.' So she is confident that he is in heaven. But Ivan"—Claudia glances at me—"was not religious."

She runs her fingers beneath the white cloth draped over the altar's edges.

"Which saint is that?" I ask.

"This is Saint Anthony, the patron of lost people and things. Forgive me, Saint Anthony," she murmurs, as she gets on her knees and peers beneath, practically looking up the robe of the saint. A moment later she flips up the corner of the cloth to reveal a small slot carved into the altar itself.

I get down beside her, slide my fingers into the narrow space. "What is this?" I say.

"I think . . . a mailbox," she says.

But whatever was there is gone.

Of course it is. Anything Ivan might have left has already been picked up—either by the so-called mailman or most recently by Ivan's killer. I slump into the front pew. So much for Saint Anthony and his lilies.

I look to Mary as though for guidance, and then at the purple flowers beside her. They are the same ones as on the hill.

My gaze shifts to the vase beside Saint Anthony. The fuchsia petals are lettuced around the edges. Fresh.

And not from Lubenice.

"Claudia," I say slowly as she pushes up from her knees. "Who conducts mass here?"

"A priest from Cres town, I suppose." She shrugs.

That could be any number of people. But that isn't the right question.

"Who was Saint Anthony?"

"I told you, the patron saint of—"

"Before that. Who was he?"

"Saint Anthony of Padua? A Catholic priest. Franciscan." She glances at me.

Ten minutes later we are speeding down the hill past miles of rocky terrain and oblivious sheep seasoning their own meat on a diet of wild sage.

When we finally reach the south edge of Cres town, Claudia slows near the cemetery.

"There." She nods toward a brick building across the street. A monastery.

It is bathed in flashing blue light, surrounded by police cars.

20

"This is very bad," Claudia whispers.

For the first time since my arrival, we are in agreement.

I exhale a breath, take stock. Three empty patrol cars mean the police are inside—except for the officer standing at the entrance beneath the crest of two crossed arms. A round window with a blue stained-glass cross is set in the brick face above it and the broad front walk is lined with trees I recognize as myrtles, each of them exploding with fuchsia flowers.

I start to get out of the car. Claudia grabs my arm. It is the first time I think I have seen her truly afraid.

"Audra, no."

"You said yourself Ivan was smart. If he meant to give me something but knew the danger he was in, he wouldn't have brought it with him. He would have left it at the chapel to be picked up and stashed someplace or given to someone he wasn't aware of. Someone in *there* knows what and where it is."

"Can't you see? Something terrible has happened here. It's too late!"

"We don't know that! You wanted to know that Ivan's faith in me wasn't misplaced. Well, I want to know that he didn't die for nothing!" I say it with more bravado than I feel. In fact, it's desperation.

She purses her lips and then nods, though I sense that she may be shaking. Crossing herself, she gets out of the car. Mutters, "Piotrek is going to kill me."

A small crowd has gathered on the edge of the street. As we reach the door, the officer—a woman—moves to block our way.

Claudia steps ahead of me to talk to her, tone as imperious as ever. She pulls her ferry pass from her pocket, holds it up like a badge.

A moment later she says something to me in Croatian as though I speak the language. And then we're pushing our way through the door.

"That wasn't horrible," I murmur, following after her.

We step into a colonnaded courtyard, the grassy middle of which has been set with chairs, as though for a lecture or some kind of concert.

I hear static of walkie-talkies somewhere beyond the short corridor to the right. Claudia pulls me down the long side of the colonnade to the left, into a reception office. It's filled with pamphlets in Croatian about some kind of art exhibit, a calendar of events. There's a door on the other end of the room, but when I try it, it's locked.

"Audra," Claudia says behind me.

"We have to find the priest who did the mass. Where are the monks?"

"Murdered."

I turn to stare at her. She's pale.

"The officer told me when she let us through. Three of them, sometime last night. It's too late."

I refuse to accept this. I go to the door and begin to pound on it. Claudia hisses at me to stop. I bang on it again.

A few seconds later the door unlocks and a monk comes into the office. He looks startled to see us, and I realize he thought we were police. He's wearing a brown robe, white belt around his waist, almost exactly like the statue of Saint Francis out front. But my attention is focused on one item: the tao cross dangling from his neck.

He says something with quiet urgency in what sounds more like Italian than Croatian, and I look at Claudia.

"What did he say?" I demand.

"Please," he says in pained English, "there has been a tragedy. I am sorry, you must leave!"

"Who conducts mass at Lubenice?" I say. "Is he still alive?"

"Pardon?" he says. Desperation rises inside me.

"Who conducts the mass? Did you know Ivan? The man living in Lubenice? Did you take anything from the chapel?"

Tell me!

He lifts his hands, looks to Claudia as though for rescue. "I'm sorry—" he says.

Claudia intervenes. I don't know what she's

saying, but all I can think is, *It's here. Ivan wanted me here.*

"Is there someone else we can talk to?" I interrupt.

I recognize the cool lilt of Claudia's voice, the way the sun through the window seems to seek her where she stands. Her skin in that light is flawless, lending her an ethereal quality that causes the monk to gape. But then something else snares my attention. At first I think it's a sound, some strain of a distant chorus that lifts the hairs on my arms. But no one is singing, of course. The next moment there is nothing in this room—not even the monk himself—as compelling as the door he just emerged from. I stride toward it and yank it open.

I push into the corridor as the room falls away behind me. There are offices to my right and left, but my gaze is fastened on what looks like a narthex farther down the hall. I skirt past an open door and then run the fifty feet to the chapel, heart thudding.

It is, I think, the most serene space I've been in since leaving my tiny cabin in Maine. Or would be, under different circumstances. But unlike my cabin, it is austere, imposing. Not meant for the unwashed world. At first glance it is empty . . . until I notice the single form seated near the front.

I pause as a figure rises from the pew. When he turns, I suck in a breath, though not at his appearance. His face is plain, so devoid of furrows, scars, or even dimples as to be nondescript. His eyes are kind, if not memorable, enough gray in his hair to put him in his late thirties. The kind of man who might look equally unremarkable in an office suit, in a T-shirt on a ball field . . .

. . . or in a monk's robes.

But it is his presence that sends me back a step.

Holy brother of God. It's a Progeny monk.

He moves toward me, the rope around his waist dangling to his knees. I swear I can practically hear the brush of his hem.

He stops three steps from me, peers intently at my face.

"Ivan said you would come," he says, as his presence hits me like a wave.

21

"I am Brother Goran," he says. His head tilts, hazel eyes rapt. Do I imagine it, or has he sucked in a small breath? "And you . . . are Audra Ellison."

"Have—have we met?"

"No," he says strangely. "I have never had the pleasure."

"How do you know who I am?"

"Because you look like your mother."

A chill passes down my arms. Just then a door in the outer hallway closes, echoing all the way to the chapel. His glance is sharp. "We can't speak here," he says. "Quickly. Come with me."

My heart drums in my temples as he leads me toward the back of the chapel and down a narrow stair to a subterranean set of rooms. An overhead light flickers to life, illuminating shelves and floor-to-ceiling cabinets—an archive of sorts, complete with a desk and monitor like some underground library.

"How did you know my mother?" I say when he has closed the door behind us.

"That is a story of another life—one I am afraid we do not have time for now," he says, withdrawing a set of keys from his pocket and unlocking a drawer.

"Is there a short version?" I say. Because at this point, I'll take anything.

To my relief he pauses, turns to look at me, if sadly. "Poor child."

I swallow. "Whatever you know about her, I'd really appreciate hearing it."

He pauses again and seems to consider.

"Your mother was . . . many different things to different people," he says. "But the things she is remembered for will never fully represent who she was. People have a habit of taking one moment, one facet of a life, and painting an entire portrait based on their own experience. We do it without exception, to everyone. To the world. To God. We assign stories to everyone around us out of our own need to feel that we understand someone or some thing. When the truth is that we don't—we can't—know anyone. Because we do not fully know ourselves." He looks at me.

"We like to think we learn people. We really only learn their stories. So here is one for you: Amerie loved rain. The way it made people huddle together—under umbrellas, beneath awnings. The way it stopped traffic. She loved the smell of it better than sun, and could smell a storm hours before it came. She said she loved that it brought her to the now. Because the moment your plans for anything are ruined, you are forced into the present. And for that one, perfect, ruined moment, she did not worry about the future, and the past was washed away."

Fat tears roll down my cheeks. He moves toward me, brushes them away with the back of a finger. And though it is the first human portrait I have ever had of my mother, I almost wish I had never heard it. It was far easier to be angry.

"If you want to know Amerie's story, the short version—which is the only one that matters—it is that she loved you and protected you with her life."

"But how did you know her? I mean, you're a monk."

"I wasn't always a monk," he says with a slight smile. "But now, you've come for something."

"You conducted the mass in Lubenice."

"That man is dead," he says, opening the drawer, "having given his life along with two others in service to our cause. But he was not one of us. His killer could not steal his memory . . . or know that he gave this to me."

He presses an envelope into my hand. "This is yours."

It is far too light. And too small to explain even the first of my questions.

"You were expecting something else."

"No. Yes. I don't know what I was expecting." There's a ruckus from somewhere in the direction of the staircase. A man's voice, and another I recognize as Claudia's. The sound brings me back to the moment as surely as a clap of thunder. Three men have died for the thing in this envelope. Four, counting Ivan.

And possibly hundreds before them.

"The diary," I say abruptly. "Does it exist?"

"If it does . . . that is the key to finding it."

But I don't want what's in this envelope to be about the diary. What I want is safety for those around me. And answers, for myself.

Footsteps on the stair. The door bursts open. Claudia.

"The police," she says, breathless. "They're questioning the brothers. With a picture of you." Her eyes, which are wild, flick to Goran.

"How is that possible?" I say, feeling the color leave my face.

"They're saying you were seen boarding the ferry last night," Claudia says. "With Ivan."

"But that's not true!" I say.

"It doesn't matter what is true," Goran murmurs, moving swiftly toward a closet. Claudia follows him with a gaze.

"And you cannot *persuade* me, friend of Audra," he says, back turned. "Nor do you need to."

"This is Goran," I say to Claudia. The look on her face is weird. "The mailman."

The monk pulls two robes from the closet, pushes them toward us. "Quickly."

I pull the robe over my head, swiftly tie the rope

around my waist. "This way," Goran says, before leading us upstairs.

"Wait here," he says and crosses the hall into an office.

I turn on Claudia. "You tried to *persuade* him?"

"I didn't know," she snaps, tying her rope. "You can't *feel* them when they've been hidden too long, or at all after a certain age. They lose their gifts, like Ivan was beginning to."

But I had felt him distinctly.

Goran reemerges and gestures for us to follow him.

"Did you come from Rijeka?" he asks.

"Yes," I say.

"I will take you myself to Merag, I know a fisherman near there. I will call him to meet us."

He leads us through a small kitchen toward a back door, but pauses before he opens it. "It is twenty meters to the car. You know what to do? I cannot do it myself."

I glance between them, confused.

"You are a man," Claudia says to me. "A monk. That is what anyone outside must see."

Goran opens the door and we step into a day that is far too bright. His stride is crisp as we follow him to the old gray Opel parked in the tiny lot behind the monastery. Ten feet from the car, a policeman steps around the side of the building and hurries after us, shouting for us to stop. I barely refrain from grabbing Claudia's arm,

213

amped nearly out of my skin. I stop long enough to fix him with what I hope is a monkish gaze.

Feel bad for your sins and walk away, dude. And quit looking at porn.

My heart threatens to fail in the three seconds it takes the policeman to wave a weak greeting and turn back the way he came.

We hunch down in the back seat of the car as Goran pulls out of the lot. I can feel the crinkle of the envelope in my pocket as he talks urgently on the phone. Claudia, meanwhile, is dialing up what I assume to be another fit from Piotrek.

"How did you know Ivan?" I ask when Goran finishes his call.

"I didn't, personally, though your mother did. And he did not know I was acting in this capacity or you would now be talking to a corpse and that envelope would be in the Historian's hands. There was a time when no hunter would harm a monk, if only for fear of his soul. Those days are gone, I'm afraid," he says, stopping at a corner. I shrink down lower, will myself to be small. Claudia drops her voice and hangs up a few seconds later.

"The envelope . . . where did Ivan get it?"

"From you, of course."

Claudia stares at me from across the seat. The car turns, accelerates down the road.

"You said your brothers were willing to die for our cause. Why? If Bathory was a monster?"

"It was a Franciscan who helped hide her illegitimate first child—a daughter—before Elizabeth's husband, Ferenc, could have the baby killed. Who ultimately brought her here, to Croatia. The brothers have hidden many of Bathory's descendants, keeping the secret genealogy of children placed for adoption by parents who could not dare raise them . . . At one time even helping those children learn to coexist with their own gifts and excessive energy in the age before pharmaceuticals."

The ADHD. I glance at Claudia. She looks like she's barely holding it together. And I admit, a marathon sprint sounds awfully soothing right about now.

"But you're Progeny."

"Yes. And so I have my own reasons for wanting to help you."

"Because you knew my mother."

"Helping you aids all the Progeny. But yes. Perhaps selfishly I wanted to see Amerie's face again."

A strange, dawning thought. How old is he—nearly forty? "Are you . . ." I'm not sure how to even ask this.

Claudia's brows lift so high they practically crash into her hairline.

"No," he says. "I don't know who your father was. Only that he died nearly ten years ago."

He turns off the road as his phone rings. A

215

moment later he pulls the car to a stop and twists in the seat.

"The boat is there, the blue and white. Quickly." We get out, shed the robes. I embrace him with so many unanswered questions.

As the boat pulls away, I look back at him once where he stands beside the dull gray Opel. Somehow I think I will never see those sturdy shoulders and that reassuring demeanor again.

22

A normal person would appreciate the vivid blue of the Adriatic, the colorful villages nestled on the coast of the even larger Krk island as we skim past, bright houses clustered like pockets of pebbles toppled down a hill. Would be fascinated with the almost perfectly round islet in the bay of that larger island, and the captain's explanation about the monastery that occupies it.

But as the captain takes it upon himself to chatter at length about the island's two-thousand-year-old walls and mile-long bridge connecting it to the mainland, all I can think is that, despite hunching against the gunwale, I feel far too exposed.

That, and I didn't have nearly long enough with Goran—the only living tie to my mother I'm aware of, and the only one capable of even beginning to answer my questions.

I pray he lives long enough for me to find my way back. The minute it's safe, I'm there.

It occurs to me then that I'm neglecting the one piece of information I do have.

The one Ivan died to get to me.

I tear open the envelope to discover a single item: a key on a loop of string. It's new and unremarkable except for an engraving on one side: SOME RISE BY SIN, SOME BY VIRTUE FALL.

I peer inside the envelope, but there is nothing else. I glance at Claudia, who has been watching me. If she's curious, she hasn't asked, and for that I'm grateful. She may be intent on punishing me for abandoning her or Katia or the underground as a whole, but she's no sadist. After being the least informed person in any discussion I've had for days, I need this moment.

I consider the engraving, but of course it doesn't ring a bell, and turn the key over four or five times in my hand.

I have no idea what I'm supposed to do with this or where it came from, let alone what it goes to. And I kick myself for not opening the envelope in front of Goran so I could ask him.

Eventually, I knot the string around a belt loop and tuck the key in my jeans.

Half a mile off the turquoise coast of Rabac, Claudia points in the direction of a beach behind a posh hotel. She makes a brief phone call as the boat motors toward an inlet just past a rocky finger. The moment we pass from view of the beach she glances at me, and tosses the phone overboard. Piotrek's fedora follows. The captain kills the motor, and an instant later she has shed her shoes and stepped onto the gunwale. Her eyes glint at me in the first hint of a real smile I can remember.

"Thank you," I say to the man, hands pressed together. His mouth gapes as a splash sounds behind me. I shed my jacket, drop my hat. "Really. We appreciate it." I toe out of my sneakers and step up onto the wale.

The water is a welcome shock. I swim hard for a full thirty seconds before looking back in time to see the boat turn south. Claudia's laugh sounds, bright as a bell across the water ahead of me.

"It is a good day, Audra!"

"Why?" I shout.

"We're alive!" She wriggles in the water, disappears once beneath the surface before striking out toward shore, and I realize she has just shed Piotrek's pants.

I laugh, as much at her audacity as in relief just to be moving and, yes, alive.

The beach—which is really more of a clearing behind the hotel—is composed entirely of pebbles; there is no white sand here. I walk gingerly the last feet to shore, breathing hard, sodden in wet clothes, my arms covered in goose bumps beneath the bright autumn sun.

A shout sounds from somewhere near the road as two forms appear on the hill. Piotrek waves, and Luka tosses down a bag. Claudia, still dripping, retrieves it, sorts through the contents, and drops a T-shirt, a pair of army green pants, and sandals with the tags still attached in my arms.

"I had Piotrek pick up some things. Come to

think of it, he probably had to send Luka." She smirks.

"You thought of everything," I say, tugging on the pants, which, to my surprise, actually kind of fit, before transferring the key, a few wet bills, and my driver's license to a dry pocket.

She shakes back her hair. "Of course."

I dress quickly, exchanging my wet shirt for the trendy-looking black one.

"Let's not tell Piotrek yet that I got rid of his favorite jeans," she says.

Five minutes later, we've shoved the bag of wet clothes between us in the back seat of the car.

Whatever Piotrek's initial reaction to Claudia's sneaking off without him, he's apparently over it. He murmurs in Croatian as she drapes an arm around him from behind, lifts her hand to kiss it as he pulls onto the road. Meanwhile, Luka has yet to speak to me.

"Find anything?" he says finally, a few kilometers down the road. His jaw is tight, the ends of his hair catching in two days' stubble.

"Not enough."

I stare out the window as we head east, remembering Goran's eyes as he told the story of my mother. Something about her affects him deeply, or did once. And I wonder if she had that effect on everyone.

I wonder, too, why I could sense him when

220

Claudia couldn't. Is it because her father, like Piotrek's, was not Progeny? Both of Ivan's parents were; surely he would have felt Goran fifty feet away, as I did. But Ivan's no longer here for me to ask.

We stop at a gas station in the red-roofed village of Delnice for fuel, coffee, and sandwiches, after which Claudia and Piotrek go in search of new phones. Luka and I find a bench in a small park just off the main street to eat our lunch in silence.

"You know," I say, picking the tomato out of my baguette, "it's not going to help for you to be mad at me."

"I'm not mad," he says and tears a bite out of his sandwich. A minute later he says, "I just don't understand."

"What's not to understand? I need answers."

"You need to stay *safe*. Staying alive is a lot more important than answers, Audra!"

"I had Claudia with me." I don't mention that I had in fact planned on going alone.

"You've known her less than a day!"

"And I've known you for what—a week?"

He exhales a forceful breath, puts down his sandwich, and looks away.

"You know," he says. "In the time we've been together, you and I have had exactly one fight."

"About your sacred duty to kill me?"

He grimaces.

"No. It was when you came back to me." He shakes his head. "Oh my God. I cried like a baby. After months of not knowing whether you were alive . . . When you came back, I said the only way to stay alive was to go on. As though I were still hunting you, and you were on the verge of finding something I was waiting to acquire. Because we didn't dare get found out. And I was happy to take every hour I could get with you for the next three years."

"Three years?"

"Hunters don't get forever, Audra. If we don't make the kill and acquire the memory in five years, a fresh hunter's brought in. And the old one is taken out."

"Taken . . . out."

He shrugs. "It makes sense. It keeps the hunter eager. It keeps the mark guessing. It takes care of the problem if we've been made. I'd been assigned to you two years before."

I quit picking at my sandwich. In fact, I've lost my appetite.

"The Scions kill their own hunters?"

"I don't think it happens often."

"What happened to 'one hunter, one mark'?"

"There's still only one hunter. He just has a different face. I wanted to keep up the ruse. Live the time we had left. You'd be on the run after that from a new hunter, but you'd be alive. I knew you could outsmart any killer coming in cold.

But you wouldn't accept that. You became obsessed with finding a way to get out from under the eyes of the Scions. I was so tired of the entire thing. Talking every day about a death sentence I wanted to forget. It was *all* you talked about. We forgot how to live, to remember that we were happy, right then. And we fought.

"You felt betrayed—even more than the day I told you what I was—that I seemed willing to settle for the time we had left. In my mind, being with you as long as I could was more than I could ask for. And more than I felt I honestly deserved. But you felt like I was giving up."

"So I found a way to die," I say.

"You were convinced it was our only option. But I was afraid. That something like we had was already a miracle and couldn't be done twice in this life. That you wouldn't want me again. That I couldn't win you again. You had much more confidence in my ability to do that than I did. Finally, I promised that even if I failed or, God forbid, you fell in love with someone else . . . I'd be there to protect you. Because that one I knew I could keep."

I stare at my sandwich.

The weird desperation that day in the Food Mart. The manic way he chased me up Lily Bay Road. Coming after me to Indiana . . .

When I look up, his expression is pained.

"I didn't come here to feel helpless. And that's

how I felt this morning. When I realized you were gone and then saw the murders on the news, I was convinced you had died in a hundred horrible ways. I know now exactly why you weren't willing to just take the years we had left. The constant worry and fear . . . I get it, and I'm sorry."

"You don't have to apologize," I say awkwardly. "It's not like I remember."

He reaches over and takes my hand between hi . "You loved me once. You don't have to believe me. You don't even have to like me, though of course I wish you did. But I'll take knowing you're alive over knowing you're mine any day." He looks up at me. "All that is to say, if nothing else, please don't do that to me again."

I say nothing. If he's playing me, I already feel like an idiot—to myself, most of all. If he's not . . . that's actually harder to consider.

So here we are, both hunted. But it's not the same. I may have months to be allowed to learn something useful to the Historian. Five years at most, under the watchful eye of a new hunter probably already assigned to me. But Luka's turned traitor. For all he knows, he has hours. He's wrong in one thing: This isn't about protecting just me anymore.

The drive becomes less scenic as we leave the coast behind. Claudia and Piotrek chat in English about the new phones they've picked up but I hardly hear them. Luka's words chase me like monsters.

You loved me once.

I try to remember if I have ever loved anyone. My adoptive parents, of course. I know I loved them. I remember putting so much care into a Mother's Day card, drawing heart after heart on the inside. *I love you, Mommy.* Waiting for my father to come home after some kind of trip that kept him away. Throwing myself at him the minute he came in the door. I don't remember them, but I remember that.

I have fractured memories of crushes—of some faceless, towheaded boy. A jock at school trying to kiss me. The faint sense that he had just eaten a bunch of peanuts. I'm pretty sure that didn't end well.

Crushes, dates, parents . . . peanuts. But romantic love?

"Well? Let's see it," Claudia says.

"See what?"

"The key."

I'm hesitant. It feels personal, attached in my mind to Goran's story of the rain, and my mother. But I pull the key out of my pocket and hand it to Claudia.

She turns it over and even lifts her shades to study it closely.

"Where did you get that?" Luka says.

I tell him the story of the chapel in Lubenice, the monastery, the monk. I feel guilty that I didn't tell him about the key earlier or show it to him first. I feel guilty about a lot.

"I don't remember you mentioning a Goran before," Luka says.

She hands it back, and Luka reads the engraving with a frown.

Claudia's tapping at her phone, apparently looking it up.

"Does anyone even use actual keys anymore?" I say.

"What does this mean?" Luka asks, holding it so the letters glint.

"No idea."

"Shakespeare," Claudia says.

Shakespeare?

"Maybe you're rich!" Piotrek says, I assume for Luka's benefit. But we all know nothing I've hidden would be so mundane as money.

"What we need are passports," Luka says, handing the key back.

"We will get those," Claudia says. "Once we meet up with friends."

"Where?" Luka says, back to playing stupid.

"Zagreb."

I glance at Luka in the back seat.

They're taking us to the underground.

23

At first sight of the old Communist-era apartments on the outskirts of Zagreb, I sink into the back seat behind a pair of sunglasses Claudia picked up in Delnice. Even Claudia seems to be keeping a low profile. Her hair, which has dried in waving curls, covers the sides of her face otherwise obscured by a pair of oversize *Breakfast at Tiffany's*–style shades. The sun has disappeared with the coast; overhead, the sky is oppressive, threatening rain.

I've spent half the car ride on Claudia's new phone reading anything I could find about Elizabeth Bathory, skimming everything from Wikipedia and History.com to the *Weird Encyclopedia* for details. Her Protestant roots and Lutheran mother. Her fluency in Latin, German, and Greek, which made her one of the most educated women of her time. That she had an illegitimate daughter before her marriage to Ferenc Nadasdy, the national hero. Apparently she was a doting mother, attended church, and refused to hand over the running of her estates after Ferenc's death.

Independent, wealthy, beautiful, and smart. A toxic cocktail for any woman of the time, made lethal by the fact that she was a Calvinist and richer than the king—who didn't dare risk her allying with her cousin in Transylvania against the crown.

There're plenty of theories about her sadism and rages. That her aunt Klara, an herbalist, was a witch (of course). That it was Ferenc who taught her how to torture lazy servants by poking papers between their toes and lighting them on fire. That the palatine, a man named Thurzo, was an old family friend and the one responsible for saving her from the death penalty after he arrested her. Possibly because he, too, was a Protestant.

As we cross the river Sava into the city, I can't help but look out at the dull gray water. I think of my mother, floating in the Danube, swollen and grotesque, if not faceless. No, the face she wears is mine.

I had thought we would stay near the outskirts of the city, perhaps in one of the nondescript and depressing apartment buildings that look like they're made entirely of concrete. But as industrial areas give way to trees and then cultivated parks, I realize with alarm Piotrek is driving directly to the center of the old upper city.

Claudia turns around to peer between the front seats at us—or rather, at Luka.

"Luka," she says, hesitating. "You understand that talking about Ivan or any of our friends who may know him . . . would be very unsafe for all of us?"

"You mean because of his involvement in the mafia," Luka says, voice low.

"Exactly."

"I understand."

"Good. We'll have time to rest at my place."

"I thought we were going to meet your friends," I say.

"We are. Tonight." Claudia's face tilts down toward my shirt. "But not like this."

We get out on a narrow street.

"Where's Piotrek going?"

"To get rid of the car," Claudia says.

We follow her through an old tunnel. There's a shrine inside locked behind an elaborate iron grate. A couple of wooden pews sit across the way, and I realize this isn't a tunnel so much as an old city gate. Three people stand in front of the shrine, gazing through the grate at a painting of a crowned Virgin Mary. An old woman sells candles nearby. To my surprise, Claudia buys a candle from her, lights it, and sets it beside several others before rejoining us.

"Now we go," she says, flashing me something in her hand: a key.

Here in the medieval city center, buildings run together like long row houses. There are windows everywhere, two and three stories high. And I wonder with some paranoia who could be watching us even now.

We pass an old church with Gothic windows and

a roof covered with two huge crests in brightly colored tiles that make it look like it was made out of Legos.

"What's that?" I say.

"If you want a tour, hire a guide," Claudia snaps.

The early afternoon sky lends the peeling plaster of the buildings a dingy cast despite their clean bisque and yellow hues. Claudia stops in front of an old door at the end of the street. The entire side of the building is covered in graffiti, like something from the inner city more than anything historic.

She lets us in and walks us down the hall to an unremarkable entrance that I am sure leads to the basement. She opens it with another key, and it does indeed reveal a narrow flight of stairs ending in a single door.

"This place is creepy," I murmur as she flips on the single bulb overhead. "Who lives here?"

"We do," she says.

At the bottom of the stairs, I notice some kind of symbol etched in the chipped paint of the frame: two rectangles sharing a bottom line like twin towers and the earth between them.

"What's this?" I say as she unlocks the door. "Nine-eleven?" She glances back at me as she flips on the lights, setting a half dozen bulbs ablaze in a crystal chandelier shaped like a flying ship.

She hesitates, glancing at Luka.

"I'm going to find the restroom," he says on cue. She points him down the hallway.

After he's disappeared, she turns toward me. "You're playing a dangerous game, bringing him here."

"I don't know what you mean."

"Yes, you do."

Does she know? Can she tell what he is?

"Commoners have no place in our world," she says.

I relax a little. "Then why did you just let him into your flat?"

"Because despite Ivan's misgivings, I knew you—better than Ivan did in some ways. He was right; you did many things that never made sense. But you always had your reasons. Even when you disappeared. I don't understand it, and I'm angry with you—"

"I'm aware."

"But unless your intelligence got erased with your memory, I believe you have a reason. And I believe Ivan when he says there was something very big that caused you to do what you did. And so I trust you. If I'm wrong, I won't be disappointed or hate you. You know why?"

"Why?"

"Because I'll be dead. And so will Piotrek. And you're the one who will have to answer for doing what our hunters could not."

She might as well have struck me.

She turns toward the doorjamb, and it takes me a minute to realize she's traced the marking with a tapered finger. "This is Glagolitic," she says. "A very old Croatian alphabet used in the liturgy."

"I thought Latin was used in the liturgy," I say. But I'm still stuck on what she said before. Am I prepared to have even more lives on my conscience?

"The Pope made an exception in the thirteenth century. This symbol is the letter V. It is also the number three."

"Why three?"

She holds her hand out like a claw. "The Bathory coat of arms has three claws on it. Our ancestor Vitus is said to have killed a dragon—like Saint George did—with three thrusts of his sword. The coat of arms shows three teeth of the dragon biting its own tail. Vitus was given the name Bator— 'brave' in Hungarian—which became Bathory. We brave, who slay the dragon. This is our legacy. It is who we are," she says, looking intently at me. "Our ancestors are also affiliated with the famous Order of the Dragon. As was Vlad Dracul the third," she adds, with a slight, rare smile.

"Vlad . . . as in Dracula, the vampire?"

She slaps my hand. "Don't be stupid. Vampires don't exist. Come."

For its drab exterior, Claudia's apartment is the poshest kind of bohemian chic I've ever seen. A red velvet settee sits beneath the chandelier ship in the middle of the living room, a leopard throw across a curved arm. The walls are hung with several pieces of what look like very old and potentially very valuable art—as well as several framed pieces of what I can only call graffiti. A kilim rug sprawls across the wooden floor beneath a tufted ottoman. There are little lamps everywhere with red and orange silk shades. Claudia systematically stops to turn several of them on.

The galley is small but modern, tiny pieces of art hanging beneath the cabinets.

"You can have the second bedroom," Claudia says, leading me down a short hallway. She flips a switch and the beaded chandelier throws a kaleidoscope of light across the ceiling. No fewer than nine brightly colored pillows sprawl on top of the red-brown comforter, which glints with pieces of mirror like an antique sari. Mismatched art lines the walls—including a piece featuring a giant red sneaker on a skinny, hairy leg. It's too vibrant to look away from and really kind of ugly, a line in another language scrawled across the bottom.

"What does that say?" I ask.

" 'And I knew that the foot of God was about to crush me.' "

"That's kind of horrible," I say.

"Piotrek painted it," she says.

"Oh. I mean it's just very . . . bold."

"I find it comforting, myself," she says, leaning in the doorway. "How many times have I felt that God was a god of crushing feet? That all bad that happened was punishment for some mistake—of even being born?"

"You don't still feel that way?"

"No," she says. "Not since the day Piotrek painted this and I cried the minute I saw it. 'I think one day you will realize that God likes you,' he said. Which made me cry more. Because it's much harder to think that God likes us than that He loves us."

I have shortchanged her, I realize, and the often-silent Piotrek. It must be impossible to have no beliefs, living as they do. As I have, too, lately. I wonder if I was ever religious, if I ever had a single thought nearly as deep during my life *before*. I recall what Luka said about our argument over whether it was better to take what life we could get or fight for more, and wonder if I'm a far shallower person today than I was two months ago.

"There are things in the closet, the other bedroom, the bathroom. Take what you want, but I suggest you sleep," she says. She turns on the bedside lamp. It is outfitted with a purple bulb. "We don't go out during the day unless we have to, as I must now if we're going to get you passports."

I catch her by the arm.

"Thank you, Claudia," I say, and mean it. She gives me a perfunctory nod.

She leaves shortly after downing a small cup of espresso with what she calls "sinful speed." "You see?" she says, as she picks up her purse. "I'm practically American."

Luka locks the door behind her as I force down half a cooling cup of coffee. There's no milk, and I'm pretty sure asking Claudia to get some would have gotten me a laugh in the face.

"How is it?" he asks.

"Horrible," I say, setting it on the table.

"Maybe she's got some sugar." He goes to search the cabinets, and I follow him into the kitchen. He's got nice shoulders. Broad, like a swimmer's.

Or a murderer's.

I remember the weight of that arm curled around me and hope to God my unconscious self—the same part of me that swam to shore for Clare's cross and crawled into his bed before dawn—is wiser than my waking mind. Because Claudia's right: I can't take one more life on my conscience.

"Hey," I say. "About last night . . ."

"You were scared. Don't worry about it," he says, his back toward me.

"I didn't mean to give you the wrong impression."

"You didn't. How about this?" he says, holding up a canister of tea. I shrug and nod, and then

235

watch the elegant hands capable of strangling someone with their T-shirt carefully fill the infuser.

"Do you play the piano?" I say on impulse. He looks up, surprise clearly written on his face.

"You remember that?"

"No."

"Oh." He laughs softly. "I told you a really embarrassing story about that once. I'm glad you forgot."

"That isn't fair."

"It's completely fair," he says, setting up the electric kettle.

"You know things about me. Personal things. I don't know anything about you other than that you were supposed to kill me."

He turns to face me, leans back against the counter.

"Okay. Ask. I'll tell you anything."

I consider him across the kitchen's small galley.

"Were you with me the day before my procedure?"

"I was," he says with a quiet nod.

"How did we spend that day?"

"We'd found this place called the Heron House outside Indianapolis two nights before. You convinced the owner that she really wanted to put us up in their only suite. It had a huge bathtub . . ." He starts to continue, stops and shifts where he stands. "We slept late. The owner brought up breakfast, and later lunch. We stayed in bed all

236

day. We didn't talk about the future, or anything from the past. You kept staring at me, said there was no way you could forget me, though of course we both knew you would."

I'm quiet for a moment. "What about the next morning?" I say finally.

"We had talked about it for so long . . . But when your cab showed up outside I didn't want to let you go. I freaked out. I broke down. You were determined. And then you kissed me good-bye and told me to find you in Maine," he says, as the kettle begins to hiss.

"I looked for you every day for a month," he says, pouring hot water into a cup. "Drove by your place a few times. It was all I could do not to get a boat and go out there. I could see your caretaker once, looking out the window. I worried she had seen me. And I waited. Till the day you showed up at the grocery."

He's just set down the kettle by the time I cross the few feet between us. The cup tips and spills as he pulls me against him, a soft sound escaping his throat.

He kisses me hard, arms hungry around me. His fingers slide into my hair. And the desperation is back without even the guise of control as he pulls me against his chest and off my toes.

He can't get enough of my mouth, my neck, my skin. "I miss the way you smell. I miss this smell," he whispers, hand cradling my head as we fall back against the opposite counter. And then he's lifting me up, my arms and knees locked around him, and carrying me down the narrow hallway to the wrong room.

"That one," I say, grabbing the doorframe, steering us across the hall.

He kicks the door shut behind us, and the kaleidoscope of stars dances on the ceiling.

"Don't sleep," Luka murmurs. He's curled behind me, nose against my ear, his fingers caught in mine.

"Why not?" I say, drowsing.

"I still owe you."

"Owe me what?"

"I made the mistake of falling asleep at your friend's flat once, where you were staying. I woke up late for work and ran out the door . . . with no idea you had drawn a purple Hitler mustache on me. With a Sharpie."

I laugh.

"I mean, you kissed me good-bye with a completely straight face."

"Wow. I'm good."

"You're evil."

I close my eyes. I haven't felt this at ease in days.

"What're you thinking?" he whispers, brushing the hair from my cheek.

"It must be tiring telling stories more than once."

"No. I love it."

After a minute, I ask, "You said I changed your mind. How?"

I feel him shrug. "You weren't a thing anymore. You weren't a belief. You had a soul. A laugh. A smell I was addicted to. A twisted sense of humor. It wasn't just that I loved you. It was that even though you were *Progeny,* you were more like me than unlike me. And then, somehow, you were more me than I was."

"So you just gave it up?"

"I went into a tailspin."

"Because you couldn't kill me."

"No. Because the Scions were the only church I knew. Their God, who wanted revenge and justice, was the only God I knew. For the first time, I didn't know what to believe."

"I'm pretty sure God doesn't condone killing."

"God has condoned killing throughout history, depending who you ask."

"That is literally so Old Testament."

He rolls onto his back. "I used to think about the story of Abraham, being told to kill his son. I spent so many nights wondering how he was willing to do it. And I didn't know what God would hate more: me not fulfilling what I had always been taught to be some sacred obligation, or me killing myself. Because that's what it was coming to. Either God would destroy me for failing, or I'd destroy myself."

I don't need to turn to study the painting behind us. The red-sneakered foot, laces tied, laughably neat, in a bow. Maybe I even see a little bit why Claudia called it comforting.

"I was in hell," he says. "I quit eating. I couldn't sleep. Worse, you knew something was wrong. You thought I was cheating on you at first, until you realized it was something wrong with *me*. I couldn't keep it secret. You knew me too well."

"Not as well as I thought, apparently."

And even now I allow for the possibility that I have just made love to a man who will kill me. I can't see it, but I have been wrong about him before.

"So what'd you do?" I ask.

"I laid my whole, messed-up heart on the table. And I knew you would leave. But honestly, I think I was more afraid of God abandoning me. For as much as I loved you . . . that thought was worse."

I'm trying to reconcile the tortured person of his story with the urgently happy-go-lucky guy from the Food Mart. I never would have pegged him as spiritual. 'Course I never thought of him as very deep until recently, either.

"You don't seem tortured anymore, though."

He turns toward me, nuzzles my shoulder. "No. I finally decided God's mercy is enough, or it isn't. It's the foundation of religion, isn't it— forgiveness? But you never really think about what that means until you have no choice but to throw yourself on that altar and pray it's enough. Forgiveness is enough, or it isn't. That is the only thing I believe anymore."

"I envy you," I say, pulling his arm around me. "I don't know what I believe anymore."

"After you came back to me, you said something about how we've both been slaves to a past we didn't know how to leave behind. The day you had your procedure, a part of me was jealous. Because just like that, it was gone. You were free."

"Maybe not as free as I thought."

"For a time you were. And I felt envious and stupidly abandoned. I didn't expect to feel the way I did."

"Losing your identity is no picnic, either."

"Your identity isn't you, Audra."

But what else is there, when your past, your roles, your upbringing and parents and culture— your very name—are stripped away? What's lef ? So far my answer has been: not much.

Eventually I doze, if only for a half hour, afraid of what my sleepwalking self might do, unable to turn off my mind.

24

When Claudia said I could use whatever I wanted in the closet, I didn't realize the sheer trove of weirdness I'd walk into. *Alice in Wonderland* skirts, pin-striped corsets, gladiator sandals, straitjacket shirts, black shorts with fringe to the ankle, velvet bodices covered with timepieces— or cocktail umbrellas or buckles—purple wigs, and masquerade masks. Miniature hats that look like shrunken-head versions of something from the Kentucky Derby. It's as though Cirque du Soleil, a goth ball, and a gaming convention all crash-landed in the same eight-by-three-foot twilight zone that is Claudia's spare closet.

"What is all this?" I say when she comes to check on me. And then I pull up short. She's outfitted in a pair of leather riding breeches, an abbreviated tuxedo coat, and a tiny top hat with a veil over a fall of pink hair.

"Clothes," she says, as though I were the village idiot. "You can't meet Tibor dressed like that."

"Who's Tibor?" I say, exasperated.

"The Zagreb Prince. Who answers only to Nikola."

"Nikola?"

"The Prince of Budapest. The oldest court."

None of this means anything to me.

"I wasn't aware that I had to look like Lady Gaga to meet him."

She huffs and starts rifling through the closet, pulling things from hangers, tossing them on the bed.

"What about the passports?" I say.

"Jester's working on it."

"Jester?"

"You didn't think I could just go pick one up at the pharmacy down the street?" she snaps.

A loud exclamation sounds from the other room. Luka. Piotrek talks over him in protest.

"You both need to change your attitude," Claudia says, getting on her hands and knees to dig in the back of the closet. She tosses out a pair of boots.

"So you want me to look like a freak."

She gets up and stares at me, indignant in pink hair, and I could almost laugh at her. She throws a pair of blood-red velvet pants with zippers down both sides at me, hard.

"It's almost ten. You'd better hurry."

I let out a long exhale as she laces me into a black corset, fits me in a purple wig. It's piled high with curls and topped with a giant black rose. She brushes fuchsia lipstick on my mouth, ties a black mask behind my head, and attaches a pair of golden chandeliers to my ears.

"Well, well," she says, looking me over as I zip

243

up the pants, almost catching my skin in the metal teeth twice.

"They fit." More or less. Good thing they stretched or I wouldn't be able to sit without popping a zipper. Claudia's at least a size smaller than I am.

"They should. They were yours," she says, tossing me the boots.

I give her a weird look, but she's rummaging through a dresser drawer.

"What happens when someone realizes they can't sense Luka?" I say, chewing my lip.

"You're ruining your lipstick! There will be too many Progeny there for anyone to realize they can't sense him." She pauses. "Stay close to him if we leave with anyone. Shouldn't be hard for you to do, I think?"

The last thing she hands me is a heavy pendant on a long chain. A bronze, three-toed talon. The Bathory coat of arms.

I turn it over in my hand. "Was this mine, too?"

She looks away. "It was your mother's. You gave it to me before you left." The hurt is there, I can see it.

"I'm sorry," I say, thinking that between her and Luka, I'm surrounded by abandonment issues varied only by circumstance, all of my making.

I clasp the pendant tightly before lowering the

chain carefully over my wig. As I do, I catch sight of the mirror and start. It's not the first time in my life I've failed to recognize myself.

I give a nervous glance around as we step out into the night. On the street, Piotrek pauses to lean on the silver handle of an elaborate cane. A black-and-white cravat is tied at his neck, his face obscured by a mask that hangs down from the edge of a top hat brimmed with feathers. Luka, apparently, has managed to hold out for the most part. He's dressed in a black jacquard tuxedo jacket over an equally black shirt, black pants, heavy boots. A thin jet tie hangs from a tight, smart knot at his throat. His mask is plain, and clings to the contours of his cheekbones. As we make our way up the street, he pulls the generous cowl of a shapeless black trench coat over his head. At first I think he looks like a hooded monk until he turns his head; from this angle, he might just be the grim reaper.

Claudia loops her arm through Piotrek's and leads us toward the Lego church. There's a couple milling ahead, a man and woman in period costume. There's another pair farther down the street—a noblewoman in petticoats, and a knight with a shield across his back.

"If we were trying to look like them, I think we missed the mark," I murmur. Luka reaches for my hand and clasps it over his arm.

"Have I told you today that you're beautiful?" he whispers. "Even with purple hair."

"Well, *you* look like a vampire."

More actors stroll down the street: a peddler with a cart, a cap pulled low over his head, a peasant woman in an apron.

Then it hits me. I can *feel* them. My pulse ratchets up a notch, so loud in my ears that at first I don't hear, let alone see, the young couple of tourists who approaches our foursome.

"Can we get a picture with you?" the girl asks. Claudia smiles and turns toward her, arm looped with Piotrek's. Her scarlet lips glisten in the wan light of a real gas streetlamp, and I blink; with the pink hair and rhinestones raining from her ears, the netting of her veil like myriad tiny windows over the pale skin of her cheeks, she's dazzling.

I almost *persuade* the girl to forget the picture, recalling what Luka said about photos and Progeny. But every one of us is masked.

Hiding in plain sight.

"Who are you supposed to be?" the girl says after snapping a selfie with them.

"Run away," Claudia whispers, before diving into a cartwheel. Piotrek tips his hat toward her just before the girl literally takes off running.

Luka glances at me sidelong.

"How can they keep from attracting attention this way, masked or not?" I hiss. "All a hunter would have to do is look for the freak parade at midnight!"

He shakes his head. "There are pop-up masquerades all over Europe," he says. "People got tired of expensive clubs, started taking to cemeteries and ruins. See those people headed toward the square?" He points toward a group of costumed partygoers.

I do, and I can't sense them at all—unlike the actors, who nod in our direction before we're even within speaking distance. Claudia skips to the peasant man's side, whispers in his ear. He chuckles, as though she's told him a joke—and maybe she has. When she turns away, something glints in her hand. She takes Piotrek's arm and pivots, pulling him around as though they were dancing all the way to the corner.

Two blocks north of the church, the streets are darker, the buildings in various states of repair— one pristinely restored, the plaster of the next one leprously crumbling away. Claudia and Piotrek pause before the beaten-up double door of a more decrepit building—a large residence that seems to extend to the corner, the windows of which are shuttered and painted over with graffiti. With a quick glance around, she fits a key into the lock and lets us in.

She marches swiftly down the hallway ahead of Piotrek, searching the walls. At the corner, she pauses to touch the peeling paint. There, faintly, is the sign that looks like two towers. And then she's leading us down the hall to the door of an apartment that looks like it ought to be condemned.

"Where are we going?" Luka says finally, his hand tight around my own.

"There is a story that there were once tunnels from St. Mark's Church to the castle Medvedgrad, where the evil Black Queen threw her lovers from the walls when she was done with them," Claudia says, eyes glinting. "There are rumored tunnels all over this area, including Visoka Street, where the new president has elected to move her residence." She smiles mysteriously and opens the door.

I hear it then: the faint pound of bass like a distant heartbeat, as though it might be coming from an apartment one building over.

Or from underground.

We follow her to the cellar, but instead of opening onto a dirty floor, the stair broadens into a tunnel—one hacked out of the original cellar, by the look of it. Electric lights are strung along a ceiling so low that everyone but Claudia has to duck beneath them. I can hear it more distinctly now, the pulse of European trance—coming from somewhere in the distance.

We walk, stooped over, for at least fifty yards until I start to worry that I might seriously have a claustrophobic attack. Just as I'm about to say

I want to go back, the tunnel ends at a door. It's obviously old, bound by iron and guarded by a man in a mask and smart black tuxedo. Without speaking, he fits a key into the lock. The minute he throws the door open on a cavernous underground chamber, we are assaulted by heavy bass. More than that, I actually have to take a step back at the sheer volume of Progeny ahead of us. It hits me like thunder, and I grab for Luka, who steadies me with an arm around the waist.

The man steps aside, head tilted as though he were a butler, but straightens the instant he takes notice of the pendant hanging midway down my chest. At first I think he's staring *at* my chest, and have just started to snarl when he steps back and abruptly bows low.

I glance at Luka, who swiftly ushers me through.

"That was weird," I say, but my words are swallowed by tech-heavy music, the beat interrupting the natural rhythm of my heart as the swarm of bodies begins to jerk, ghoulish beneath a shuttered strobe.

Is it my imagination, or have people turned to stare? One, and then five, and then twenty. They haven't stopped moving, but the laughter I thought I saw in thrown-back heads gives way to frozen masks swiveled in our direction.

I look around, expecting to see a bar, but there's no such thing—just a tattoo artist working on a costumed figure reclined in an old barber's chair in the corner. I get it; the pulse of so many Progeny in one location is more intoxicating than any cocktail, but in none of the usual ways. Goose bumps rise on my arms, climb to my shoulders like an army of ants.

Luka pulls me close, and I imagine, more than hear, him telling me to breathe. But every time I do, I feel as though I'm inhaling the electric pulse in choking particles. Purple lights flash over the chiseled ceiling until I feel like they're going off behind my eyes. Exposed flesh all around us lights up in glowing tattoos: three claws on the shoulder of a woman, tearing skin down the bare chest of another. The dragon, eating its tail, constricting the neck of another in an ultraviolet choker.

Ahead of us, Claudia has thrown herself into Piotrek's arms, arching back so far it's a miracle her wig hasn't come off. A scaled dragon, invisible until now, dips into her décolleté. She drops her arms back like a blissed-out rag doll as a Mad Hatter in red stockings takes Piotrek by the shoulders.

Luka pulls me toward him, and the beat is undeniable, infectious, far too demanding. The only thing that feels better at all is to *move*. The lights go out completely, fluorescent lashes, masks, and fingernails glowing in a bobbing frenzy in the pitch-black around us. I hold tight to Luka's neck. His trench coat is missing. He's warm, clothing already damp beneath my arm. Tension, fear, and confusion have welled up in me at once, and I feel it all sweating through my pores like a demon that must be exorcised here, now, as the strobe shocks the black cavern back to life.

It does not stop. *I* cannot stop. I spin around and find myself face-to-face with a Greek comedy mask, a cap with bells falling down over pale, gilded cheeks. He kneels so close to me I fall onto his back. Hands lift me onto a set of shoulders. I flail once and close my eyes. I am floating, a dozen hands grasping my arms, back, and legs. And for the first time since I woke up in the Center, I do not think of danger. I do not think at all. There is only the beat of surrender, and breath and bliss. I open my eyes on a ceiling raining blue light, the strobe flashing like lightning.

Amerie loved rain . . .

And for that one, perfect, ruined moment, she did not worry about the future, and the past was washed away.

I barely feel my feet touch the floor, belatedly realize I have landed on my toes in the boots with the precarious heels that should have crippled me by now. But I feel no pain. There is nothing but this rapid burn of everything I have been carrying with me for far, far too long.

I am alive for the first time since I woke up in the Center's clinical white room. Perhaps ever.

I don't know how long I go like that—a half hour, an hour, two.

The Mad Hatter comes to cup my face with a smile. She kisses my cheek before melting away. Claudia grabs my hand, pulls me through the thinning press. And then we are rushing into a tunnel, up a stair, and onto the street. Piotrek veers left onto a main thoroughfare, all but abandoned this time of night. There's an old blue tram rolling toward us. He leaps up onto the outer step, and Claudia has followed suit. They're out of their minds, I think, even as my foot finds a hold on the second car, my fingers fighting for purchase as if I were a climber on a sheer rock face. I glance back, purple hair in my eyes, to find Luka laughing at the end of the car.

We let go several blocks east and run down the side of the street. Piotrek jumps up onto the post of a chain fence, teeters, then balances like a ballerina. I laugh and then gasp as Claudia leaps for him. He hops at least five feet to the next post just as she lands where he was perched a mere second ago, and then Claudia's chasing him the better part of a city block from post to post, one long stride at a time.

"He's crazy." Luka laughs, and I nod in agreement. But my heart races with them as we run to catch up.

On the very last post, Piotrek jumps into the street—right toward an oncoming car. I scream, too late, as he skirts across the car's roof, landing on his feet with an audible chuckle. The car screeches to a halt.

"That was you," Claudia says, her finger pointed at me. And only then do I realize my mental shout for the driver to *stop!*

By the time we find ourselves back in the city square, the sky is indigo, threatening dawn. That can't be right.

"I know a place," Piotrek says, slowing to a walk. We're at least a mile from the upper city on a narrow side road. He leads us to a tiny restaurant. The windows are dark, a lone light shining from a back room, maybe the kitchen itself. Piotrek slides his mask up, presses his forehead to the window. When nothing happens, Claudia turns to stare intently through the window beside him. A minute later we're admitted by an older man who welcomes us as though we were expected—even though he's still in his nightshirt.

By the time we sit down I feel the soreness of my feet. My lower back aches. My ears are still ringing.

I sigh and slump back in my chair as the proprietor comes with coffee, not even caring what Piotrek is apparently ordering for the table.

And then I smile up at the ceiling. A laugh rises from my chest. Claudia removes her mask. She looks spent and sated at once.

Luka groans.

"A night like that could kill a man," he says. And I doubt he's feigning his fatigue.

The proprietor's wife, a plump woman in her sixties, emerges a few minutes later with sugar and a pitcher of thick cream. She's still in her dressing gown. Piotrek murmurs at her, catches her hand and kisses it. She blushes, and then laughs like a girl.

"I miss surfing in Hvar." Claudia sighs. "A splinter of the court used to meet near the coast about a year and a half ago. We'd drop clothes on the way to the beach. Swim until dawn. Go surfing in the morning."

"We surfed?" I say.

"You didn't. We did," Claudia says. "You were a miserable surfer."

"That can't be right."

"Pio, didn't you have to give her mouth-to-mouth at least once?"

"She loved it," he says, sliding a lazy smile my way.

"Hey. We never saw Tibor," I say belatedly, a weird languor like fatigue taking over my limbs.

"No. But he saw us," Claudia says.

"Everyone was costumed. How could he know I was there?"

She leans in, her eyes shining.

"Audra. *Everyone* knows you were there."

254

• • •

Luka and I stagger into Claudia's flat just before dawn, shed shoes, jewelry, masks. Claudia and Piotrek arrive a short time later, having taken a different route home.

Claudia chatters in incoherent exhaustion before disappearing down the hall, the two cups of espresso she's just made forgotten on the counter. I swear I hear her bump into the door of the bedroom.

"Good night," Piotrek says as he retrieves the espresso, a tiny cup in each hand. He pauses just long enough that I think he might say something, but then tilts his head and strides down the hall after Claudia.

I am by now more spent than I can ever remember being. And though I know I will be sore tomorrow, I am, for the first time in weeks—possibly years—at peace.

Luka peels off his jacket, loosens his tie.

He's obviously exhausted, but I know he is acutely aware of my slightest movement, the breath I have yet to exhale. I have felt his eyes on me all night.

In three strides I'm across the room. My mouth finds his. His arms tighten around my waist.

"I think," he murmurs, lifting me off my feet, "that you're going to kill me."

We return to court that night. And then the next, and the next. I wake every afternoon to a ringing

255

in my ears, the echo of electronic music still drumming in my veins, and rise in anticipation of the frenetic melee.

We've acquired a minor court of our own: namely, a girl named Ana—the Mad Hatter of the first night—and her sibling, Nino, who is half as vocal as Piotrek and twice as crazy. The only two to ever share their faces let alone their names with us. They've crashed here with us the last two mornings, collapsing on the living room sofa, only to disappear sometime around noon.

I've come, by now, to recognize each of their trademark persuasions: Claudia, with her haughty demands, casting the desire to please her like a spell. Piotrek and his unspoken ability to make anyone feel beautiful. Ana, with a fragility that would make the most feeble old lady leap in front of a truck to save her; and Nino, with his danger. By now I've seen more than one policeman hightail it away from him with a glance, including last night after he rode a stolen skateboard down the funicular to the lower city.

"He's going to die," Piotrek said, blinking into the darkness—before he shrugged and followed suit.

But it's Ana who finds the gentle place in my heart. For every way that Claudia is sharp, Ana is soft. For every word Claudia says, there is a mere cant of Ana's eyes. Polish, like Piotrek, she is a waif of a girl, a sparrow in Cosplay boots with precariously high heels, tremoring like a leaf on a stem.

"Nino's going to marry me at Christmas," she says, touching a thin silver ring on her finger. She can't be more than sixteen. But for all his lunatic ways, Nino is a different man around her. Gentle, near-reverent, as though she were not a kooky girl in striped leggings but a paleMadonna with anime eyes, always yelling for one of us to "look after Ana," before embarking on his next crazy stunt.

"Are any siblings actual siblings?" I say to Claudia one night.

"A few," she says. "But blood relations are rare in Utod circles. Most of us are orphans, after all."

In all this time, Tibor has yet to make himself known. I don't care. For the first time since I woke up in the Center, I feel that I am home.

"You know, there are bigger courts," Claudia says one morning as we eat cold pizza after Luka, more haggard by the night, has already collapsed in bed. She has reclaimed the sofa in the absence of Ana and Nino, and stretches like a cat.

"Bigger than Zagreb?" I say around a mouthful of food.

"Budapest is bigger. So is Moscow. We should go. Court's moving in a few days, anyway."

"Moving where?" I say, slightly panicked.

She shrugs. "It changes. There's a communiqué that goes out every month in the homeless magazine."

"A print magazine?" I say. She nods. "Isn't that risky?"

"There's a code if you know where to look," Piotrek says, slouched against an armchair on the floor. "The magazine is sold in every Croatian city by the homeless, who keep the profits. Do a good deed, find a safe place. Because we"—he lays a hand on his chest—"are the ultimate homeless."

"Who puts out the magazine?"

"The Franciscans," Piotrek says. "Our truest brothers for centuries, which is a scandal when you consider that Erzsebet Bathory—Elizabeth, as you say—was a Protestant. A Calvinist, even. And that the Habsburg king, a Catholic, became Holy Roman Emperor before her death. Tsk tsk."

"Does the Church know the extent of the Franciscans' involvement?"

"They are not so involved today, except as helpers."

"But the monk, Brother Goran, who gave me the key . . ."

"This is the first I have ever heard of a Progeny

monk. But who is to say what is happening with those Ivan knew before he died? Who could ever understand Ivan, or those he ran with?"

But I have heard the same said of my mother. And of me.

"The Scions are far more powerful today than the Church," Piotrek says. "What can a few Franciscans do to them? Yes, a few may be murdered. But even the Scions fear for their souls. The Church is well funded by the rich Dispossessed," he says, wiggling his brows.

"You won't get to heaven like this, Pio," Claudia says.

"I am Utod. My heaven is here," he says, spreading his arms.

"This isn't heaven," Claudia says, sitting up. "And we can't go from court to court forever. Even Ivan said as much."

I glance down at my plate, no longer hungry. It's the first time we've talked about Ivan in days. I've been all too willing to forget the questions he left behind—including my reason for dying.

Piotrek shrugs. "We can go to Istria for a while, if you like."

"I don't want to go to Istria. I want to *live,*" Claudia says, shrill.

"I've actually never felt more alive," I say honestly.

"You call this living? Scurrying in the dark like rats?"

"I thought you loved court!" I say, feeling strangely betrayed.

"Look at me," she says. Her hair is askew, her makeup smeared. In her Queen of Bloody Hearts getup, she looks vaguely like a crackhead. "I'm eighteen. I feel forty. Some days I wake up and wish I hadn't."

I glance at Piotrek, waiting for him to intervene. Leaning against the armchair, his back is bent like that of an old man.

"I say we leave, see the world!" Claudia says.

I glance between them. "You can't be serious?" I say.

"Of course I'm serious," Claudia snaps.

"Where shall we go?" Piotrek says with a slight smile.

"São Paulo," Claudia says. "Madagascar. Egypt."

"Mother Russia!" Piotrek says in a thick Russian accent.

"China," Claudia says.

"China takes money." *And passports,* I think— a thing Luka inquired about earlier today. In private, I wondered aloud why we needed them at all, given my success at the passport agency.

"You can't *persuade* a check-in kiosk or a customs camera," he said. And I had to give him that.

"Money is easy to get," Piotrek says. "We are Utod. The world is our orchard." But his expression is weary.

"Oyster," I say.

"I don't like shellfish."

"So it's settled. China," Claudia says. "What will you do about Luka?"

Do I imagine it or do she and Piotrek look at me at once?

"Bring him with me, what else?"

"Suit yourself," Claudia says after a beat, untangling her legs onto the floor.

A few moments after she has gone down the hallway to collapse into bed, Piotrek rolls his head toward me.

"She gets this way every few months. Wanting to leave like a restless lover."

"Do you ever? Leave, I mean."

He shrugs a shoulder, eyes half-lidded. "For days. A week, maybe. At most, two. But we always come back."

"You don't want to see the world?"

"Of course. But for as much as we say we want to live, we are far too good at merely existing. And the underground court is that, because it means safety. And so we create our own world, every night. Again and again." His gaze is distant. He sounds as tired as he looks. "Claudia believes that life is short. She wants to consume it. But you cannot consume life in safety. And in the end, we want safety more, even, than life."

I think, not for the first time, that maybe this is what it's like to have a terminal disease. To know

261

that every minute is just one in a limited and dwindling supply and that you'd better squeeze some life in while you still have the choice. No wonder the image of my mother in the rain has never left me since the monastery. The moment is all we've ever had.

He rolls to his side, gets up, and then pauses. "But she is right. Perhaps we should go a few days early. Wait for court in the next city."

"We can't leave," I say. "At least not yet. We haven't gotten our passports." And the truth is, I no longer care if we get them at all.

"I will contact Jester tomorrow," Piotrek says, before ambling down the hall.

To my relief, Jester is silent. Claudia sings the next evening as she powders her face, all talk of China forgotten.

25

Pounding on the door wakes me, impossibly, from sleep. My limbs are leaden, weighted to the bed. I glance at the old digital clock across the room on the dresser: 5:07 P.M.

I push up in a panic, look around me. My clothes are where I left them, a black star of a mask, a riot of blond braids splayed across a hat that sat last night like a sinking ghost ship on top of my head. It's the outfit I laid out while asleep the morning before. Aside from that single night of closet raiding, I've apparently been too exhausted to experience any new sleepwalking adventures . . . at least as far as I know.

I stretch an arm across the bed, find it empty. I never heard Luka rise.

"Audra!" More pounding. Claudia. I untangle myself, trip from bed.

"What?" I say, hoarse. I yank open the door. Claudia stands there in a plain black sweater and pedal pushers, Audrey Hepburn glasses on her head. It's bizarre, seeing her in something so normal—possibly her weirdest costume yet— until I recall her penchant for watching artists in the park on weekend afternoons.

She holds a phone toward me.

"What's this?" I take it from her, realizing I

never washed the makeup off my face, including the feathered eyelash that clings like a dead spider to the corner of my eye. I peel it off, stick it to the doorjamb, and take the phone from her. Squint at a single line of text:

T says: Bring the talon tonight.

"Who's this from?" I say, confused.

"Tibor, through Jester."

I give her a weird look as Luka appears in the hallway. He's freshly showered, wet hair tucked behind his ear.

"Tibor wants my pendant?" I've worn it every night. Have not missed the eyes that stray toward it each time I arrive, the words spoken to cupped ears behind the pounding music. Or the following our predawn wilds have acquired as we spill from the underground well before first light. If they—or any of the faceless others—know who I am, they've said nothing about it. Or at least not in front of me.

"No, Audra. You. You're the talon."

"Okay." I glance from her to Luka. Apparently I'm failing to understand something.

"Maybe he's gotten the passports," Luka says, though I know he's really asking a question. "It has been nearly a week."

In fact, I've hardly noticed the passing of the days, which have blended together into one long night at a court that has extended from Visoka Street to the nearby Tuskanac forest.

But Claudia is clearly shaken.

"What are you worried about? You're friends with him, right?" I say. Made up every night, surrounded by a court full of frenetic Progeny, she's always appeared more glamorous than life and older than her years. At this moment, however, she looks like a scared eighteen-year-old.

"Not exactly," she says, looking pale. "I've never met him. That I know of."

"I'm curious to meet him," I say lightly. After all, Luka and I came here for safety. It can't hurt to make his acquaintance—the fact that I've smuggled non-Progeny contraband into his court notwithstanding.

"Audra," Claudia says, grabbing me by the arm as Luka excuses himself. Her hand is cold. "Be careful."

"I will." I'm always careful. We all are. "What's the worst that could happen?"

"I've seen him send people away. Or worse, to Nikola for judgment. They don't come back."

I think of my own disappearance. Of Katia's, and Ivan's. Claudia is used to people leaving her life. And I know that her bitchiness the day I met her in Opatija was nothing deeper than hurt. I kiss her cheek. "I'm not leaving," I say.

But as she goes out to the kitchen, it's my turn to be uneasy. Tibor knows me, or of me. These are Progeny, with the same blood I have. And my mother is an underground legend. But Luka is the enemy. Is it possible Tibor knows or suspects what Luka might be—what he was?

The thought works at me until my cavalier attitude about meeting the Prince of Zagreb is all but eaten away.

A few minutes later Luka steps inside the bedroom and quietly closes the door. I drop the clothes in my hand, lean into his chest.

For days, everything has been perfect. Too perfect. From the frenzy of court and my heightened awareness of Luka's every glance to his weight against me in bed at dawn. One long night of delirium and desire.

Luka's right; a week is a lot longer than passports should take. Not with a man supposedly on the inside.

Luka touches a kiss to my shoulder, inhales the scent of my neck.

"Don't come tonight," I say.

"They'll notice if I don't and know you're protecting me."

Piotrek, Claudia, and I have been careful to flank Luka each time we enter the underground and in every dash throughout the city with others. Claudia has done this despite her doubts, and I am grateful.

"If I leave to meet him, don't follow me."

"Audra—"

"You can't! And if you see anyone trying to single you out, get away." When he says nothing, I add, "Promise me."

"I promise. But only if Piotrek goes with you."

I nod. I can live with that.

"Trust me when I say I have a whole new appreciation for what it means to be you," he murmurs.

I let out a slow breath, not wanting to remember.

A half hour ago, I was in the clutches of a heavy sleep and beautiful dream: Luka and I were together in a small flat and it was morning. He was sipping coffee and I was drinking tea, each of us on a laptop. That's it. A stunningly mundane morning with no threat of death, without looking over our shoulders. We were online, checking news and e-mail, maybe a blog. Something I can't fathom today, where the burner phone in my pocket becomes a ticking time bomb with each successive use.

I glance toward the rumpled bed, where he held me through the night, curled beneath the covers. The sight of it makes the dream fade more quickly with each passing moment. Especially in this subterranean room; the flat in my dreams was filled with windows.

By the time we leave, my heart is trilling against my rib cage like a hummingbird's. I adjust my mask, brush back the chains of a gold hairpiece protruding from my ornate blue wig like chopsticks stuck in a bowl of chop suey.

My kimono offers little defense against the first chill of fall, and I imagine I have difficulty breathing in the wide obi lashed around my middle. Luka takes me by the elbow to keep me from stumbling on the cobbles. He's dressed all in black, as he has been every night, a long coat brushing the tops of his boots.

"Remember," he murmurs. "You're valuable—very valuable—to them."

I nod, twine gloved fingers with his.

Claudia, ahead of me in an elaborate peacock mask, has been silent all evening. The bustle of her short skirt rides her rump like a beehive before cascading to the ground behind her. In fact, the whisper of her hems behind her clicking heels is all I've heard from her since leaving the flat.

She's said Tibor has been known to send people away. Has she already written me off for a second time? I don't miss that she's clinging to Piotrek's arm as though an invisible hand might snatch him from her side at any moment.

We've gone to court by a different route each night. But even without the whispered instructions from the Progeny actor—tonight, a medieval priest—I would know the general direction blind. Can already sense those gathered deep in the hillside of Tuskanac forest from here.

I stare, dumbfounded, the moment we enter.

The court has nearly doubled in size.

But there's something else. The tenor of these caverns has changed. The electric pulse that buoyed me onto shoulders just last night has coalesced into one heaving drone. The frozen expressions of the masks seem macabre and menacing, the eyes behind them fixed in a single direction: mine.

My first thought is that I should never have brought Luka with me—that I need to get him out.

My second is that it's too late.

The strobe sputters like an erratic flashbulb. Someone grabs my arm: the Jester, his comedy mask exchanged for the leer of tragedy. I shove him off, but he raises a finger, wags it back and forth. And then the lights black out and his mask transforms into a glowing skull.

Hands seize mine, force them behind my back. I struggle and then stumble as I am dragged through the melee.

I shout for Luka, scream for him to run. But the music drowns me out and there's the Jester's finger, fluorescent as his skeletal teeth, wagging in front of me like a metronome.

The temperature cools as I'm hauled into a tunnel, music fading till I can hear the breath of my captor.

"Where are you taking me?" I shout. My voice echoes, the ground is uneven beneath my feet. I wrench around, catch sight of my captor's mask.

A gilded gladiator. The scabbard of the short sword at his hip does not feel like plastic.

He says, roughly near my ear, "Stop fighting. I'm taking you to Tibor."

I'm escorted through a carved wooden entrance guarded by two centurions, into a strangely lit chamber.

The entire back wall is filled with television screens. They flash with electric blue light and the chaos of the cavern I have just come from. The court, from ten different angles, zooming in on masked faces at intervals. One screen dedicated to the entrance, empty except for the butler. The last shows the tunnel I just came through.

A figure rises from a carved chair to my right. He's dressed in striped pants, top hat askew on his head. Jet hair hangs on either side of a horned red and black samurai mask past the shoulders of a long topcoat. A cat-o'-nine-tails is coiled at his hip, and, like the gladiator's sword, it does not look fake. He steps forward as I enter, the most sinister ringmaster I have ever seen.

Tibor.

"And so the prodigal daughter returns." His voice is as wiry as his frame. He opens his arms and frowns when I make no move. "You do not remember poor Tibor? No, of course you do not."

But he is not the only one in the room.

"Who's there?" I demand, looking around us.

Tibor audibly sucks in a breath.

A moment later a shadow emerges from behind the bank of screens. His cloak is far too reminiscent of Luka's grim reaper the first night, black hood drawn over his head. His mask is utterly white and featureless, only the eyes alive.

"Do you believe me now?" the figure says, before turning toward me.

"Hello, Audra. I am Nikola of Budapest."

26

Nikola. The Prince of Budapest.

Inexplicable trembling takes my arms. It doesn't help that I've had no chance to burn the nervous energy building up all evening. Or that there's something unnatural about his tone, as though his larynx were made of metal.

"What's this about?" I say. Because I'm pretty sure it isn't passports.

"Sit," Tibor says, waving a hand toward the chair. I don't move.

"How do you like court?" Nikola says, as he takes the empty seat, which only serves to make me feel like I'm somehow being interrogated. Now I see that a small device is set in the round opening of the mask's mouth, disguising his voice.

"It's fine, I guess." But the allure of the anonymity, the freedom I knew here, is already fading with its sense of safety. For the first time in days, I am keenly aware of the key around my neck, practically burning into my skin. Of every unanswered question I managed to set aside and then forget altogether in the masquerade that has been my existence in Zagreb.

"See how it has grown at the whisper of a single name," Tibor says. *"Audra, Audra, Audra!"*

"And yet I do not believe you are aware of the implications of your return," Nikola says.

"I guess not," I say.

"It was very cruel of you to die," Tibor says, picking a piece of lint off his pant leg. "I have a personal ritual when we lose one of our own. I hang a small plate etched with the name of the departed on the wall of my hovel. I did this for you as well. But then ten days ago Ivan informed me that my ritual was premature. So I took the plate down"—he mimes the action neatly—"and put it in a special drawer. For later. Little did any of us realize what you had accomplished in the act of your so-called death. At least at first." He begins to applaud. "Bravo, Audra."

This is the Prince of the Zagreb underground? The man is a lunatic.

"It wasn't an act," I say.

Tibor lays a finger against his masked cheek. "Ah, yes. The memory you shed like a scab. Which begs the question, why? What could be so precious that it must be so protected—even from us?"

"I'm sure I don't know," I say.

Right now I want two things: to find out why Nikola is here, and to get out of here as soon as possible. In fact, I wouldn't mind accomplishing them in reverse order.

"Ivan was a great fan of yours," Tibor says lightly. "His faith in you knew no end."

"So I've been told."

"And then it got him killed."

His head snaps toward me. In an instant, he has crossed the space between us and grabbed me by the throat.

"WHERE IS THE DIARY?" he shouts, full force, an inch from my face.

I claw at his hands, grab at his face as he hauls me across the floor.

Nikola is on him within seconds, and sends him hurtling toward the wall. I fall to my knees and then my hands, sucking in air.

"Touch her again and I'll have you shunned from your own court," Nikola says quietly.

Tibor spits, the edge of his mask askew, which only makes him appear more deranged. "It won't matter. Don't you see? She has killed us all!" And then he begins to chuckle, the sound more than slightly manic.

"What do you want from me?" I rasp.

"Audra," Nikola says, blocking me from view of Tibor, "we want what you knew. What you forgot. The thing you are protecting . . . it is a weapon. One we need."

"Sorry. I can't help you."

"But you can. And you must," Nikola says, getting down in front of me.

"I don't think you understand. It's gone. Whatever it was, I meant for it to disappear with me and it did!"

He shakes his head. "The Audra I knew was fanatical. A zealot."

"I think you have me confused with my mother."

"Oh, no. You would never have done what you did had you not found something of great interest to the Historian."

"Which means it needs to stay buried!"

"No. Which makes it of greater interest to *us*." He leans closer. "Had you stayed dead, your secret would have died with you. But now that the Scions know you are alive, all that has changed."

"Everything's changed," Tibor echoes, leaning against the wall. His eyes gleam. "Perhaps they will kill us all tonight!"

"I can't help you," I say, pushing back onto a knee.

Nikola straightens, paces several steps away.

"How is your new sibling—the commoner?" he says.

In an instant every misgiving I had about tonight turns to cold, clammy fear. I follow his gaze to the bank of screens as they zoom in and then coalesce into a single image: Luka, searching the crowd in the cavern, no doubt for me.

"They never have quite the same . . . rapture as the Progeny at court."

How long have they known? Is it possible that they know what Luka is, or has been? Sweat rolls down the inside of my kimono.

275

"He's not a part of this!"

"Why don't you hear us out?" Nikola says. This time I get up and sit when he gestures toward the chair.

"You came for protection. For you and your sibling. We don't care that he's common. Do what you like. But safety comes at a price. Recover what you buried and give it to us. Do that, and we will protect you from any ramification the Historian may visit on you. The entire court will. You will be its queen."

The truth hits me like the flash of a strobe. They've let me come to court just long enough to taste safety. But they never intended to let me stay. And now they won't hide me unless I resume whatever mission they thought I was on.

They don't want me. They want my mother. But if I was ever like her before, I definitely am not now.

I'm shaking so hard that it's an effort to merely sit still.

"Ivan himself said that if I had found the diary I wouldn't have stopped until I ended this," I say through clenched teeth. "And unless there's something someone hasn't told me, that's the only hope there is!"

"Is it?" Nikola says strangely.

"What more can there be?" I demand.

"That . . . is what we would like to know."

"What makes you think I found anything at

all?" I say. "Maybe I was tired of this game. This whole life. Maybe I just wanted to *live.* Did you consider that? Wanting to *actually live?*"

"No. It was the last thing you cared about. Just *living.*" Nikola says it like the word is dirty. "Tell her."

"Tell me what?"

"Something happened before you disappeared," Tibor says, giving up his pretense at madness altogether. His entire voice changes, dropping in tenor. "For more than a year, you were fanatical. Obsessed. You wanted to know everything about your mother. Anyone who knew her. Wanted anything that was hers. It was unsafe for you and Nikola to meet, though you visited court in Budapest on several occasions with Katia and Andre." He looks down, seems sad at the mention of their names.

He shrugs. "Not because you were in love with life at court, or because you wanted safety. But because it was your mother's life, or so you thought. But then something happened. Two months before you disappeared, you began to change. I thought that the Utod way of life had begun to wear on you. Some of us do go crazy, you know," he says wryly, looking up. "You began to stay away more and more. You became secretive. You were gone for weeks at a time without a word. When I saw you, you were exhausted. Preoccupied. I could see it in your eyes. You were on a holy quest."

"Don't pretend you knew anything about me," I say. But I'm calculating. By the time frame he's talking about, I knew what Luka was.

"Oh, but I did know you," Tibor says intensely. For the first time I realize that his eyes are a turbulent gray glittering with intelligence. That there is something wounded about his expression.

No. If he says we were involved, I think I'll actually vomit.

"You don't even know, do you? He didn't tell you." A soft laugh. "My brother—my true brother—was your adoptive sibling. Your protector. You and I were *family,*" he says.

"What?"

"You don't even know who I'm talking about, do you?" he says, sounding suddenly disgusted.

I glance from him to Nikola.

But then I do know.

"Ivan," I whisper.

"You broke his heart!" Tibor shouts. "What right did you have to leave as you did? To let him think you were dead?"

And the answer is: I don't know.

My mind is reeling, tilting like a madhouse. Why would I do that—to Ivan, a sibling sworn to protect me?

"He defended you," Tibor says. "To the court,

to me. He never stopped protecting you. Saying you could only have good reason, that you were shielding us all even as you disappeared. I called him a fool and worse. Ivan *died* without ever knowing what your disappearance was for!"

I feel sick, hearing those words. Amped as I am, it's all I can do not to lean over and vomit.

"You have two great objectives at this moment," Nikola says. "The first is to stay alive. The second is to recover what you knew. For your own sur-vival. For ours. The Utod cannot survive another generation in this age of digital surveillance, of DNA genealogy. This genera-tion will end it—all of this, once and for all . . . or die. *You* are the key to that. You always were."

I reel away, tug on the obi around my waist, trying to breathe.

I cannot do what they are asking. Even if I wanted to, what do I have to work with? A single key, a cryptic line. And while my bond with Ivan is a revelation to me, it does not come as a surprise. His contact was the only fail-safe I left myself. Now that he's gone, anything he might have known about me or my so-called mission is in the Historian's possession along with the rest of his memory.

Ivan tried to warn me before he died. And I chose not to listen.

Sick guilt washes over me again. Not just for his murder, but for what I must have put him through with my disappearance, the news of my death—the phone call out of the blue announcing my resurrection just a week ago.

And what have I been doing ever since? Dressing up and raving myself into a stupor each night and making love to my former hunter.

And the sad truth is this: I might even be able to give Nikola what he is asking for now, had I defended Ivan half as well as he defended me.

"Recover what you knew," Nikola says, "and we will keep you and your common sibling alive."

But I hear his implied inverse much more clearly: Fail and both will die.

I think of Claudia's statement just this morning about running away to China and wish now we had gone immediately. Why didn't we leave?

The passports, of course. The ones we have so far been unable to get replaced by Tibor's lackey Jester.

And then I let out an incredulous exhale.

"You," I say. "You had our backpacks stolen."

Tibor shrugs, like it's some joke I've taken too personally. "So what?"

"We are prepared to do far more," Nikola says.

"Yes, like die. I heard you," I snap.

He leans forward.

"Every few years, there are stories," he says quietly. "They show up in the news, much abridged, of course. Tragic deaths, suicides.

The real circumstances circulate through the underground. Of Utod, on the run from hunters. Men and women valuable to the Historian for their memories of names, faces, the whereabouts of other Progeny. Let alone the location of something so singular as the diary. Progeny who, facing impending assassination, fell into gravel crushers. Dove off cliffs. Ate bullets that destroyed their brains to protect such details from harvest. I loved Amerie. I was her sibling for nearly a decade. It was my job to protect her. But it was my job as well to protect those she knew. The fact that so many lives were not immediately taken upon her death is no coincidence. The fact that you lived to learn who you are is no accident. That was the depth of her commitment, Audra. And that is the depth of mine. To you, and to our kind."

"My mother drowned," I say slowly. "Her body was found in the Danube."

"Her body was found in the Danube. But she did not drown. She had been doggedly pursued for weeks. It had gone too far, she said. And she was right. I found her before her hunter could, which was by then only a matter of time. I protected her—and those she loved—as I had sworn to do. I made certain she died a hero, unwilling to become a villain in death."

I am very still, the echo of his whisper in my ears.

"You're saying . . ."

But I don't need him to repeat it.

I am staring my mother's killer in the eye.

"And so I make you another promise. If you cannot find the thing that caused you to disappear, which I believe was something greater, even, than the diary . . . or if you *will not* find it . . . we will do you the favor of killing you before a hunter can." He glances toward the television screens. "But we will dispense with those closest to you first."

27

For the first time I wonder if it's possible that I faked my own death not just to escape the Scions but to avoid being killed by my own kind.

Get out.

Get Luka, Claudia, Piotrek, and run.

My life, right now, is at least precious to them. But if Nikola suspects for a minute what he is, Luka will never step foot outside this court alive.

I force myself to ignore the television screens. Tibor and Nikola, I know, are waiting for an answer from me. The right one. Never mind that I have no way of finding what they want aside from a key that could open anything from a mailbox to a pair of fur-lined handcuffs. I need to get the others out alive, but Luka and I will never escape Europe without new passports.

Tibor sits, stone still, against the wall, his eyes sliding this way and that. But his gaze is very, very lucid as it darts between Nikola and me.

Is it possible he had no idea that Nikola killed my mother?

"So you'll protect us if I give you what you want."

"Yes."

"And kill me before you'll let a hunter take me if I fail."

"If it comes to it."

"But kill my friends if I refuse."

Nikola is silent.

"How can I do what you're asking when you haven't been completely honest with me? You say you care about Utod survival. But all you really want is power."

Nikola actually laughs. "You're young. You know nothing about power or the decisions that go with it. The consequences. I tried to convince Amerie to terminate you in the womb. You made her vulnerable. But she would not be dissuaded. When you were born, she took you to a foundling box in a Budapest hospital where women with unwanted children or, in her case, children they could not raise for obvious reasons could be left anonymously. She knew you would be cared for, adopted out to a good home. And that, God willing, one day you would find your way to her again.

"But everything she did from that point on . . . it wasn't for any of us. It was for *you*. The hope of you. You were her ruin. And she was nearly ours. When you found us the first time, a whole generation reared on whispers of her believed themselves inspired. And they were! They would end this war. I thought, here at last is the fulfillment of everything Amerie fought for. I was willing to accept I had been wrong. Then you disappeared, and the underground shattered in your wake. Do you think I reveled in being right?"

"Ivan believed in her," I say, daring to glance at Tibor.

"Ivan has always needed something greater than himself to believe in. God. The universe—these, I will grant him. But I have never under-stood his blind faith in you," Nikola says. "It killed him in the end. Yes, I ended Amerie to save us all. I will answer to God with full knowledge. But you killed Ivan in ignorance. Tell me, which of us is worse?"

But this is not about Ivan, who is already gone. It's about Claudia, whom I dare not abandon again. And Piotrek, wholly committed to her. And Luka, who gives his loyalty too staunchly.

"What I had was so dangerous I thought it best buried forever," I say slowly. "Knowing that, are you sure you want it found again? I may not be the reincarnation of my mother, but I'm also no idiot." I slide a glance to Tibor.

Nikola chuckles. "Look around you. The court is full of misunderstood genius in every form. It's in our blood. We are a court of savants. Brilliant. But shortsighted. I cannot allow you to ruin all that we worked for a second time. Nor for those inspired by a face—your mother's, yours—to be so misled. Find it, whatever it is, and deliver it to me. I will do what must be done."

I exhale a long breath through my nose as though about to answer against my better judgment.

"Ivan's last act was to get my fail-safe to me. I'm surprised he never gave it to you, Nikola, after he heard I was dead."

I let the insinuation hang in the air. I need Tibor to doubt him—enough to help me.

"A good thing," Nikola says. "Or I would have no need of you now. You have one week."

"Fine. I'll need passports, money."

"You don't need passports, as you will not be leaving Europe," Nikola says. "Money, you will receive before you go. We will keep the commoner."

Panic surges up within me.

"Did it ever occur to you that I have a common sibling for a reason? He, at least, won't give up his memory of me to the Historian if he dies!" I say it with far more conviction than I feel.

"Yes, you have a point. Keep your sibling. You see how easy this is? You act as though we are enemies, when, in fact, we are here to help."

"I never needed your help the first time, Nikola." I get to my feet. I need to get Luka and the others out of here.

"Enjoy your last night at court," Nikola says. "I trust when we speak next you will have much to tell me."

But I know as far as he's concerned, our conversation won't be over until I hand him the thing locked away by the key—probably along with my own head.

* * *

It's all I can do to move evenly past the guards, to keep from running down the tunnel.

To gaze steadfastly at the camera until I've passed beneath it.

The minute I enter the thundering cavern, I throw myself into the mob in search of Luka.

I'm painfully aware of the cameras—can see them now in the corners, on the wall, perched atop a bank of lights. The eyes that track me, human and electronic.

A hand grips mine and I spin, ready to shove its owner through the crowd, but instead I come face-to-face with Luka.

My breath leaves me in a shudder of relief. I have to force myself not to throw my arms around him even as my legs, jerky with adrenaline, threaten to give out.

Luka nods toward the way we came in. But to leave this minute would be an accurate display of my abject fear. And I just can't give Nikola that.

There's another reason I'm unwilling to go. Because I am strangely elated. Yes, what I did was foolish. But we're all adrenaline junkies here, in some form or another. And after cowering and scurrying from the corner of one country to another, it feels good—so good—to have stood upright for a moment. I am high with the kind of adrenaline that comes with stepping out on a narrow ledge. And by God, while I'm there, I'm going to dance.

I leap up into Luka's arms and he catches me at the last possible instant, his responses jarred to catlike life, clutching my legs to his chest as I throw my arms toward the lights overhead with a shout.

I have no idea what I'll say to Claudia. She'll hate me, maybe, when I tell her we can never come back. Thinking about this only makes it worse, and the need to move more essential until I'm caught up on the shoulders of a fiery phoenix with flames on his mask and arms.

I know that feeling, of rising from ashes. Of stumbling on reborn legs that have forgotten how to stand. Of threatening to set yourself—and everyone around you—on fire.

I thought I had to find answers. I thought I had to find safety. I have neither answers nor safety—less of each, in fact, than before. But I am alive. Right now. And for this moment, at least, I am done with dying. With anonymity, which is its own form of death. My face already conceals more than I will ever remember of who I am.

In the periphery of my vision I spot a camera along the wall. Tibor and Nikola and who knows how many others, monitoring an underground more tightly controlled than the streets above.

With a sweep of my arm I tear off my mask. Toss it high over the milling mass of Progeny.

288

The gold hairpiece gets flung against the wall. Last of all the wig, hurled directly at the camera. It snags, obscuring the lens. I don't care if my hair is mashed, or if the scar from my procedure is visible through the patch of hair behind my ear. In fact, I hope it is.

Luka swiftly pulls me down. He's shouting, and though I can't hear him, I make out the shape of his words.

What are you doing?

The music drives on, but all around me people have frozen in place like pillars.

I want to announce, maniacally, that the rumors of my death are greatly exaggerated. I laugh, but no one around me is smiling. It is a private joke between fate and me. I will soon be disappearing, for good this time no doubt, and the Historian already knows I am here. The charade, at least for me, is over.

Luka tugs me toward the exit. Farther back, Claudia and Piotrek are worming their way toward us through the stunned mass, Ana and Nino in their wake.

I turn back at the door one last time and, after winking to the nearest camera, bow grandly before Luka drags me out by the arm.

The butler in the cell outside stops us as we make for the main tunnel.

"This way," he says, leading us in a different direction. He slips a package into my hand. And then we rush through a narrow passage to come up into a decrepit building.

When we emerge onto Visoka Street, I turn my face to the starless sky.

It is raining.

We range farther through the city than we ever have, Claudia chattering in outrage and then awe at my actions earlier. The outrage, I expected. Even anger. The awe, well, I didn't see that coming.

"It's like you gave fear, life, everyone the finger," she says with relish. "I wish Ivan were alive to see it!"

Me, too.

Claudia talks about how some girl dancing next to her started to scream the minute I took off my mask as though she had seen a dead body.

She might have, I think.

We end up on the edge of the city, where we race up a fire escape, free-climbing the last story to the rooftop to take in the lights of Zagreb. And I know it's the last time I'll see them.

"How many Progeny are in the city tonight, do you think?" I say.

"Two hundred," Claudia says.

"Three," Nino says.

"And they're all talking about you," Claudia says.

Luka reaches down and takes my hand. Our

heads turn in unison at the sound of running steps. Nino, sprinting for the edge of the roof. I scream, and Luka lets go of me to hurry after him. I follow suit, already afraid of what I'll see. But before I reach the edge I hear Nino's whoop from somewhere below. Luka stops on the edge of the roof, shakes his head. A second later, Piotrek blazes past us. Ana pulls off her shoes and lobs them one at a time onto the neighboring roof before following suit.

Claudia catches my arm when we're the only ones left.

"You met him, didn't you?"

"Yes. Not just him. Nikola was there, too."

Her eyes widen.

"Luka and I have to leave, Claudia. And so should you and Piotrek." I give her a slight smile. "It's time for that trip to China."

Shouts from below, calling us.

"They want you to find it, don't they? What you forgot."

"If I don't, they'll come after us."

She nods, squinting toward the east, which is just turning the color of denim. "Ana and Nino can go where they like. But Piotrek and I . . . we're coming with you."

"Claudia, I can't find it. Whatever it was is gone."

"We stay together."

"It's not safe!"

"Screw safe! We're family."

"You can't speak for Piotrek."

"He'll tell you the same thing himself when we get back."

And then she's running off the edge of the building.

Thirty minutes later, Nino has hijacked a Vespa, which he plans to take to some skateboard park.

"It's his new thing," Ana says with a laugh before climbing on the back. I'm going to miss her.

"Meet us at the flat before dawn. It's important," I say before they speed away.

We leave Claudia and Piotrek to talk in private near a low bridge over the river, where I know she'll end up diving into the muddy water. A last burn before we pack up and go. But I can't fathom jumping into even a tributary of the Danube. Not after my conversation earlier tonight.

Instead, I *persuade* an off-duty cabdriver to drop us off near the funicular. I've been silent all this time, Luka worrying his lower lip between his teeth. Now that we're finally alone, I begin to shiver violently in the rain.

The moment the cab pulls away, I collapse to the wet pavement with a shudder.

"Audra!" Luka slides an arm around my middle.

"He killed her."

"Who? Killed who?"

"Nikola. He was there tonight. With Tibor. He killed Amerie. He killed my mother!"

Luka pulls me to my feet. But I curl in on myself, sobbing. Finally, he just lifts me into his arms.

I can smell him even in the rain. The scent that is a part of him as much as his eyes. His hands are strong—enough to kill—but gentle as they hold me to his chest. He touches a kiss to my temple as he carries me into the building, down the stairs of Claudia's flat.

"We have to leave," I say. "When Claudia and Piotrek get back."

"All right."

He doesn't bother to get a towel, wraps a blanket around me after he's peeled away my wet clothes, setting the package beside the bed.

His hands know me. His mouth knows me. And, impossibly, his heart knows me, too.

Better than my own.

I lift my face as though he were sun, rain, air. Tell myself there is no future and no past. Nothing but the soft sound of his groan. The ragged hiss of his breath. The whisper, when it comes.

I love you, Audra.

Words are eternal.

The moment, however, is not.

293

28

"Someone else just got back," I say.

We lie, limbs twined, after the final burn of the night. It's nearly dawn. I felt the first couple return hours ago. I can hear them, talking in the front room.

Luka smells like sweat and skin. I know this scent, though I don't remember it. I love it—and him. I know that, too, though it's only been days. But experience is not love.

And I am done with logic.

We talk in the darkness of the purple lamp, and I tell him everything. He's quiet the entire time.

"I haven't been afraid since the day you walked into the Food Mart," he says at last. "Not really. Not until now."

Claudia's words ring through my mind:

I want to live.

I straighten against Luka's chest, lift my head to look at him.

"Then we'll go until we aren't afraid," I say. I roll toward the package on the bed stand, tangled in my obi.

Luka's fingers light on my spine.

"Audra . . ." he says strangely.

I peer inside the package and then curse. It's full of cash, no passports.

"What's this, on your back?"

I crane around, not knowing what he means.

A scream erupts from down the hall. At first I think it's an obscene laugh, or a screech from the kitchen, maybe the coffeemaker. Until it comes again, horribly human and hysterical.

I shove my arms into Luka's damp dress shirt and run into the front room after Luka, who is still buttoning his jeans.

Ana is swaying on her feet; Piotrek grabs her by the waist. Claudia, pale and frozen, holds her phone in a shaking hand.

"What's going on?" Luka says.

Claudia turns the phone toward me.

I cup my hand around hers to steady it. A picture on the screen—a video. A human form, bound and badly beaten. I take in the angle of the shoulders, stymied by the blackened eyes and swelling cheek. But I recognize the aubergine jacket, which I last saw riding away on a Vespa.

Nino.

I turn away. But I can't unsee it, or stop staring even after it's gone from sight. A groan from the video. He's alive, if not conscious. And somehow the sound makes it worse.

"Nino never showed up," Claudia says faintly, holding the phone out for someone to take it. Luka does and, mouth grim, turns away to replay the video.

"Why? Why? Nino!" Ana cries, splintering my heart.

And I know, without being told, that this is because of me.

I convinced Nikola I needed Luka. Thought as soon as we left we'd all be safe. But the Prince of Budapest never meant to let me go without collateral.

How long have they been watching me? How easy was it for him to see my soft spot for Ana, for whom the moon rises and sets on Nino?

"Which of them did this?" Piotrek demands.

"Nikola," I say, hoarse.

"Where would they take him? He can't be that far."

"Listen." Luka turns up the volume. Drone of an engine.

I move toward him, force myself to watch the full twenty-two seconds from the beginning, to take in the dark interior, the jostle of the phone recording the video, the metal floor beneath him. "He's in a semi trailer. He could be any-where."

I press my fingers against my eyes. One toss of my mask. A grand-bow exit. Claudia's wrong—I didn't give the finger to everyone, just to Nikola.

This is my fault.

I take it all back—the bravado, the insinuation. The accusations, the snark.

I have to find Nikola. To say I'll do it. I'll find

it and give it to him, say I'm sorry—whatever he wants to hear.

Claudia's phone rings in Luka's hand. She stares across the room at it, face stricken.

"Answer it," I say. She takes it from him as one in a trance. Answers, and then holds it toward me.

"It's for you," she whispers.

I snatch it to my ear. "Who is this?"

"Audra." Tibor.

I move out of earshot of Ana. "Where's Nino?" I hiss.

"Is it true what you said?"

"Yes," I say, not knowing what he's even referring to, trying to replay the conversation now jumbled in my head. "Isn't it obvious that he's playing you? We just got a video of Nino beaten half to death in a truck! If you think for a minute that I'm going to do anything to help you—"

"I didn't know about your mother. What Nikola said about murdering her . . . Progeny don't turn on their own."

"Nikola's a killer, Tibor. Criminally insane. Where's Nino?" I demand.

"I don't know! I just heard that he was taken near the edge of the city."

"Then tell me where to find Nikola."

"You don't just find Nikola! He finds you! Forget Nino. He's as good as dead."

I spin away, out of earshot of Ana. "Don't say that!"

"I'm sending you Jester. It's the best I can do."

"I don't want Jest—"

The call clicks off. I stare at the phone and then throw it across the room.

When I turn, even Piotrek's face is white.

"We have to go," I say.

We leave ten minutes later, Luka practically carrying a catatonic Ana to the car.

"Where?" Piotrek says as we leave the old upper city.

Behind darkened glasses, I mentally search the map I saw in the back of the in-flight magazine. The Budapest court, once our next destination, is now last on the list somewhere below Afghanistan. Which leaves Bosnia to the south, Slovenia to the north, and Italy to the far west, given our lack of passports.

"Go north," Luka says.

No one speaks. Ana sags against the corner of the back seat beside me, doped up on something Claudia gave her. Whatever it is, I wish I had some, too. I can't stop shifting, my legs too restless, my skull pounding so hard I think I may be sick.

Luka lays his arm around me, but it doesn't help. I am replaying my conversation with Nikola last night, my unfortunate exit from court. Wishing I could redo it, sneak out the back, that we had all left within the hour. I cannot erase the image of Nino beaten nearly beyond recognition. Between him and Ivan, I wonder if I will ever be free of guilt.

Hell must be like this.

So this is what it has come to, the search that first brought me here: all of us in a crowded Skoda on the run to nowhere.

This time there is no mention of the mafia, no talking around what we are in front of Luka, and Ana is too doped to notice.

"Audra," Luka murmurs near my ear sometime later. Claudia and Ana are dozing, Piotrek fixed on the road, his gaze miles away. I lift my head, realize belatedly that I must have dozed, too.

"I think I know what goes with your key."

29

We stop a couple hours later at a hostel in Graz, Austria, where Piotrek books us a six-bed dorm room under the name Franz Müller.

We promptly pull the shades, put Ana to bed. Sometime after the others have gone to sleep, Luka gets up, rummages through the pack Claudia loaned us, grabs the little pad and pencil off the desk, and gestures me into the bathroom.

Inside, he switches the lightbulb in the fixture with the purple one from Claudia's flat.

"What are you doing?"

"Take off your shirt," he says.

"Seriously?"

"Just do it."

I tug the back of it over my head, and Luka swivels me away from the light.

"Can you see this?" he says. I glance back in the mirror.

"What is that?" There's a line of six symbols glowing down my spine like some alien street sign. None of them are familiar, but something about the boxiness of the figures is.

"I just noticed these this morning."

"You know every scar on my body and you've never seen these before?"

"It's not like I've seen you under a black light

till this week. Didn't even notice them until this morning. Look. They're sharp—can't be that old."

He starts to copy them onto the pad. I strain the other way in front of the mirror, flipping the images in my mind.

"I think I know what that is," I whisper and tug his phone from his pocket.

I search "Glagolitic script," filter for images, and locate a chart of characters.

"Write this down. Z . . . B . . . G." I search out each one, comparing boxy consonants, archaic vowels. "E . . . A . . . D. The last one's not on there."

He makes a face. "Zbgead something? Not Zagreb . . ."

"Are you reading up or down?"

"Down. Up spells something daegbz."

"The same characters also stand for numbers." I search through the chart. "Try 9 . . . 2 . . . 4 . . . 6 . . . 1 . . . 5." I glance up at him. "That mean anything to you?"

"924615 . . ." he says. "924 . . ."

For a minute I think he actually pales in the black light's purple glow.

"What?"

"I just . . ." He nods toward the key dangling from my neck. "Claudia said that was Shakespeare. I never saw you read Shakespeare."

"Maybe you don't know me as well as you

think," I murmur. Why do I feel like there's something he's not saying?

"Better than you do. Let me read that?"

I hold the key up, and he searches the phrase on the phone.

"Measure for Measure," he says. I pull my shirt back over my head. But something's bothering me, scratching at the back of my mind.

I squint at him as he reads: "A story of 'morality and mercy.' Sounds eerily familiar," he mutters, and then hesitates. "It's set in Vienna."

"Vienna."

"Austria. As in a few hours away."

"We're in Europe. Everything's a few hours away. It's practically New England."

He frowns.

"I'm joking. Not really."

"Who uses keys anymore? Old-school banks, maybe. But why would you need a key if you have a code? What if this key's more about what's on it than what it does?"

"So it's telling me where to go, not how to unlock something."

"Maybe. Meanwhile, if this is what you picked to remind you where it is—"

"I'm an idiot. Because anyone could have figured out the same thing. Seriously, a Google search? That's my level of encryption?"

He gives a wry smile. "You have to admit, this does sound like your humor. 'Some rise by sin, some by virtue fall.' A jab at the Scions and claim to Bathory's innocence in a single line."

"Just in case it landed in the wrong pair of hands?" Apparently I've had my mouthing-off problem for a while.

"Audra," he says slowly, "you *could* potentially find what Nikola's after."

I cross my arms around myself, not sure how I feel about that. And suddenly I have a very unwelcome thought.

And if you're with me, then so could you.

I had thought my reservations about him settled. Literally put to bed.

"We don't know what the other symbol is," I say.

"Yet. Maybe Claudia or Piotrek has seen it somewhere."

I'm quiet.

"Audra . . ." He takes my hand. "I'm with you, whatever you decide. Wherever you go." He kisses my fingers. But there's strange conflict in his eyes.

"Just do me a favor," I say.

"Anything. You know that."

"If, by some chance, you really are with me for a different reason . . . take the key. You have the code now. Don't hurt anyone. Just go and do what you have to do and leave us alone."

He looks as though I've struck him. And I hate myself for what I just said, but I can't help it.

Because I can't stand the thought of one more life on my conscience—all because I chose to trust the one person I really want to believe more than anyone.

"What does it take to prove myself to you?" he says, his voice breaking. "That I'm not after what everyone else is, even though I'm the most logical person to want it?"

"I don't know," I say and wish that I did. He takes me by the shoulders and kisses me—roughly, with rising desperation, fingers encircling my arms. I welcome it, wanting it to expel every fear inside my mind. Instead, tears squeeze out the corners of my eyes.

"I *love* you, Audra," he whispers. "Don't you get it?"

I love you, too.

And that's what scares me.

I pull away and leave him there, return silently to bed.

A minute later, he steps out of the bathroom and quietly puts the lightbulb away. But I know I've hurt him. I know it, and I can't help it.

And I know, too, that Ana's not asleep.

30

I lie in my bunk a long time, trying to make sense of the symbols, the letters or numbers they represent. Pounding against the empty storehouse of my memory for anything to do with Vienna, Shakespeare, sin and virtue, even rearranging the words and then the letters of the cryptic line on the key.

Why did I go to the trouble of having those symbols permanently tattooed on my body? To put them in a place that only a lover—near a black light, no less—would see? Something meant to be revealed under the right circumstances—Claudia's flat, the dark strobe at court. Something there, if I needed it, its discovery contingent on my return, but invisible under normal conditions.

The pants in the spare closet were mine. Did I also put the black light in that lamp?

A fail-safe. Like the numbers in the tao cross and the key I left Ivan for safekeeping, assuming we'd both be alive.

In the end I decided that the fact Nikola wants it so desperately is reason enough for me to deem it Bad. That we stand a better chance of surviving in some remote district of Mongolia or Siberia—assuming we can finagle a border crossing—than anywhere having to do with the Bathorys.

But what of those we leave behind? Four lives have already been lost. For all I know, Nino's might already be the fifth. No wonder I erased mine to bury it all.

Sometime midmorning, I spot movement on the ladder of the bunk beds across the room. Ana steps from the last rung without a sound, a blond-haired wraith in a white T-shirt.

"Can't sleep?" I whisper. She looks up, dully.

It kills me to see the stars gone from her eyes.

"Come on," I say, holding back the covers as though she were twelve. She climbs in beside me and cries against my shoulder until it's wet, clutching me like I'm the last strong thing to hold on to in a storm.

My mind is disobedient in sleep. The last symbol, the one nothing at all like the boxy Glagolitic characters and set apart by a small space from the others, is littered through my dreams.

"Audra, get up."

I open my eyes on Claudia, in a blunt-cut black wig, bangs hanging down to her shades. "We have a problem."

"What?"

"Ana's missing."

I rub my eyes. "What do you mean missing—" I stop at the sight of a leggy, olive-skinned brunette with shoulder-length dreads sitting on one of the low bunks against the wall. She's clad entirely in purple, from her dress to her tights and knee-high boots, an open laptop at her side.

"Who's that?" I demand.

"That's Jester," she says.

I stare, dumbfounded. *That's Jester?*

The new arrival gets up and comes over. There's something different about one of her legs—the angle of her knee is slightly off—and only when she's kissing my cheeks in greeting do I realize it's prosthetic.

"How'd you find us?"

"I tracked Claudia's phone," Jester says. Her accent is unmistakably French. "Isn't it exciting?"

"Tracking a phone?"

"No! That Tibor has declared war against Nikola and thrown his lot in with you. He sends his regards, by the way," she says, dropping several German passports on the bed beside me.

"What do you mean Ana's missing?" I say, staring at them.

"She said she was going for coffee, but that was hours ago. Piotrek's looking for her."

Across the room, Luka's scratching a pencil over the pad on the desk. A few seconds later he holds it up. It's covered with imprints from the sheet above. The last symbol from my back, drawn again and again and again.

"The top page is missing." He strides over and pulls the neck of my shirt aside. Instinctively, I reach for the key. But I already know it's missing.

"She took the copy of the symbols and their translations from my backpack," Luka says grimly.

"What symbols?" Claudia says.

In my anger, which is only a thin disguise for the fear turning my fingertips to ice, I round on Claudia. "I go to sleep for what—three hours? And crazy Tibor declares some war against Nikola, *she* shows up with a laptop as though none of this is bad enough that we need a digital trail, too, and Ana goes missing with a drawing of the symbols on my back. What genius felt the need to draw them over and over anyway before she ran off with my key?" I demand. "How many different ways can we try to get ourselves killed?"

"Audra—" Luka says, gesturing at me.

I glance down at myself, and then at the pencil in my hand.

My sleepwalking activities have returned. That, and I'm such an ass.

"What symbols?" Claudia says, as Jester's laptop chirps.

I go into the bathroom to splash water on my face as Jester practically sprints across the room.

"I found her," she calls out. In the mirror I see Luka and Claudia sit down on either side of her to stare at the screen. Claudia covers her mouth with a hand.

What now? I don't think I can take any more of sucking so bad at being on the lam.

"She's in Budapest."

I stride out to the bed and sit next to Luka. "How do you know?" There, on the screen, is camera footage of a woman coming up out of a subway station in a pair of shades and what looks like one of Claudia's wigs. Her face is covered with electronic dots, an image of her on a window to the right.

"How did you get this?"

"Jester has certain skills," Claudia says. A minute later she's on the phone with Piotrek speaking in clipped Croatian.

Jester's a *hacker?*

"Where's she going?" Luka says.

"She's on the Buda side near the Danube," Jester says with obvious dismay. "No, no—"

"No what?"

"Gellert Hill. She's going underground," Jester says, typing frantically.

"Then we can find her."

"We're about to lose her."

"You just said you know where she is!"

"There's a whole world under the Buda Hills! A church, bunkers, a complete World War Two hospital. Hundreds of cave systems, some kilometers long! Why do you think tracking Nikola is so difficult? Even the city doesn't know everything that's there. The Budapest princes have intentionally kept entire systems secret for centuries, going so far as to steal the city's survey of the caves beneath Castle Hill in the late eighteen hundreds. As far as anyone knows, it disappeared and has never been found."

"You think Nikola has the survey," I say.

"Undoubtedly. It is the reason the Budapest court is the safest and most famous in the world. It has been the safe haven of the Progeny who found their way to it for years."

"So Ana's looking for Nikola," I say. With the key and a copy of the symbols on my back. "But you're saying she may never find him. That she may never see the light of day again!"

"Unless he reached out to her first. Look." She points to the screen. "These are not the movements of a girl wandering aimlessly. She knows where she is going."

And as I watch the specter on the screen, she's right; I've never seen Ana so resolute.

"Why would she look for Nikola?" Claudia says.

"To exchange information for Nino." I get to my feet, fingers digging into my hair.

"She'll be underground in minutes," Jester says. "I can try to trigger a fire or smoke alarm near the church, but then they'll know something is up. They'll be that much harder to find."

"No," I say, getting up. "Let her go."

"She's got your key!" Claudia says.

"Her fake key," Luka says quietly.

But that's not all Nikola will have if she reaches him.

He'll have Ana, too.

I squeeze my eyes shut, fists pressed to my head.

It won't stop. It will never stop. Who will be next? Claudia? Piotrek? Or will they go straight for Luka?

Claudia was more right than she knew that first night when she said it would have been better if I'd stayed dead. At the time, at least, she had been talking about the Scions—not our own blood.

Piotrek returns and listens, grim-faced, to Claudia's rapid account in Croatian. Luka asks if there's someone in Budapest close enough to intercept Ana, but she has since disappeared.

I get up, grab my jacket. "Let's go," I say.

Luka, watching me all this time, closes up our bags.

"She could be anywhere underground by the time we get to Budapest," Claudia says.

"Not Budapest," I say, shouldering my backpack. "Vienna."

Because the only way I'm going to have any-thing to bargain with is to get to it first.

We skirt down the back stairs to the first floor. Just outside the common room Piotrek slows and nearly stops altogether. The television in the corner drones on to no one. Two girls at the center table sit engrossed in conversation, the guy in the corner oblivious to all but his laptop. Luka veers toward me without slowing.

"Move. Don't stop," he says, taking me by the elbow.

Too late. Even after he walks me swiftly out the side door to the car, the television screen is embedded in my memory.

Filled with a picture of me.

31

Sitting in the back of the Skoda, I might be in shock.

"What did it say?" I ask, my voice steadier than I feel. I can picture every letter of the caption, but it's in German.

"They found Nino's body. You're wanted for his murder," Piotrek says. In the back seat, Luka reaches for my hand.

I close my eyes.

Did Nino bleed out on the floor of that trailer, or did they kill him? Did he die alone—or at Nikola's hands?

I try to block the images, but they play out with brutal detail, nearly as though I had witnessed them.

What will happen to Ana now?

"They're calling you a serial killer," Piotrek says. "Saying you killed a man in Croatia last week."

Beside me, Claudia stares out the window in silence. I wonder if she's thinking how close to the truth it is, calling me a murderer. It doesn't matter that I never drew blood, could not have possibly inflicted that kind of damage on a man Nino's size. He and Ivan both are dead because of me.

The resolve I felt ten minutes ago has frayed to a single thread. And I know if I allow myself to think about Ana—fragile, so lost without Nino—I will come completely undone.

"Turn here," Jester says from the front seat, laptop open on her knees. "We need to switch cars. I'm lining one up now."

"Why are you doing this?" I blurt out. "Tibor volunteered you, but you don't strike me as anyone's lackey."

" 'Lackey'?" she says. Claudia translates. I had no idea she spoke French.

"Tibor's been trying to gather information on Nikola for years. It's something of an addiction to me now. I am sorry for you, but this is a gold mine to me. Katia was my sister."

"I need a chart," I mutter. "Between 'siblings,' real siblings, and love interests, the underground's worse than Arkansas."

Piotrek frowns in the rearview mirror. "I don't understand."

"Does it seem strange to anyone but me that other Progeny are willing to kidnap or brutalize their own for Nikola?" I say. "For someone willing to kill his own people?"

"He is the Prince of Budapest," Claudia says quietly. "He is very powerful. More so today, as he's become so elusive. He's more a myth than a man to most Progeny—practically a god to young Utod like Ana. You're the only person

I've heard of, other than Tibor, ever speaking to him. And yes. Every prince has the authority to remove any Progeny he considers dangerous. Now you understand why I was afraid."

"So court is safe as long as you don't stand out enough to get killed."

"I've altered your facial nodes in the police database," Jester says. "It may help for a while. Meanwhile, here is the news article: 'Audra Ellison, wanted for the murders of Nino Kolar and Imre Tomić and the kidnapping of fifteen-year-old Ana Gudac.' "

"Kidnapping?"

"It says you drugged and kidnapped her after murdering her partner in a fit of jealousy. There's no mention of anyone else by name. Only that you may be traveling with others."

At least I've been singled out. It isn't a guarantee of anyone else's safety, but for now, at least, they're not in the news.

I don one of Claudia's wigs before we leave the Skoda at a car rental lot and switch to a larger Peugeot kombi complete with expressway stickers.

Fifteen minutes later, Jester's got the etching of the last symbol on my back propped against her laptop screen, where she's re-creating it by hand, muttering at every bump through a construction zone.

If Jester cracks that symbol, I will finally know

what I've been protecting all this time. The thing that Nikola and the Scions alike want desperately enough to kill for. A weapon, Nikola called it. Evidence that most likely proves Bathory's guilt—why else would I have erased it? What makes Nikola so sure, then, that he can use it against the Scions?

But right now my biggest question is how to wield that same weapon against him.

"You said you've been gathering information on Nikola for years," I say to Jester. "Like what?"

"Anything. What courts he appears at. Who his confidants are. Few have the courage to openly oppose him, but Tibor has never trusted him. Not since the rumor began that Nikola wanted to make a census. You can imagine the kind of alarm that would create, how dangerous that would be in any hand—even one of our own. Nikola argued that the Historian already has such a census in the form of a genealogy dating back centuries. Or, at least, that has been the rumor forever. Every time a hunter makes a kill and harvests a memory, a little piece of that puzzle gets filled in for the current and previous generation. It's how they know to assign new hunters to marks as new Progeny are discovered."

"A death map," Claudia says.

"With such a genealogy the Scions can trace bloodlines for hundreds of years to the children of Elizabeth we descend from: Anastasia, who was illegitimate, and Pál—the only male to pass the legacy, which he received from Elizabeth herself. The Franciscans kept such a thing for us once until the practice was abolished, two hundred years ago, when the genealogy was stolen and many Utod died."

"What could Nikola possibly gain from a census?" Luka says. "Except for the potential to wipe out an entire underground?"

"Just that," I say. "The potential to wipe out an entire underground."

But why?

"No, there is more," Jester says. "Because the legacy is passed through the mother, the children of Elizabeth's illegitimate daughter are more powerful than those of her legitimate son. But they are also far more rare. They were the highest-priority targets of the Scions for centuries, the most hunted of the hunted. Tibor believes that Nikola is searching for some missing remnant of Anastasia's line."

"More powerful how?"

"No one knows. The bloodline died out or went into hiding nearly a century ago." Jester lifts her shoulders. "But Nikola's been obsessed with it."

Could that be what Nikola thinks I found? Some remnant of that line? Maybe it's never been the diary after all!

"For what purpose?"

She shrugs. "Who knows? He's a madman."

"And Tibor isn't as crazy as he lets on," I murmur.

"No. On the contrary, he's frighteningly intelligent, with a deep ability to understand the psychology of others."

"Crazy or not, Nikola's no idiot, either. How did he become Prince of Budapest, anyway? How does anyone?"

"A matter of connection and charisma."

"All the Progeny have charisma," I say.

"Yes, but the underground is the ultimate experiment in leadership. You know who the true leaders are—others talk about them in mythic terms. People follow them, if only out of curiosity. Why do you think I am here?"

"You said yourself: because of Katia."

"For the excitement, no? We can't all jump off high buildings," she says wryly. "And everyone is talking about you for days now. We Utod have our own pop culture, being comprised mostly of young people. You are a celebrity."

It's true that Progeny culture—court itself—is practically a cult of youth. In that way, I suppose, the legends about Elizabeth Bathory have lived on—forever young, charismatic, beautiful . . . and just as walled up as ever.

"Nikola was nothing, once," Jester continues. "But he was afraid of nothing. That will get you far at court. But it was becoming close to your mother that put him on the map."

"How?"

"He became a zealot. Much as Amerie was rumored to have been. And zealots are idolized at court, because they are filled with passion. They are alive. They are out doing zealot things! Like having their memories erased."

"If you're here for fame by association, I strongly suggest you rethink your motives," I mutter.

A blip sounds from Jester's computer, and a large gold version of the logo she entered off my sketch balloons onto the screen.

"Aha," she says. "Here it is."

I had forgotten about the computer, searching in silence all this time. Now, at sight of the symbol, I think I might be ill.

Luka's hand tightens around mine as though sensing the sick lurch in my gut. He's been quiet, no doubt upset at what I said last night. Maybe even reconsidering his promise to protect me no matter what. And while I selfishly hope that's not the case—would be lost, actually, if he left me now—a part of me can't possibly blame him.

I also feel guilty for wanting him to stay when I know Ana is somewhere on this earth alone.

"This is the Glagolitic symbol for life," Jester says with some surprise. "And . . . it is also the logo for Der Tresorraum in Vienna—a private vault unaffiliated with any bank." She taps the screen and looks back at me. "How did you know it was Vienna?"

"Luka figured it out," I say, glancing at him. But he is tense, and silent.

Auerspergstrasse, Vienna, is lined with Baroque buildings, their columns set into outer walls, elaborate banisters trimming the roofs. Rich, yes. But not at all how I pictured the setting for a high-tech vault. I check my wig in the rearview mirror, make sure that a section falls over my face. It's weird to have long hair, to be nearly my natural color again.

"This vault offers anonymous safety deposit boxes," Jester says. "You cannot get this even in Zurich anymore. However long you took the box out for—one year, ten, thirty—it wasn't cheap. But here is why you did it: There's no identification required. Just your pass code and biometrics."

"I don't like this," Luka says. "Nikola had no choice but to let you find it. He can't fake your biometrics."

"Which means I'll be fine," I say. *At least until I get in.*

Piotrek looks into the mirror at me. "We will let you and Luka out on that side street and circle back in fifteen minutes, and then every five after that."

"I'm going alone," I say.

"You can't," Claudia says. "Luka, don't let her!"

But he does not insist. An effort, I know, to

try to prove his motives. But his jaw is twitching.

"We've already passed more traffic cameras than I can count," I say. "And for all we know, Nikola's got someone watching the building. A second person is just another opportunity to identify one of us. I'll find a different way out, meet you there on the back of the block," I say, pointing to Lange Gasse street on Jester's screen.

"There's a hotel on the corner," Jester says. "We can meet there. You're on your own till you get out; I don't dare try to access their system while you're in there except for emergency. Remember what I said about the cameras. Alter your stride if you can."

"Call at the first sign of trouble," Luka says, something frantic in his gaze.

"I promise," I say, and mean it.

I slide on my shades as we pull to a stop and quickly get out, belting Claudia's borrowed jacket around me. I can *feel* them pull away, leaving me strangely bereft and all too conscious of the fact that I am, for the first time in days, alone.

I turn the corner and walk past the Auersperg palace at a swift clip, pretend to answer a call, my hand cupped around the microphone, obscuring my mouth and cheek. The section that is Auerspergstrasse is only two blocks, but it's part of a much longer thoroughfare regulated by cameras. The fact that Parliament is visible a block east from here just past a roundabout doesn't help.

Der Tresorraum might as well be a bank or even a museum by the look of it, except for the modern glass front doors. Not what I would have expected for a vault. I carry on my fake conversation as I pass beneath the camera at the entrance.

The interior is sparse, at modern odds with the Baroque architecture out front. A receptionist sits behind a desk in an anteroom beside a large steel statue that looks vaguely like a spiral tunnel.

"*Kann ich Ihnen helfen*?" the man at the desk says as I pocket my phone.

"Do you speak English?" I say.

"Yes, of course. May I help you?" he says without smiling. I wonder if he can hear the pulse pounding in my ears.

"I'd like to access my box."

He rises. "This way, please."

He escorts me through a door, which he opens with a key card. Down the hall past several secure corridors, he admits me to a windowless chamber. It houses nothing more than a desk, the woman sitting behind it, and the unmistakable entrance to a giant vault set in the adjacent wall.

The woman gestures to a pad on her desk. "*Bitte*," she says, and I assume by the outline on the screen that I'm supposed to lay my hand on it.

I wonder if she sees that my fingers are trembling, the moist smear my palm leaves against the screen.

And then a lock clacks on the vault's steel door, and she crosses the room to haul it open for me.

The "vault" is nothing but a large room housing two counters, each with a metal plate in the middle and a standing touch screen.

"There are two rooms in the back for your privacy," she says, pointing like a flight attendant.

The skin of my neck feels clammy against the wig. I don't take off my shades, having noted the cameras throughout the vault. So much for anonymity, I think, moving swiftly to the nearest counter as soon as the woman is gone. I select English, key in my code as it prompts me. Tap my fingers on the counter. Wonder, for the first time since Jester's search, if the Glagolitic symbol for life on my spine was just that—a reminder to live. If the numbers above it mean something else, have no correlation to this place whatsoever.

The plate in the counter abruptly slides open. A biometric thirteen-by-fifteen-inch box arrives on an elevator platform. I stare at it for a long moment before picking it up. It is surprisingly light, but it might as well weigh a ton. It carries the mass of multiple lives and has cost me my past and possibly my future as well.

I carry the box to one of the rooms, which lights up as I enter, and lock the door behind me. Set the box on the table, remove my shades. Sink into the chair.

My mouth is dry as I press my thumb to the pad, and a part of me actually prays that it will not open.

But God doesn't hear that one.

It chirps, flashes green.

I slowly lift the lid.

32

The oversize envelope inside is nearly two inches thick. I lift it out, fumble with the old-fashioned string.

A leather journal slides out on a stack of papers. The book is worn around the edges, the ties that bind it stiff from lack of humidity.

I know I should shove everything back in the envelope and go. But I also know it could be hours before I have any semblance of privacy; I can't fathom processing any of what this is— let alone what it might mean—in front of an audience.

I coax the ties open, flip through the journal, which is nearly full. A small photo drifts onto the table, and I pick it up. A newborn in a yellow outfit. I turn it over. It's marked *"Audra két napos."*

My breath escapes me as though I've been punched. I have never seen a picture of myself this young. Where did I get this, who took it—and where?

Photo between the fingers of one hand, I turn to the front of the journal.

The first twenty or so pages are a list of notes in my handwriting.

Born Vojvodina 1981 mother: Serafina
father?
Belgrade: 1992–December 1994 (Bosnian
  war)
1995: lover—Marton ___?
. . .
Budapest 1997–1998 Prince: Attila
1996: Nyirbator
2001: Attila killed
2002–January 2003: Budapest Prince:
  Andrik
2005: Returned Budapest? Tamas killed?
2008: Zagreb Prince: Imre
2013: Bratislava 2x
2016: Croatia ___?
Died August? Body found near Csepel
  Island, Budapest

I blink, heart stuttering. I had been tracking someone.

My mother.

I scan back. Find the name Imre. Remember the caption the night of Ivan's death, his name given on the television. Was Ivan once Prince of Zagreb?

The next two pages are a list of contacts at four European libraries, including the National Hungarian Archive, followed by what have to be nearly fifty pages of notes on Elizabeth Bathory, with portions boxed or circled:

Witnesses either did not actually witness Elizabeth in the act or unsure

Elizabeth not allowed to speak on own behalf

Respected nobles accused of procuring own relatives to serve E.'s household, turned blind eye OR willingly sacrificed girls for hope of conviction against her

(Did she do it or not??)

Elizabeth: Protestant (Calvinist), King: Catholic

Bathory/Nadasdy holdings: thousands of acres, 20 castles

E. husband Ferenc, national hero, BANK-ROLLED CROWN. Debt too large to pay back. Ferenc dies, E. begin litigation against debtors INCLUDING ROYAL TREASURY.

King can't risk action against national hero—turn entire country against crown. But can against a widow

King calls witnesses from E.'s own holdings—nobles, court officials. E. made loans to servants, paymaster, castellan, squire, court master. THEY ALL OWED HER MONEY. ALL TESTIFIED AGAINST HER.

Palatine Thurzo (Protestant) charged to protect her before Ferenc dies. Move for no execution. (Keep E.'s property from ceding to Habsburg crown in full, prevent precedent of crown claiming Protestant property)

1611: E. walled up at Cachtice (Slovakia). CROWN'S FULL DEBT CANCELED, portion of lands cede to crown. All documents sealed. Treated as though E. "never existed." Husband's reputation as war hero intact

KING CROWNED HOLY ROMAN EMPEROR 1612.

Holy crap. I'm an ancient conspiracy theorist.

I thumb through several pages of names I don't recognize and what look like hand-copied records. There are several more pages labeled "Budapest," "Zagreb," "Bratislava," "Bucharest," "Belgrade," with names of what I assume to be court leaders or members.

Why would I do this—catalog their names like this? I think back to Jester's story about the genealogies. This journal is dangerous to every person I've listed.

Is this what I had erased from memory—a record created in naiveté? A list that, once written, I could not unsee?

I pause on a page filled only with questions, such as: Who was Ismeta's sibling? And then: Imre = Tibor's brother?—Yes. Goes now by "Ivan."

My eye catches on two successive lines:

> Ivan and Nikola falling out. Amerie sides
> with Nikola—WHY??
> Amerie dies 16 months later

I scan ahead to several pages filled with names and death dates—and a seeming list of those who died in quick succession after their passing:

> Tamas (April?) 2005
> June: Zsolt
> October: Attila II, Silus
> December: Judit, Braco (suicide, memory
> unrecoverable)

But something happens after the last of those. About ten pages have been torn out.
And then this:

> Audra,
> It's me. You.

The skin rises on my arms.

> We can't have this (journal) anymore.
> There is too much here, too much that
> you were not meant to find. Too much,
> too much. And you have too much—too
> much love, too many questions. Too much
> sorrow . . . and too much joy.

I tried to find her for us. She was gone by the time I got to Europe.

Ivan helped me find the journal (hers—what's left of it). I'm keeping this all together. Were it up to me, I'd burn it all. I've already seen it—it will never leave my brain now. Which is the problem.

I think I know what I need to do. It's pretty horrible. Dying would be easier, I think—for us, at least. But not for Luka. Not for the secret that does not go in this book, or any book. The one you'll die for.

I'm rambling—you'll think you were an idiot back in the day. I'm rushing, that's the problem, because I'm leaving tomorrow for Bratislava and one last shot at the diary. Nyirbator, maybe, if I have time, but everything's backward. The entire story is backward. Can't write too much here while I'm still on the move—everything will end up with the Historian if I die now at any rate (big bonus day for that a-hole), but at least if these pages are taken by the Utod (you know who you are, traitors), they'll have to figure part of it out for themselves. But then Luka will be free and all he'll have to deal with is his grief.

I love that man. I love him, love, love him. The first time he told me he loved me, I didn't hear it. And I waited so long to hear it, too. He waited to bring it up again for weeks because he thought he had upset me.

He's patient and good and gentle. Don't let it fool you: He'll kill for you. Don't let him. Kill for him, instead, if you have to. One of you has to live.

He's buying us a ring if we (you and I) live through the next few months. I'd call that an incentive to stay alive.

I sit back hard, dumbfounded. Blink, grab the envelope, pull it open to peer inside, and then upend it.

It falls into my palm. A ring with a simple row of little diamonds.

I slide it onto my finger. A perfect fit.

We were engaged??

I flash back to Maine, recall the desperation I took then as him trying too hard. His manic will to rescue me from Rolan, get me safely to the underground . . .

His reluctance to let me come here alone.

I flip forward several pages, reading quickly.

Me again. You.

I couldn't stay long enough in Bratislava. I'm running out of time so fast, the sun's practically moving from west to east . . .

I don't know how I'm going to bring it up to Luka. I know what I think I have to do. It isn't selfish—it's maybe the least selfish thing you'll ever have done. And now that I think back, we were pretty selfish even just a year ago.

I'm so sad. I'm going to treasure these beautiful, beautiful hours. Do you know what Luka said to me before I left?

"I love you more every day. When you go to bed tonight, know that you'll be even more loved tomorrow."

The last night I was with him before I left, he sighed against my neck and said he loved the smell of me. And I understand what he means, because sometimes I wish I could inhale him, breathe him into my cells.

Now all of that is going away. I have never cried this hard.

I flip to the next page. It's the last in the journal.

Audra,

So here we are. I'm at a crossroads, and you, reading this, are where I was months ago. Different date, same person . . . same impossibility.

Life is beautiful, Audra. I know it doesn't seem like it, with everything. But it is. And it is new. Katia said something the last time I saw her that I will never forget (or I will, so I write it here): Heaven doesn't come tomorrow. It's here now. You don't have to die to get there.

I hope I don't lose that thought along with everything else. They say your life flashes before your eyes when you die . . . I really hope it does.

I'm writing another note after this one. It's for you. It'll be the first one you get from me. With hope, the only one. It's short and sweet (miracle, isn't it?). I can't say everything I want to—haven't even been able to here. And I've decided I won't talk about Luka in it. You know why? Because I want you to have the joy of falling in love with him all over again. I think I could spend my whole life doing that.

Ask him what he has to tell you when it's all over. But it has to be over. And if you're reading these words now, it won't be until you finish what I started. I'm so sorry. I tried.

The worst part is I can't write it here. I can't write it, and I can't tell Ivan. It would be so simple if I could just tell Luka everything I need you to know . . . but I know what they'll do to him once they think he knows anything. And while they can't take his memory, they'll make him wish they could.

Protect him. He'll take a bullet for you without even blinking. Don't let him. He is good. Proof of God, and a better person than I am. But maybe you are, too.

If you're reading this, you know what happens next. It's August and I swear I can hear the symphony playing at the Wolkenturm. I wish we could have a long, good chat, because I have so much to tell you. But more than that, I wish we all had more time.

I just heard last night that Katia is gone. It's all coming down.

Go back to the beginning of our story. I'm giving you everything I dare. You know what you have to do.

Give my love to Luka.

Me (You)

P.S. Don't trust Nikola. He's in league with them.

I stare at the far wall, so many questions slicing through my mind at once they may actually mince it to pieces. About Nikola, about Luka and me, what I had hoped and failed to achieve in Bratislava. About the story I'm supposed to go back to.

But most of all, what I'm supposed to do with it all.

You know what you have to do . . .

But I don't. And though there's still a pile of loose pages I haven't even looked at, I've had all the revelations I can take for the moment.

I glance at the clock in the corner. I've been here too long.

I tuck the baby picture inside the journal and start to put everything back in the envelope, but pause at the sight of a sheet folded multiple times. It's worn and yellowed, but that's not what's caught my eye. It's covered with names, some of them fuzzy where the ink has faded, some of the letters retraced more recently. One of them, in new black ink, is mine. Luka's is written below it.

I carefully unfold the sheet, laying it over the biometric box and envelope; it's the size of a newspaper centerfold and twice as fragile, crumbling at the corners.

Rows and rows of names are scrawled across the page in progressively faded ink. There, near the bottom, is mine and Luka's. My mother's is a row above mine, alongside an empty box. Above her: Serafina, paired with the name Petar Todorov. Some kind of family tree?

No.

I jerk back from the table the instant I realize what this is.

A kill map. Progeny and their known murderers.

So many names, each of them the tiniest representation of a life . . .

Ink has bled through in several places from the other side. Heart thudding, I turn the page over.

A chart in the vague shape of a Christmas tree occupies the bulk of the sheet. At the very top are twelve names I don't recognize, faded with age, their letters redrawn. The next tier contains fourteen names, and the next level twenty. There are other notes beside some of them in what appears to be Hungarian that I can't make out. But several of those lower down, I can: "Hungarian army," "Red Army," "Hungarian Social Democratic Party," "Socialist Federal Republic, Yugoslavia," and more recent labels including "media," "police," "tech," and the names of several global banks, each accompanied by a city ranging as far west as the United Kingdom and as far east as Turkey.

A chill crawls down my spine as I realize I am staring at the evolution of the Scions . . .

The birth of a massive cabal.

There's a single line down the right side of the page, separate from the rest, connecting a progression of circles. Some contain names I don't recognize, many are blank, only a few with dates. The succession, I assume, of the office of the Historian.

The last circle is very new, in crisp black pen. It is empty except for a year.

This one.

At the top of the page the title THE REAL SERIAL KILLERS is scrawled in my handwriting.

I have to be holding the most complete map of the Scions in existence.

Now I know what Nikola was willing to kill for.

33

With shaking hands, I cram everything back into the envelope, tie it up tight.

How much of this does Luka know? Have I shown him this grisly chart?

I glance at the time and panic. Tuck the envelope into the waist of my pants beneath my sweater and tie my coat over it, put on my sunglasses.

I don't even bother to return the empty box to the counter.

"Good?" the woman in the room outside says.

Now that I've emerged from the vault, my phone begins to ping with a series of incoming texts, piling in one after another, and then with the chime of voice mail, again and again.

"Yes, thank you. But I, ah—I felt like my taxi driver was asking me a lot of questions about this place, what people kept here."

Take me out the back way you go to your car.

"Yes. Come with me," she says, as though this is not an unusual request. "I will escort you another way."

I follow her at a brisk clip. I need to leave this place—and Vienna, and Europe, for that matter. We all do.

But almost overpowering my urgency to leave is a desire to get back to Luka. To see and touch him. To say that I know now and believe him and I'm sorry. To ask him for the story of us and the things we said to one another . . .

To tell him that the woman I was before sends her love.

He has kept his promise. He has been relentless in his love. I glance down at my hand, realizing I never took off the ring. Moreover, I don't want to. Even after knowing him only a few short weeks—at least as far as my memory is concerned—I can actually picture him picking it out.

The woman leads me down a back hallway, which she accesses with her key card.

With her back to me, I pull the phone from my pocket, unlock it. Texts spill onto the screen:

From Luka's number: *Are you in?*

Ten minutes later: *Accident on corner— access blocked out front. Do not come down Lerchenfelder Strasse.*

From Claudia's number: *Luka's freaking out.*

And, most recently, from Luka: *I'm coming in if I don't hear from you in the next 10 min.* That was seven minutes ago.

I send a quick note that I'm on my way as the woman unlocks a back door.

"Here, to the path," she says, opening the door and gesturing me toward a green common area filled with trees and the occasional bench in the middle of the block.

I glance out. "Thank you," I say.

"Miss Ellison?" she says as I step past her.

I start to answer and then halt.

She should not know my name.

My head swivels just as she reaches inside her jacket.

Adrenaline fires my veins—but instead of the gun I imagined, she produces only an envelope. "What's this?" I say, taking it with unsteady fingers.

"In case I miss."

The pistol lifts in her other hand. I leap to the side with a scream. The shot fires, and I throw my entire weight against the metal door, slamming her back.

I sprint for the trees, ears ringing, phone clutched in one hand, envelope in the other.

The entire interior of the block is enclosed by the buildings that line it. To my distant right, a skywalk leads to the parking garage across the street. Bad choice. I sprint across the grass, connect with one of the narrower paths toward the northwest corner, where I saw a hotel on Jester's map.

Open the door. Open the back door. Come out for a smoke, a walk—just open the door!

I'm running full force, throwing every persuasion I can think of ahead of me, not knowing who might even be in the building, let alone on the ground floor. Just before I reach the back entrance, a woman in a maid's uniform steps outside. I barrel past her, into the hotel, through a laundry into a small kitchen. Emerge into a red and purple bar area, veer into the lobby.

I look back and find a balding hotel clerk staring at me in astonishment.

"*Guten Tag*," I pant and shove out the front door to bolt across the street, blood pounding in my temples.

My phone rings in my pocket.

"They know," I say, breathing hard against the phone. "They were waiting for me to get it—"

"Where are you?" Luka demands. Sirens sound somewhere in the distance, and for a disoriented moment I can't tell if I'm hearing them from the street or through the phone.

"Lange Gasse," I say, veering right. "Headed north."

"They've got us blocked—" I hear a car door opening. "I'm coming."

I tear down the sidewalk looking for a back street, an alley between buildings—anything to stay out of sight.

"Keep going north. Don't stop. Are you being followed?" I can hear his steps pounding the pavement, words jarred with every stride.

I glance back, but I'm running so fast I can hardly see. "I don't think so."

"There's a hotel a few blocks up, on your left."

I can't get the image of the woman with the

gun out of my mind. The angle of it was, for a split second, the perfect kill shot. I start to hyperventilate, vision spotting.

"Audra? Audra! Find a place to get your bearings. You're going to be okay," he says, and I nod, though I know he can't see it. I duck into the doorway of a café, just enough to get out of sight, to calm my burning lungs.

"You're okay. I'm almost there."

My next breath is a ragged sob.

"One more block. You're going to make it." And it sounds like he's slowed as well.

I look down and actually see the envelope clutched in my hand for the first time. I tear it open.

The note is brief.

> Do you think you can escape Vienna without being followed? Bring the contents of the box and the Scions will let Luka live. The offer expires at midnight. He will be dead by morning.
> N.

An address in Budapest is printed at the bottom.

Like that, the breath I just caught is knocked from my lungs.

Don't trust Nikola. He's in league with them.

"Audra? Are you there?"

I squeeze my eyes shut, nod. "Yeah."

342

"Keep going."

I shove the note in my pocket, push out of the doorway with a glance behind me, and jog to the end of the block, wiping my cheek on my sleeve.

"I see you. You're almost there."

"I see it," I say, nearing the Art Nouveau building, an ornate crest over the front entrance. A hotel car is waiting outside.

I need that car! A few seconds later, a doorman comes down the steps, waves the car forward.

"Get the doorman to hail you a cab," Luka says.

"I did. It's pulling up now—I see it."

A pause, and then he says, "I'm almost there."

The doorman steps up to get the door, and I slide in without a beat, and then across to the other side. I feel as though my nose is dripping. My hand comes away red. I search around, wondering if I'm injured, but no. I've run so hard my nose is bleeding. The driver hands me a tissue, and ten seconds later, Luka slides in after me.

Go. Go. Quickly.

And then we're pulling away down the street and I don't even know what direction we're headed because I've thrown myself into Luka's arms.

34

"I'm never leaving you alone again," Luka murmurs against my hair. We've called the others, who ended up abandoning the car in the traffic jam, which Jester's convinced was orchestrated, and told them to meet us in Zurich in two days.

"The good news is that the cameras at the vault don't record video, in order to keep it anonymous," Jester said.

Not that it matters now.

And then we directed the driver the other way. East, toward Bratislava. It's too close to Budapest for my comfort, but it's the largest nearby city with an airport. From there, I don't care where we go.

"I think Claudia knows we're not meeting them in Zurich," I say.

Luka strokes the hair that isn't really mine and murmurs, "Then she knows you want to keep her alive. It was coming to that, anyway."

Yes. I want to keep her alive. And with the others headed to Switzerland, I can at least concentrate on the life I'm concerned about right now: Luka's.

The driver glances at me in the rearview mirror—has done so twice in the last minute.

I'm not her. Maybe I resemble her, but now that you look . . . no.

"How did you do that?" Luka says.

"Do what?"

"Get the doorman to hail your cab before you even got there."

"I don't know. The same way I got the maid to let me in the back door of a hotel, I guess."

"So you . . . called it in?" he says strangely.

"I guess. I must be getting better."

"I've never heard of that. I don't think that's normal."

But nothing about this is normal.

I realize then that he's staring at something, and follow the line of his gaze to my hand.

He's very still, and for a moment I just listen to the hard beat of his heart through his chest. It's strong and steady as the arm wrapped around me, if a little faster than before.

I lift my fingers, the diamond ring throwing fire from the sunset behind us.

"So, um . . . guess what I found."

"Yeah," he says and rakes his hair back. "About that."

His tone catches me off guard, and it occurs to me that maybe I shouldn't have made assumptions. For all I know, we—or even he—called it off. Can I blame him? Four weeks ago I didn't even know who he was.

"I told you a few months ago—"

"It's okay," I say, twisting it off.

"No." He catches at my hand. "Wear it. If you

want to. I never got you the diamond I said I was going to. I never got the chance."

"Oh. Well, I still want that," I say.

He takes the ring from me, slides it slowly back onto my finger, and then studies it so long I don't know if he's looking at the ring or the finger it's on.

"When I gave you this, I said it looked like a princess ring," he whispers. "Perfect for you."

I think of what I said to myself, about Luka being good. Proof of God, even, in this godless mess.

He pulls me closer in the back seat, wraps both arms around me. The edge of the envelope digs into my side.

"So how big of a diamond are we talking about?" he says.

I lean back against him. "Oh, big."

"Maybe I shouldn't have said anything," he murmurs.

"I did leave myself a note to ask you about something when this is all over."

He shakes his head. "Figures."

We've had so little levity—the truest laugh I ever heard from him was back in Maine, when he thought we were free and I knew no better. I close my eyes, envision the wine aisle of the Food Mart, the Mad Moose on the south side of the lake, the feral ducks gobbling up fries. I pretend, for just this moment, that the note in my pocket does not exist. That I am not plastered on television screens, wanted for murder.

That Nikola has not threatened to kill him by morning.

I catch myself admiring the ring on my finger, and I can't help but think of Ana. I instantly feel guilty. What right do I have to be happy when the one thing she wanted—a life with Nino—has just been taken from her? When I don't even know if she's still alive?

"Why didn't you tell me?" I say.

He exhales a long sigh. "How do you spring that on someone who doesn't even know your name? Who doesn't know if they even trust you?"

"I'm sorry," I whisper. He pulls me tighter against him in response.

"It's not your fault, you know."

"I found a lot of crazy stuff," I say quietly. "Do you know what it is?"

"No," he says. "Not all of it. And I know this is hard to understand, but I didn't want to. You were so preoccupied trying to find a way out that even when you were with me, you weren't with me. I felt like I'd lost you way before you went to that Center." He lays his cheek against the top of my head.

"In the end it didn't matter, because you did find a way. And if all went as planned, we would never need to talk about it again. But the other reason I didn't ask for details is because I knew you had things of your mother's. And . . . given what I came from, and how she died—or how we thought she died—you deserved to have whatever piece of her you could. Pure. Untainted by my past."

I was right, in my letters to myself. He is gentle. And I don't need a diamond to believe it.

Protect him.

"You're stronger than you know," he murmurs against my hair.

"I don't feel strong."

"You are. You're the strongest person I know. Not to mention scary smart."

I lift my head to look at him. God, he's beautiful. I can't imagine what this has been like for him. Were the situation reversed, it would shred my heart to see no recognition in his eyes for me.

"I left you alone," I say. "I did it for us, I know, but I left you. And I took your friend and your lover with me. I am so sorry, Luka."

He reaches up and covers his eyes, his expression twisting beneath his fingers.

"I'm so sorry," I whisper and clasp his face between my hands, kissing the tears that roll down his cheeks. "And I love you."

He pulls me against him with a sob, arms locked tight around me, and buries his face against my neck.

"You're the strong one," I say softly. And I mean it. Because of the two of us, he is the only one who could weather what he did and survive. Even after falling in love with him again after so short a time—perhaps the greatest gift I have ever given myself—I don't think I could go through losing him and come out alive.

And I get why he was willing to take those three years. And why I fought for more, unwilling to *just* survive.

Now we'll be lucky to have even that.

35

It's early evening by the time we arrive at Letisko Airport in Bratislava.

"This won't work," Luka murmurs.

"It has to," I say, combing the bangs of my wig down toward my eyes.

"Audra." He catches me by the arm. "We can still turn around and leave."

But that's the thing. We can't.

I *persuade* the ticket agent to bump two other passengers from the last flight to Liverpool, which is as far as we can get on anything tonight. Which is to say, not far enough. I suggest, too, that I actually resemble the photo in my new German passport, which looks nothing like me.

Past the ticket counter, I pause to assess security. The agents who can be persuaded. The cameras that can't. They're not my only problem; an entire terminal full of passengers waits beyond the checkpoint.

"This is crazy," Luka whispers. "There's too many. You can't do this alone."

It is crazy. Jester, Claudia, and Piotrek together wouldn't take this on. But I don't have a choice.

I present my ticket and passport to the agent at the front of the line. Ignore Luka as he does the same behind me. Take the envelope out from

350

beneath my sweater. Lay it, along with my shoes, jacket, and phone, on the conveyor belt. That is the hardest part: watching it pass from my possession. So simple and old-fashioned on that moving belt. So much trouble over a stack of papers. So many lives lost, families ruined. So much blood spilled.

Too much.

By the time we get through security, my nose is bleeding again. I retrieve the envelope, hurry to the bathroom, where I tuck it back beneath my sweater once I've gotten the bleeding to stop. I also take the opportunity to flush the note from Nikola down the toilet.

I stay there as long as I dare, head tilted back against the stall, eyes turned toward the ceiling. But I know Luka is waiting and I don't dare let him out of my sight for long.

We move quickly through the terminal, sequester ourselves near a window at our gate. No one in a twenty-foot radius is looking, far too preoccupied with phones, children, conversations. *Anything. Anything but me.*

I don't have to try to keep my knee from bouncing; there's no spare energy for the jitters. I turn my face against Luka's shoulder, a wad of toilet paper held to my nose.

"How are you doing this?" he murmurs, holding me tightly against him.

I don't answer. My head has begun to pound.

"Audra, you're going to give yourself an aneurysm," he says tightly.

I actually wonder if he's right.

"It's worse if you talk about it," I say.

He pulls me tighter against his chest, holds my head in his arms.

"I was thinking," he says, "maybe we go from Liverpool to Dubai."

"Dubai?"

"We'll get you a burka, make this whole anonymity thing a lot easier."

I exhale a soft, pained laugh. But it's not my anonymity I'm worried about.

"Whose idea was Maine?" I murmur.

"Yours," he says, and I can't help a small smile.

When they call boarding at last, he has to help me up.

By the time we get in line I'm swaying on my feet. His arm tightens around me. A woman behind us offers him a bottle of water. She thinks I'm sick. And I am.

Waiting in our seats on the plane is the worst. He lays his head atop mine, which is resting on his shoulder. I close my eyes and hold his hand.

I want to hold it forever.

I wait for the remaining passengers to straggle on and fumble for overhead space, for the tone to indicate that the door is about to close.

At the last possible second I unbuckle my seat belt and push up unsteadily.

He clutches me. "Where are you going?"

I cup my hand to my face, say I'm going to be sick. It's not the first time I've told that lie.

He reaches for the airsick bag.

"No," I say urgently. "Not here."

I hurry past the flight attendants to the galley, grab a stack of napkins. Glance back at Luka's stricken face.

Throw a last, massive persuasion behind me.

Don't let that man off the plane.

The next second I'm out the door and sprinting up the jet bridge as fast as I can. Crying.

I'm almost to ground transportation when my phone starts ringing. I ignore it, hail a cab. The phone is relentless.

Finally, I shut it down.

36

I close my eyes in the back of the cab, a tissue shoved up my nose. Head pounding, face swollen—from tears, *persuasion*. From life.

We drive past a field of windmills, giant turbines blade-silent against the gray sky. I pull the envelope from the waist of my pants, clutch it in my lap, and watch windmill after windmill go by.

It takes everything I have not to reassemble my phone. To call Luka, tell him I love him— again, again, and again. But not to say I'm sorry. I've had a shroud of death over my head since the day I was born, but he—he has to live. There are so few things of real beauty in this world. It cannot afford to lose one more.

Nausea and dizziness roll past me, leaving me wasted in their wake. I pull the tissue from my nose, glance at the envelope. Steeling myself, I loosen the tie, take out the stack of papers.

I carefully unfold the Scion map, lay it out on the seat beside me. And that's what it is: a map of the organization through the ages, the chronicle of its power. The circles toward the bottom of the expanding tree are mostly blank, some of them filled only with the name of a financial institution, a government agency, or a surname.

I don't know how this information was collected, or how reliable it is. Can only imagine the cost of adding even one name to its morbid genealogy.

The lineage of the hunted on the other side is far more tragically complete. There's a pen clipped to the seatback in front of me. I take it and care-fully fill in the name of my mother's killer:

Nikola, so-called Prince of Budapest. Traitor.

Though it may end up in Nikola's hands, it will at least show the truth.

I turn my attention to the rest of the assortment on my lap: several pages, worn and folded, my name written on one side. I unfold and smooth them out. Notes, penned in Hungarian, the English translation added more recently in the margins:

Trial documents sealed by Habsburg
    court—discovered by Jesuit priest
    1720s
Thurzo wife multiple visits to E. 1612.
    ← steals E.'s jewelry each time
    (payment???)
E. daughter Katalin visit—living at
    Keresztur? at time
2 weeks before E. dies, priests Andras
    Kerpelich and Imre Agriensy come
    to witness will from **Esztergom
bishopric**

> Buried Cachtice—NOT removed to
>   Nyirbator.
> Lamosz Cemetery Budapest? No—no
>   longer exists
> Trnava, Slovakia

I gather that these are the details of Elizabeth's visitors as she lived walled up in darkness. The potential burial site of her body, which as far as I read was never found.

This isn't my handwriting—whose notes are these?

I flip through page after page like this, translations of the original notes written from the margins into the corners in thick, broad curves, and feverishly across the back. At least I wasn't the only one seemingly obsessed.

The last three pages are penned in the same hand, their rushed and sprawling lines solely in English.

Audra, my heart, my love . . .

This is a letter addressed to me. I rifle to the last page.

It is signed "Amerie."

These pages, like the others, were written by my mother.

I read with shaking hands.

Audra, my heart, my love . . .

How do you put a lifetime on a page?

The day you were born I felt more alive than I had ever been before. On the day that you look into your own child's eyes, you will understand what I am saying: that I saw the face of God.

I had never known such love, such gratitude and humility, as the moment I held you. Such purpose, and fire, as the instant I let you go. Determination to change the future that pulled us apart.

In another life, I would have told you stories about your grandmother and made you dumplings, which are the only thing I ever learned to cook. I would have held you every night until you would no longer let me. We would have laughed and sung songs and played hide-and-seek. And I would have left you treasures as my own mother did when I was old enough to find them.

I would have told you everything I knew about your father, whose name was Tamas Vargha. The most noble man I ever met.

We would have fought, I am sure, over your independence, which I would have been fearful to grant you. Wanting to protect you, which I think, aside from love, must be the biggest instinct a mother has.

I did not know my own mother until I was the age you are now as I write this—eighteen. I knew her only a year before she was taken. I see her face before me every day, trace the faint lines of her mouth with the finger of my mind. I have always been like that, never forgetting anything I have seen, and so the image of your face—dangerously provided too few times throughout your life by a mutual friend—has always been in front of me. You are beautiful.

I hoped that we would begin a new life together one day. I will hold out hope until my dying breath, but you should know I have sworn to leave the Scions nothing. Having stolen you from my life, they will not benefit from its memory.

Maybe you resent me or even hate me for the fact that I had to leave you. Or maybe you have some vision of me greater than anything I can live up to. Nothing you do or have done or are could possibly fall short of my vision of you. You were perfect when you were born. You are perfect to me now. Perfect, even in your mistakes. Nothing—not even you—would ever convince me otherwise.

I seal this letter with several notes and hope I have time to give them to Imre. He knows to give them to you, and will not dare to look at them in order to protect them. You are too old by now for songs and I cannot hold you. But I leave treasure for you. Find it. Live. Let my life's work be my humble offering for all the years I could not be the mother I hoped to you.

I love you, Audra, and will have many things to say to God about my loss of you. But many more to say for the gift of you.

Amerie . . . Mother

It is dated three years ago.

I read the pages again and again, searching every word for the cadence of her voice. Aching to hear it.

At last I cover my face out of sight of the driver, and sob.

We are fifty kilometers from the outskirts of Budapest by the time I fold her letter away and look again at her soaring notes. Churches, some of their names scored out. Names of people and estates written at various angles across the page where she ran out of space. The names of those who visited Elizabeth in her imprisonment, and took her last confession.

The next things in the stack are little pieces of paper like the kind you tear off a cube. I recognize Luka's handwriting across all three of them, their lines short—the kinds of notes you leave on a countertop, on a refrigerator, or by a bedside.

I love you, Princess.
—L

Do you know how beautiful you are?
—L

One more day. I'll be the man waiting at the altar.
—L

I stare, frozen, at the last note in my hand. The paper beneath it is a marriage certificate.

37

I'm married.

I glance at the date on the certificate: September 24. Last year.

Why didn't he say anything? Why, when he saw the ring on my finger and I thought we were only engaged?

Because as far as he knew, I had seen everything in the vault. And then I deserted him on the plane.

I fumble for the phone, power it back on, and pray it still has a charge. When it comes to life, the screen floods with text messages and voice mails. I dial Luka's number. He does not pick up.

No. Of course he doesn't. With any luck he's on his way to Liverpool. But I know he would never have willingly stayed on that plane without me, would have fought to follow me. In which case at least he doesn't know where I am or what I'm about to do.

I page through Luka's texts, sick at heart.

> Where are you?
> Audra, don't do this.
> Please. I can't lose you again.
> Audra?
> I love you.

His voice mails are the same.

Don't do this. I love you. I can't lose you.

But I am the one who cannot lose him.
And I have no intention of dying.
"Excuse me," I say to the driver. "I need to make a stop."
The next call I make is to Claudia.

38

The numbered gate on Csónak Street is painted like that of any residence below Castle Hill on the hilly Buda side of the Danube. It is by now nearly 11:00 P.M. The street is quiet, only the occasional car or biker passing by.

I step into the light of the lone bulb positioned at the top of the old stone arch and glance straight up at the camera. Ignoring the intercom, I pull off my wig and shades.

A moment later, the gate audibly unlocks. I push it open, step into the tiny overgrown courtyard, and reach the front stoop just as the door opens.

A diminutive man in a sharp tuxedo opens the door and gestures me in. A mask with a curved, beaklike nose obscures the upper half of his face.

Of course.

He doesn't speak as he escorts me through the foyer to the back of the house and down two flights of stairs to a small chamber that widens into a broad tunnel. Nor do I ask where he is taking me as I follow him through a series of corridors lit by a string of electric lights, past grottoes with multiple exits in the ancient subterranean maze.

By the time we arrive in a cavern shored up with ancient brick, I can hear the drum of that industrial drone. Can sense the Utod gathered in this underground hive.

Trilling laughter echoes from a neighboring tunnel that glows like a great yellow eye. A second later a woman trips into the cavern as a man catches up to her, gold rings gleaming on his fingers. She's short-skirted Baroque, down to her creamy stockings and bow-tied boots. A second woman in a powdered wig stumbles out of the passage after them, skeletal teeth glowing faintly on red-rouged lips. There's an air of richness about all three of them, as though *this* were the truest noble court, the one in Zagreb a thrift-store imitation. But they fall silent the moment they see me: unmasked in the cargo pants and shirt I've worn since yesterday. I feel the heat of their eyes on my back as the butler leads me away.

By the time we reach a corridor lined on either side by stone pillars topped with rough-hewn heads, I am certain I am in chambers as old as the earth itself.

The sentinels are replaced farther down with human versions robed in black. Their white masks hover in the shadows between electric torches, seem to float without bodies at all. At the end of the corridor: a carved double door attended by two robed figures, white faces turned toward me in frightening uniformity. It is the same featureless mask and robe Nikola wore to court in Zagreb, a thing of nightmares, multiplied as though by mirrors. They are so still I wonder if they even breathe . . . until I see the eyes of one follow me.

My skin crawls as I move past them.

Not all of them are Utod.

The white-faced forms swivel inward as I pass. The last two open the doors. I walk directly into the chamber—and the presence of Nikola.

He stops me, five steps in, with a lifted palm. And I see the round voice box set in the mouth of his vacant mask. But he is not alone.

A robed figure lights a candelabra on a narrow altar behind him along the wall. The massive top half of a face protrudes from the stone above it, the forehead obscured by a primitive crown. The carved lids of the eyes suggest a squint, but their stone sockets are empty.

If there are cameras in this court, they are not kept here; there is no hint of modernity in the room and, other than the altar, no furniture.

"Did you know . . ." the figure at the altar begins, startling me.

It is a woman.

She's also common. She moves elegantly from one taper to the next, fingers encased in black gloves.

"That long before these caverns became shelters and prisons . . . they were a hunting ground? In a time when that was all there was. Hunters. Hunted." She sets the last taper in its cradle and turns toward me as Nikola moves aside. "And now here we stand, millennia later, you and I."

She's not just common.

She's a hunter.

Don't trust Nikola. He's in league with them.

Do the revelers in the tunnels outside have even the slightest idea? How much arrogance does it take for a *prince* to host hunters within his own court?

And how much deceit?

"I have what you want," I say.

"I'm glad," she says. "I'm so pleased you're here, Audra." Her English is perfect, with only the barest hint of an accent.

"I'm sorry, have we met?"

"Only in the broadest sense." Her eyes lift. They are pale, nearly amber. "Though I feel I know so much about you. So very much, from so many sources, so few of them firsthand. Ivan, of course, most recently."

I blink.

And then I realize that this can be only one person.

The Historian . . .

Is a chick.

My mind revolts. The Historian, a woman? What kind of irony—and twisted misogyny—is *that?*

"You're surprised," she says mildly.

"I thought you'd be taller."

My thoughts, meanwhile, have careened from order. Thinking I'd be meeting Nikola, I was prepared to hand over a single item: half of the Scions' map. The other half is with Piotrek, to be delivered to a location for pickup once Claudia reports I have arrived at a pub on Kazinczy Street alive. Preferably with some kind of guarantee that Luka will be safe wherever in the world we go.

That, at least, was the plan.

Which is all moot now.

Now any one of these robed figures could kill me—shoot, stab, strangle, garrote me on the spot—and retrieve the documents from my fading memory without ever seeing them in person.

I tamp down the rising tide of panic that threatens to take out my knees.

"I have part of what you want. I won't receive the location of the other half until I arrive across the river, alive," I say, making this up on the fly. "And just so you know, I haven't seen the entire document. So I don't know what's on the rest."

She steps closer. She's a few inches taller than I am and peers down at me. "So audacious," she inhales, as though with strange wonder. "So fearless. I see her there in your eyes."

I recall the empty circle in the succession of Historians, drawn with crisp, new ink.

"You wouldn't know since you came to this job *after* Nikola killed her," I say, lips curled back from my teeth.

"Clever girl," she says and holds out her hand.

I pull the folded paper from my pocket. Slap it into her palm.

She doesn't even bother looking at it but walks directly to the candelabra and holds it over the nearest taper. I gasp and lunge for it, but Nikola is on me in an instant.

"Where's Ana?" I hiss.

"I'm sure she'll turn up. Somewhere," he says, the electronic voice sinister. And even though I squeeze my eyes shut, I can't block out the vision of her floating, like a pale Ophelia, in an eddy of the Danube.

I lash out with an elbow, crack him hard across the chin. His head snaps back, the mask slips up his face.

I falter at the sight of that nose, the unremarkable mouth. The line of that jaw.

I don't need to see his eyes to recognize his face.

Goran. The monk from Cres island.

Ivan's death. The monastery where the monks came from to retrieve whatever items Ivan left beneath the statue of Saint Anthony . . . the key to the box only I could open. Each thought slots into place in quick succession as Nikola pins me to the ground.

Never mind that he's got sixty pounds on me; the breath got knocked from me before I found myself cheek to cheek with the floor.

"Is anything you said to me the truth?" *The story about my mother? The rain—her regret and her love for me?*

But my mind has already raced both back and ahead at once. Is prepared to hate him for stripping the one memory anyone has ever given me of my mother. And to believe it anyway, even if he laughs in my face.

"Did you know," he says hotly against my ear, "that these caves once served as the prison of Vlad Tepesh—from whom Ferenc, our early father, learned the art of impaling his enemies?"

"History lessons from you? That's torture."

He twists my arm so far around I actually wait to hear it snap. "History teaches us who we are."

"If the past is all you are, you better hope to God you never lose your memory!"

"You may not understand this," he hisses, but what I do, I do for the protection of this court. This safe haven for those who come here to remember who they are."

"They aren't remembering who they are!" I shout. "They're forgetting! Or did you not notice that everyone out there is wearing a mask?"

"They are alive!"

"Yes—walled up alive, just as she was!"

He lets go. I shove myself up. And then his fist lashes out so fast it sends me sprawling.

"You're just like her," he spits.

My ears are ringing, two torches blazing on the wall where there had been only one. I lift my hand to my mouth, tasting blood.

"Enough, Nikola. Leave us."

I sense more than see Nikola hesitate before striding to the door. It falls heavily shut a second later.

I stagger to my feet with a rolling wave of nausea. Try to assess the figure less than eight feet away as she casually withdraws a pistol, clicks off the safety, and sets it on the altar. My eyes drop to the weapon.

"Let's not be primitive," she says. "Even if you reached this pistol before me, my successor is already appointed. You would die within seconds, your memory would be harvested, and my guards would no doubt feel compelled to take out half the population here tonight. Nikola, such that he is, would no doubt find a way to survive . . . and where would that leave us?"

"You just let a man hit me and you're talking about primitive?"

"If you were a man, would it be more acceptable?"

Slowly, she comes into focus. The side of my face is already beginning to swell, and the outside of my eye with it.

"I brought you what you wanted," I say.

"A chart with a few names? That is what Nikola wanted. I have given him something better in exchange for the honor of meeting you."

"And what is that?"

"A limited truce."

"He didn't bring me here. I did."

"Yes. You are a woman who brokers her own fate. I've heard about such a woman before. You are so like her."

"Everybody's heard about my mother."

"I mean Bathory herself."

She leans a hip against the altar, gestures in the direction of court. "Every woman out there is her, in some way or another. Some genius. Some beautiful. Some sensual. Some brash. Each of you endowed with one sin for which she was punished, like the shattered shards of a single stone."

"Her sin was that she wouldn't be bullied," I say, working my jaw and thinking I might not vomit after all.

"She was impolitic at the least, a traitor at worst. And she was crushed by the same power with which she abused others. Her sins were plenty. But I haven't come to debate with you. Several years ago, Nikola recovered some pages of your mother's."

"This is news to me."

"I believe you have several more pages as of

371

today. More accurate ones. Or the real ones. It's very possible Nikola's were planted to mislead, as we have not been able to make sense of them. But more likely they only made sense to her because of how her mind worked. Her Progeny mind . . . so like yours. She was rumored to be very close to finding something before she died. I would like you to find it."

"Yes. The map. I just gave you half of it!"

"I believe there is something more."

"The diary."

"Yes. I believe she encoded its whereabouts in her notes and that only you will be able to make sense of them."

"The diary's a myth! The so-called diary is the map you just *burned* a part of!"

"Myths have their foundation in truth."

I give a short, incredulous laugh. "You want me to find King Arthur's sword while I'm at it? The Holy Grail?"

"I don't care what you find, as long as you deliver me that."

"I can't do it," I blurt.

"And yet you will," she says. "Or Luka will die."

"You don't understand. Even if it's real, the notes don't make any sense!" I say, scrambling for purchase, my mind already rushing ahead— to China, Madagascar, anyplace on this planet we can run, fly, or swim, as we should have done a week ago. All of us.

"Look," I say. "Nikola is Utod. He actually knew her. He took her life. Let him earn his truce with you. Send him on your quest. I'll give up the notes . . . in exchange for Luka."

She lowers her head, and for a moment I think she might actually be considering it. But then I see that she has pulled something from within her robes. A phone. Without a word, she places a call.

"Put him on, please," she says.

The screen blooms to pixelated life. She turns it toward me as the camera pans to a bloodied Luka bound to a chair.

39

It happens in car accidents. Everything slows, seconds like delayed heartbeats. The closest object in hyperfocus . . . everything else fallen away.

Except this is no accident that can be averted with lightning-quick reflexes. My attention snaps to the gun in her other hand, but I have no control over what happens on the other end of the screen.

"Luka, please say hello," she says.

Luka doesn't move. For a horrible moment, I actually think he's dead.

She lifts the gun and points it at me.

My own face stares back from the tiny screen in the corner.

Luka's head lolls with painful effort. His face is purple, hair matted to a bloody crust on the side of his skull.

"Audra, get out of there." His voice is a rasp. He squints through eyes swollen nearly shut, but then lifts his head a little more. "What have they done to you? What have you done to her?" he shouts, bucking against his restraints, and this time he's rewarded with a sickening punch.

I scream and scream, and can't stop. He's trying to say something, but I can't even hear him.

The screen clicks off.

At some point two of the robed men have entered the room and restrained me. I lunge for the phone, the gun, the Historian herself, my arms twisting in their sockets.

"I can't do it!" I scream, over and over. But what I am really shouting is Luka's name, my fear, my guilt. This is my fault. He will die, and it is all my fault.

"You have five days," the Historian says, before they drag me out.

40

They do not take me out the way I came in but through the court itself. A strobe-lit nightmare pounding through my skull.

But all I can think is: If Luka dies, it'll be because of me. If that happens, I don't want to remember. I can't remember and live with it. I'd rather die.

At some point the throbbing ebbs from my ears, if not my head. I see them, belatedly, like an image delayed in long-distance transmission from my eyes to my brain. The masks turned in my direction, mouths agape at my uncovered face—or in recognition, or both. Is this what Nikola wanted? His court in uproar over Amerie's daughter returned from the dead? My resurrected self appearing to the frenetic masses? If only they knew I was being escorted out by two hunters—that the Historian herself is within their sanctuary.

He accused me of leaving the court shattered in my wake once before.

I could show him shattered.

But I won't live to take revenge on Nikola. Because, like Luka, I am as good as dead.

We emerge from the underground labyrinth via the stairs of a darkened building and exit through a utility door. The night air assails me, and I begin to shudder between the hands holding me by my upper arms. But not from the chill.

One of them throws his cloak around my shoulders. I find this gesture of kindness ridiculous. Laughable. I shrug the cloak to the ground.

Somewhere across the river Claudia is freaking out; it must be well past midnight. I wonder if she'll ever be able to forgive me for leaving her a second time without a word. I don't dare contact her and don't know how to say good-bye.

As we descend a narrow walk on the edge of Castle Hill, I lift my head. From here I can see across the dark Danube deep into the Pest side of the city. It would be beautiful if the waters weren't ominous, if the city weren't filled with ghosts.

A car pulls up, and one of the men with me opens the door. For a minute I harbor the wild hope that Luka will be there, waiting in the back seat. But of course, the seat is empty.

I slide in, mute, not bothering to shut the door, so that one of the men has to do it before he slides in front. The second man waits as though to be certain I won't try to bolt. But I have no more fight left in me. He turns back as the car pulls away. The man in front is still wearing his mask. I must be coming unhinged because I find it slightly hysterical that a *hunter* is wearing a mask in front of *me*.

"These are the papers," the driver says and hands me an envelope. I stare at it uncomprehendingly, and then recall I'm supposed to be on some fool's errand to find the diary.

I take it finally, if only to bide my time until I can ensure they'll never be able to harvest my memory. I will not share with them a single moment that passed between Luka and me. How to find Claudia, Piotrek, Jester. The precious few words my mother left me.

I take it, too, because the writing inside is hers. And then—perhaps for that same reason—I open it.

The pages are similar to the others, sentences running up some of the sides, curving along the corners where she ran out of room. Some of the information is familiar, though the dates are incongruous.

The Historian was right: This set is a ruse.

"Where do you want to go?"

I want to go to Luka. Barring that, to the Danube, with its icy waters.

"Csepel Island," I say, throat raw. Do I imagine it, or does the man in the passenger seat tilt his head, slightly? Perhaps he knows it's an unlikely place to hide a diary or the lifework of a woman who knew her time was short.

Or perhaps, in a sense of ironic congruity, he recognizes it as the location where my mother's body was found, floating in the water.

The car winds south toward the river. Somewhere near the inner city, before we have even crossed the bridge, the hunter in the passenger seat points toward a road and murmurs. The driver responds in Hungarian, irritated, but then pulls off onto a side road toward a park. Because of course I won't be allowed to die without some kind of abuse or molestation first. I steel myself for the fight to escape, to reach the river with my dignity, at least, intact.

The minute the passenger removes his mask, I know that possibility is gone.

I recognize that profile from nightmares. And now that I'm looking at him, the shape of that ear.

Rolan.

Before I can grab the door handle, he lunges across the front seat for the driver. Bashes his head against the window with a sickening crack. The car careens toward a grassy lawn and crashes up a curb, the driver's head bouncing against the steering wheel. I shove myself across the seat as Rolan grapples for control of the car. The instant it slows I heave the door open, pitch onto the lawn so hard it knocks the breath from my lungs. The ground tilts. I crawl to my hands and knees, fight to stagger to my feet.

"Audra!" He grabs me by the shoulders. I twist away like a wild animal, claw at his face.

"I'm trying to help you!" he shouts, shaking me.

"Killer!" I spit. "You killed Ivan!" A hysterical sound rises within me, and my feet come up off the ground, kicking at nothing.

"I did *not* kill Ivan." He shakes me again, drags me back several feet until I notice the form of the driver sprawled on the ground. His face is covered in blood. So much blood—so much like Luka's. Like Nino's. I have seen too much blood, too many killed for one lifetime, let alone the space of these short days.

"Get in the car!" he says, but I'm struggling to break free—until his next words stop me cold.

"If you want to save Luka, get in the car *now*."

It's like the tendrils of a nightmare that will never end. Death at every signpost, blood on the pavement. Rolan at the wheel.

"I saw you on television. You were there. You killed Ivan!" I am beyond composure, if not logic. The curse, perhaps, of my Progeny brain.

"I was on the ferry when his hunter killed him. I didn't get to him in time. I tried to revive him," he says tightly.

"To take his memory!"

"If I killed him, would I have been anywhere near the body by the time the police arrived? Think, Audra!"

I squeeze shut my eyes, press my palms tight

against them. It makes the swelling on my face hurt even more. I welcome the pain. It gives me focus.

The car on the television screen, abandoned on the ferry. The body still in it. The police. Rolan's face in the pixels. The voice on the phone.

Hallo, Audra.

But it wasn't Rolan's.

"Someone answered his phone after he was dead."

"It was gone by the time I found him or I would've used it to reach you." He's speeding down the freeway, south, for lack of any other direction.

"You came to kill me in Maine," I say.

"I did *not* come to kill you. I came to protect you. They were suspicious after your death—had already tracked Luka to Maine, pegged him as a traitor. They were coming for him and would have found you. I volunteered to take him out, but I came to the States for you."

"You let me believe he was trying to kill me!"

"I had to get you away from him. To remember who you are. It was the only way to keep you alive."

His hint that my adopted parents were in danger. His willingness to return me to the Center and retrieve my records. To kill Luka.

And now I have effectively killed him myself.

Everything I have done. The details of a life,

381

obliterated. All for a single month of peace. In the end, all for nothing. I have saved no one.

"Why are you doing this?" I say wearily. "I know what you are! And there are no such things as Watchers."

"Not by that name, no. But we have watched for centuries. Sympathetic to the Progeny plight. Without the resources to take down the Scions of the Dispossessed—until now."

I shake my head. "Sympathetic to the plight . . ."

"We were monks, Audra."

I give a harsh, abbreviated laugh. "I've heard that one before."

He's silent.

"I just saw you kill a man!"

But now I remember Rolan murmuring while I was still in hysterics over the sight of the body. I had thought it Croatian, Hungarian.

No. It was Latin.

"It has taken generations for us to make our way into the ranks of the Scions," he says quietly. "To mingle bloodlines with families ancient enough for us to become the thing we have hated. I called us 'Watchers' more aptly than you know. We saw our course as a necessary evil, and broke from the order that we loved with the knowledge that this day would come. The Progeny will not survive another generation. Not just because of the Scions. Nikola's gifts are gone, but he is still ambitious. He'll deliver

382

his own before giving up power. Few Progeny who live long enough ever reconcile losing their gifts. They'd rather be hunted than be common."

My head is spinning.

"If you've been planning this for centuries, why didn't Ivan know about you?"

"And risk exposure with a single harvested memory? We've been, by design, as unknown to your world as you are to the common one around you. Renounced as heretics by the sect we served, cut off even from them for the things we meant—and had—to do. But we never forgot who we were. And we waited, in anticipation of a day like this. It's time for the Scions—and princes like Nikola—to be held accountable."

"And you and your 'Watcher' friends are going to do that."

"No. You are."

This time my laugh is genuine.

"Except that you're failing to realize one thing: unless you and your brotherhood of evil monks knows where the diary is—do you, by the way?"

"No."

"Then I've got nothing. Even if I managed to somehow find and deliver it, you and I both know the Historian would never let Luka or me live. And that's assuming the diary even exists."

"I believe it does, that it is the key to ending

this, and that you have more to bargain with than you know."

"Yeah? Like what?"

"You aren't just Progeny, Audra. You're a direct descendant of Anastasia."

"Her first daughter? The illegitimate one?"

"Yes."

"I thought they all died out."

"Not all of them."

I think back to the conversation with Jester. Nikola's census. And then I know: Nikola isn't trying to chart the Historian's so-called death map. He's trying to locate more descendants like me.

The children of Elizabeth's illegitimate daughter are more powerful than those of her legitimate son.

My ability to sense Ivan and Nikola. To *persuade* an airport, to project suggestion ahead of me on the run . . .

"Your brain is brilliant. Your gifts are stronger. They fade later in life. Or at least . . . that's the theory."

"No one's lived long enough for you to know," I say dully.

"Your line has been hiding for centuries. That it survived at all is testament to its power, Audra. There was a massacre two hundred years ago, when the genealogy the brothers kept was stolen. That wasn't the work of Scions. Anastasia's line has been hunted by a faction of princes for generations in an effort to keep you out of the Scions' hands."

"You're saying it was an inside job. That the Progeny are killing their own."

"Is that really so surprising, given what you know?"

"Then why did Nikola bring me to the Historian—why, when he killed my mother?"

"I don't think he killed your mother."

"You think she killed herself rather than be used as a pawn by either of them."

"I'm speculating, but I don't think he did. I do know this: You're a great prize to the Scions. Do you know what they could do with someone like you?"

"Then why not just take me? Why send me after this thing?"

"Because whatever it is, it's even more valuable or threatening than you are."

I close my eyes. But every time I do, I can't stop seeing Luka beaten nearly to death. Can't stop thinking of Nino, who didn't survive. I would gladly trade the gifts and power Nikola seems to crave so much for a common life without them, surrounded by the people I love. Given the choice now, I wouldn't take a single step further.

But I am not surrounded by those I love. And I have been unable so far to protect them.

My mother failed in this regard, too.

385

Something nags at the back of my mind. The incongruences in her notes. If her mind was like mine, she would never have needed to write notes at all. Or having done so, could have destroyed and retained the information.

Unless they were meant as a message to someone who could make sense of them, who thought like she did.

Someone like me.

"Is there any possibility they'll let Luka live?"

"I suppose that depends," Rolan says quietly.

"On what?"

"On you."

41

If I never see this stretch of highway to Bratislava again it will be too soon.

Claudia is in hysterics at the thought of me with a hunter. It's 2:00 A.M., and I've asked her to dispose of the envelope I left with her somewhere safe, if such a place exists. Or to burn it if it doesn't. Pain twists in my chest at the thought of losing those few precious remnants of my mother. Of Luka.

"Whatever you do," I say, "don't open it, don't read it, don't even feel it, or you'll end up in the same position I am."

My mother's notes—the ones Nikola found— are spread across my lap, but I am convinced, once again, that they are a red herring.

Jester seizes the phone from Claudia.

"Where are you? We're coming there."

"No. Get out of the city. Stay safe. Set up shop. I'll need your help."

An hour later I'm just trying to hold my brain together. To summon meaning from the inconsistencies between Nikola's collection and mine. To decode the numbers (or letters) tattooed on my back in case they served a dual purpose. To trace imaginary roads between the Bathory family estates, scattered like pebbles across the Austro-Hungarian empire. Searching, all the while, for patterns until my mind is as cluttered as one of my mother's pages.

I ask Jester to research the burial grounds of the Bathory relatives, the conspiracy theories about the location of her body, which has never been found. It's got to be near the last place she drew breath, at Cachtice in modern-day Slovakia, northeast of Bratislava.

"But it wouldn't be a church, I don't think," I say. Her name was unholy at her death.

"And Gregory Thurzo's wife—find out where she might have gone. She systematically stole Elizabeth's jewelry on her visits—maybe she took something else out with her. Her husband is the one who lobbied to keep Elizabeth alive. And find out where Elizabeth's daughter Anna lived and was buried. She visited her mother regularly at Cachtice."

"I'll look," Jester says. "But do you know how many family records—archives, anything— exist after Elizabeth? None. They were serious when they said it would be as though she never was."

Even as I disconnect, I know a theoretical diary could have ended up anywhere. Smuggled to her cousin the prince in Transylvania to plead her innocence. Destroyed by Elizabeth's sons-in-law or Pál's tutor and guardian, who managed

Pál's share of the estate—at least until it was stripped from him. Burned in frustration by Elizabeth herself.

I have to remind myself that there was something—*something*—damaging that I hid as effectively as Elizabeth and her elusive diary.

I comb through the connections between Ivan, Nikola, Amerie. The princes of the courts they frequented, their birthplaces, religions (all Catholic), and the sites of their deaths. Ivan, I am convinced, was purposeful about the location of his death, if not his death itself. Amerie, purposeful about her death.

We've just crossed the border into Slovakia when I say I need caffeine.

"I can't think anymore. I'm going crazy."

It's the second time I've made Rolan stop. The first time was at a tiny café on the outskirts of the city just so I could hold still long enough to regain some semblance of rational thought. But now the images are racing like frames of an old-fashioned film—too fast for my consciousness to grab hold of. And I know Rolan is struggling, his mind not wired for the Progeny disdain of sleep.

He stops at a gas station, goes inside for coffee. A police car pulls into the station, parks across the lot. I study the officer who emerges from it until he glances in my direction, though I never persuaded him to do so.

Does he recognize me, know I'm wanted for murder?

I'm more innocent than Rolan in this fact. But I'm the one who will be convicted if I fail.

Five days. So little time. And I don't even know what to look for once we get to Slovakia—or where to go from there if I fail.

A line from my journal tugs at my thoughts.

> So here we are. I'm at a crossroads and you're where I was months ago . . . I couldn't stay long enough in Bratislava. I'm running out of time so fast, the sun's practically moving from west to east . . .

I'm pinching my brows together when Rolan gets back in the car.

"I got you some coffee with your cream and sugar," he says.

As though I haven't heard that before.

"West to east from Bratislava," I say.

"What?"

"I went to Bratislava first, said I would get to Nyirbator if I had time, which I did not. That everything was backward. That the entire story is backward."

> Life is beautiful, Audra. I know it doesn't seem like it, with everything. But it is. And it is new.

"It isn't where Elizabeth Bathory died," I say.

"Then where?" Rolan says, setting a tray with no fewer than three coffees on the console.

"I don't know!" I pull my hair. "It isn't where she died. She died in Slovakia." But she was born in Nyirbator—literally "New Bathory"—due east of here, in Hungary.

"Turn around," I say suddenly.

He looks at me for a hard minute and then starts up the car.

We stop in Esztergom, just within the border of Hungary, for a few hours' sleep after Rolan almost goes off the road and I barely alert him in time.

Just before dawn, Rolan's phone chirps. He rubs his face and taps in his code and then, after a moment's hesitation, glances at me.

"What is it?" I say, feeling instantly ill. Have learned, by now, to fear the worst.

"Luka's still alive."

"Let me see," I say, reaching for the phone. When he hesitates, I shout, "Let me see him!"

It's a photo. Luka, in the back of what I recognize as a semi trailer. Just like Nino, blood drying on his face.

"Send a message to the Historian—"

"I don't have direct access to her."

"Then send it to whoever you report to."

He glances at me warily.

"Tell him to convey this up the chain of

391

command: I want proof of life every twelve hours. If I see one more bruise on Luka's body, I will take a running leap off the next building into traffic. Tell them I said that even if you manage to stop me, they can't get from my memory what I, myself, don't know."

With a quiet nod of understanding, he makes the call.

Four days left.

42

East of Hungary's great plain, the village of Nyirbator looks like what I imagine the Ukraine to be: eastern European and nonaffluent. Car repair shops with names like Zolt and Attila dot the corners, and the best-looking restaurant in town takes prime real estate in the tiny square. As for us, we have had a diet of nothing but coffee since we left Esztergom this morning.

"The Bathory family home is a museum now," Jester says on speakerphone. "Gutted, except for a few wax figures. Tourists hardly even go there." I can hear her keyboard clicking in the background.

"What else?" I say, rubbing my eyes.

"There's a mausoleum . . . a new walkway with a bunch of sculptures of Stephen, who became the Prince of Transylvania and King of Poland. It runs between two churches Stephen built with spoils after defeating the Turks . . ."

"Tell me about the churches."

"Both built by Stephen Bathory. One Minorite—"

"What's that?"

"The Friars Minor—the minor brothers," Rolan says quietly. "Franciscans."

"It's been rebuilt," Jester says. "It burned down. It isn't original."

"What about the other one?"

393

"The other one . . . is Calvinist."

I glance at Rolan.

"Elizabeth was a Calvinist."

"The Bathory family is buried there. The churches are near one another," Jester says, sending directions.

We come to the Minorite church, and I look up at its ornate red-striped exterior. Except for the adjacent museum, it's the same shape and size as the Calvinist church farther up the hill.

I insist on peering inside the reconstructed sanctuary in case something catches my eye, stirs a memory. An image. A shape. A smell. I'll take anything at this point.

The minute we step into the interior I reel back, overloaded by the gilded altars, the icons, the shape of the pews, the figures of saints.

"We'll never find it," I say. My pulse is a cudgel in my head. "It could be anywhere. Anything. In a drawer of the office. In the bookshop. A hollowed-out arm of a saint—"

I struggle to catch my breath, an iron band closing around my lungs. My mind won't stop, is traversing the museum, charting churches, diagramming the walkway between them, juxtaposing saints . . .

Rolan takes me by the arm, pulls me out into the air.

"This isn't it," he says.

"How do you know?"

"She was a Protestant."

I shield my eyes with a shaking hand. "The Franciscans helped her!"

"They helped her child."

"Why, when she wasn't even Catholic?"

"Because they believe in direct interaction with the world. Feeding the hungry. Clothing the poor . . ."

"Protecting the Progeny."

"Protecting the Progeny."

We trudge up the hill, past the wooden bell tower separate from the church itself. It is labeled with a large sign: BATOR.

Bathory.

Near it, on an outdoor pedestal, sits a bust of Stephen, the placard in Hungarian.

I begin to tremor. I am surrounded with Bathory images, land, conquest, and history. And, in the absence of sleep and a good burn, I am falling apart.

We enter through the carved side door. Gothic windows stretch up the walls of the church. The sanctuary is airy, modern, and white except for the wooden joists that split apart like palm fronds to spread into a magnificent lattice across the vaulted ceiling. It is too clean, too sparse, to offer a hiding place for even the least tainted soul, let alone an artifact as morbid as Elizabeth Bathory's diary.

An entrance near the back of the church opens

395

into a whitewashed room. In it: a single marble sarcophagus with an ornately carved lid.

The dragon biting its tail.

Stephen Bathory's tomb.

There are only a few other things of note in the chamber: a knight carved in a slab of red marble that looks as though it was formerly broken in two. A stone crest—the dragon again.

That is it.

I clutch my head. Nothing makes sense except the ticking of the seconds, the precious hours we spent driving here. Nearly two of five days . . . gone.

I almost miss the slight figure of the man who comes to inquire of Rolan in a voice so soft it's as though he has only a short breath to speak each sentence. He is thirty, if that, his thick glasses making him appear older.

The comb-over doesn't help.

I don't have the concentration to try to hold a conversation, turn away as Rolan speaks with him. Not that I'd understand them anyway—they're talking in Hungarian.

Meanwhile, Luka is somewhere in a semi trailer, bleeding out for all I know.

Just beyond the last row of pews, I press the heels of my hands to my eyes. I refuse to replay the last words we spoke, or to dwell on how strong his hand was, holding mine, the way he smelled. I force myself to focus, to speed and calm my mind at once. But I can feel the tears seeping down my cheeks.

"Audra," Rolan says. I hear him as though from a distance. Because I am praying a petition that is both plea and demand at once, in a deafening mental scream.

"Audra!" Rolan says.

My eyes snap open. But he is not standing there with a diary, or with a long-hidden lockbox. Or with a map of local landmarks that somehow form a dragon, three teeth like the center of an *X*.

"I am Pastor Tamas," the man says, so quietly that I squint, as though doing so will help me hear.

"Welcome to our church," he says. I glance desperately at Rolan. I am not here for the indoctrination tour!

"The pastor says this was once a Catholic church," Rolan tells me. I blink at him, sure my expression is blank.

"Yes, it is Calvinist now since the sixteenth century," the pastor says, before launching into something about the freestanding bell tower outside.

I glance down at my feet, at the marble beneath my sneakers, rebuilt in the lifetime of Elizabeth.

"There are thirty-three monks buried under the main church floor," he says, following my gaze. I back a step. I've never understood the practice of burying priests or prominent elders beneath the floors of churches in a holy minefield of souls. Of entombing poets, patrons, and artists along the walls, or far below in crypts.

My first thought is that I hope we don't have to break through a slab of marble to find the diary—or whatever it is—that will save Luka's life.

My second is that I will do it, single-handedly, if I have to.

My third is sheer astonishment at the morbidity of the Christian faith. Of the dying Jesus on the Minorite church cross. Of the execution cross itself. The bodies beneath the floors, entombed in walls and stone and beneath the earth outside. Death, everywhere.

"You will see the story of our salvation in the windows," the pastor says. "There are none along the far wall—a reminder that we must turn away from darkness . . ."

I've just decided there's nothing here, am already thinking ahead with panic. We can't afford to cross the map from eastern Hungary to Bratislava again. How many times have I zig-zagged through the ancient borders of the Austro-Hungarian empire in my past life—and into Wallachia and Transylvania in modern-day Romania as well? How long can I do this and hope to accomplish anything before I lose Luka for good?

A single whisper: *Please.*

"The tree of life," the pastor says, pointing to

the paned window above the organ pipes. He turns to the window adjacent to it, the first of several along the length of the church, gesturing to each in succession. "The serpent, by which man was tempted. The flower of our Lord Jesus Christ. The water of baptism . . ."

I go very still. Glance sidewise at the row of windows along the southern wall.

"The fire of the Holy Spirit," the pastor says, "and the Holy Trinity."

The Trinity window, which is not at the very end of the concave apses over the altar but on the angle just right of it, is composed of three circles built into the top of the window's Gothic arch. At first glance it is the same as the other windows. On the second, it is not. At the top of the baptism window, the circles are elongated into drops. In the next, the drops invert to form the petals of a flower.

Inside my skull I can almost hear my eyes clicking from one window to the next.

Rolan asks the pastor some question, his voice more gentle than I ever imagined it could be.

"West to east," I say, my words echoing slightly.

I'm running out of time so fast, the sun's practically moving from west to east . . .

The pastor pauses.
"What?" Rolan says.

"The story. In the Bible, it starts in Eden." I'm no biblical scholar, but I'm pretty sure of that much. "The tree of life," I say and point to the window at back. "The serpent in the garden," I say, pointing to the next window, the first on the long adjacent side. "All the way through Jesus to baptism, the Holy Spirit, the Trinity . . . the salvation story goes that direction."

"Yes," the pastor says softly, kind enough not to scorn me as an infidel or the religious village idiot.

"That's the south, isn't it?" I say, pointing to the long, windowed wall.

"That is correct," the pastor says.

"But the sun goes from east to west. It goes along that side . . . from east to west," I say, looking at Rolan.

"The sun *tells the story backward.*"

It does not end in morbidity. It is not mired in death. The story, once told in the unnatural succession . . . naturally goes backward. From the Trinity just right of the altar to the tree squarely centered on the back wall.

It has to end in life.

I glance up toward the slant of sun through that fourth window throwing panels of light against the darkened wall. And for a minute I feel that the droplets in that pane are about to fall, to rain down on my upturned face.

43

The window is abbreviated by the organ pipes to a mere third of the size of its siblings. Near the top of that Gothic frame, the panes curve up like a bowl or a crescent—or the limbs of a tree. A circle floats above it, a single golden fruit. I blink, and the crescent branches are a pair of arms, lifted to the sun.

The vertical panes form tiny squares where they meet the line of the "ground" the tree grows from. They are inset with the same gold glass. I stare at them long enough to see them separate from the rest of the window.

Three. Like the teeth of the dragon. The Trinity, the holy number of the Progeny. Three, the Glagolitic symbol like two towers sharing the same line of flat ground. Like the three vows of poverty, chastity, obedience.

The images flash, rotate before my eyes. This time I juxtapose them with the curving lines of script arcing across the pages of my mother's notes—so like those Gothic arches. I shuffle them in my mind, lay them out on an unseen canvas. Not the pages of contradictions, take those out. Not the front of the one with its uniform lines. Eight left. Two across, four high. Switch two. The back of this one instead of its front. This one turned upside down, the curving translation connecting to the end of the page beside it.

They form the Gothic arch, a tree like this, two limbs lifted as though to the sun.

A sun floating above the crescent, a golden island of light.

Rolan, beside me, is murmuring something.

"What is it?" I say.

" 'Be praised, my Lord, through all Your creatures, especially through my lord Brother Sun,' " he says. "Francis of Assisi."

The orb on the pages falls away, leaving only the curved arms, so like the Franciscan crest. The arms fall away, and the sun floats like a perfectly round island. The elements reassemble, forming the tree of life.

I glance toward the lattice at the top of the church, created, the pastor said, to draw the eye upward.

Thank you.

Outside the wind has picked up, bringing in a string of clouds.

Three days left.

44

We have driven nearly a full day straight. We have spoken little in the last few hours; even my frantic calls with Jester have subsided to only the occasional text. The three of them—Claudia, Piotrek, Jester—are safe for the moment.

Luka, however, is another story. The most recent proof of his life arrived less than an hour ago in the form of a video. He was so still I thought it proved nothing at all—until one of his captors kicked him into consciousness.

One of you has to live.

"Rolan?" I say, glancing at him. The cuff of his sleeve slides back from his wrist as he rubs his face, exposing a double-barred cross tattooed on the inside of his wrist. It's similar to others I've seen except that the lower bar is shorter than the one above it.

"Yes?"

"You're a monk. But you're a hunter. For real. Aren't you?"

His expression is grim. He carries with him burdens beyond my knowing, not the least of which was the body we left near Zagreb.

"Yes," he says finally. And then: "We were monks. I am not much of one now, if I ever was. Not much of a believer, either, sometimes. I have become the darkness I have hated."

"I'm sorry," I say and think of the long side of the church, devoid of windows but invariably lit from the other side. Of Luka, the night he claimed forgiveness was enough or it wasn't. And I hope that it is—enough. For him. For Rolan.

For me.

"I need you to do something for me, Rolan."

He glances at me, and it is the first time I have seen anything resembling apprehension on his face.

"If something happens—"

"I'll protect you. To my dying breath."

"I know you will. But I'm trusting you to do something else," I say. "No matter what we find, we both know they're not going to let me trade it for Luka and leave with him, alive. And I won't be their pawn."

"What are you saying?" he says, voice rising in alarm.

"If something happens to me, Rolan . . . I want you to take my memory."

45

Even from here I think I smell sage blowing down to the sea from the hills.

In the time since our ride from shore, the Adriatic has shifted from turquoise to lapis beneath the morning sun. Now, as we arrive at the almost perfectly round island of Košljun in the Bay of Punat on Krk, it is on a sea of jade.

There's a monk waiting by the jetty. Rolan tenses, not wholly trusting what we may find even here, though Jester has assured him that she spoke with the monastery from a secure line. When the boat docks, however, he makes no move to follow me ashore.

"They would not welcome me here if they knew what or who I am," he says. "I will wait here. Keep your phone on."

I tell myself I should take it as reassurance that he is not with me only to kill me the moment I lay eyes on whatever I may find here. But as the monk meets me, I am full of nerves. The clock is ticking, each minute too brief. And we have a long road to take in the two days before us.

"I am Brother Daniel," the monk says to me. "It is an honor. I have been expecting you, hoping you would arrive in my lifetime."

But my attention has gone to the statue of Saint

Francis in front of the monastery. He is taming a wolf. I instantly remember the picture I drew on the flight from Chicago—the German shepherd, which was not a dog at all but a wolf in the circle I recognize now as an island.

Somewhere, in the course of the letters written to myself, *before,* I had deciphered this location.

Why had I never come?

As we enter the monastery, I glance up at the crest over the door, note the crossed arms, the tao cross behind them. The banner over them both is Glagolitic.

"What does it say?" I ask Daniel as we pass beneath it.

" 'Peace and good,' " he says, as we enter the shade of the courtyard's colonnade.

We pass down a locked corridor to the last of a series of storerooms. It is sealed with a biometric lock.

He actually trembles as he opens it, and I feel for him, this man with the responsibility of curating secrets like a collection of poisons.

"What I am about to show you has cost many lives," Daniel says, bolting the door behind us as an industrial light flickers on overhead. "As of this week, I am the last living guardian of this information."

My heart is drumming, and twice I think it may actually stop as he unlocks a series of drawers and begins to produce handwritten letters, testimonies, personal accounts, and news articles, some of them so old that they threaten to crumble, others printed as recently as months or weeks ago. Each of them goes on a long, broad table that can never accommodate the weight of so much corruption. A story of slow rise from peasant beginnings fueled by ambition and revenge.

I sit down to read.

It takes hours. Too many. And I actually shudder to think of Nikola at the monastery on Cres just days ago, so nearby.

And then I remember Rolan, waiting all this time.

"What about the heretic monks, who infiltrated the Scions?" I ask. Daniel looks at me in surprise.

"There was a rumor over a century ago that several brothers from the monastery in Romania had made a vow to achieve such a thing," Daniel says, unlocking another drawer. "A secret, fanatical sect, condemned as heretics before they disappeared. But that is all I ever heard of it, many years ago."

By noon there are enough names to fill in several more circles of the Scion map—destroyed, in part, by the Historian, still fully intact in my head. And the picture is far worse than I realized, the Scions' influence extending into the upper echelons of the European Union, Interpol, the IMF, and governments as far east as Asia.

I sit silent, eyes hollow.

The last item Daniel lays on the table is a thick, bound book.

"This is the true diary," he says, spreading his arms to encompass the entire collection around us. "We have committed to collecting and protecting its growing tale for centuries, moving it from monastery to monastery at great risk to ourselves . . . in the hope that one day the entire story may be brought to light. Your mother worked tirelessly to complete the most recent years of this account. It is the reason she never allowed her memory to be taken, lest the work be exposed, or destroyed. And here"—he touches the book—"are the names and stories and relations of all who have died, with as many details of their lives as we have been able to gather. It is a more complete genealogy of the Utod than that in the Historian's possession."

I hesitate, and then open its cover. Turn to the back. There is Ivan, with more pages of information on his early life than I would have thought possible. And Nino is there, the date of the newscast announcing his murder penned in recent ink.

My breath catches.

And there is Ana. Her birthdate and biological and adopted parents. Nothing of her love for Nino or her otherworldly eyes that provoked such fierce adoration from others or the steely loyalty sheathed in her waiflike frame.

Her death is dated four days ago.

Sometime later I recover enough to ask how many brothers have died protecting this archive.

"Seventy-nine," Daniel says. "Nothing near the losses suffered by your bloodline through the centuries. But they were precious to us, and each life was given gladly."

"What about the diary of Elizabeth Bathory?" I say. "Does it exist?"

"If it does, I have not seen or heard of it, except in legend. And if it does, it has no power to end the killing. Only the truth, now, can do that. As for Elizabeth Bathory . . . God judged her long ago."

"The truth won't stop anything," I say, incredulous. "Nothing is going to stop this. They're too big!"

"You can stop it," Daniel says quietly.

Rolan said the same before I saw any of this, and I laughed in his face.

"With what army? Do you even know who the new Historian is? Her name? Anything?"

"No. Not yet."

I look around me with growing despair. Even if I took all of this back with me now—what would that do? How do you prosecute, let alone police or convict, a cabal? What did my mother, anyone—I most of all—expect to do?

And then it hits me. No wonder I gave all this up. Chose to forget it. To have it removed from my life as effectively as I removed myself from this one.

To live.

Because this will never stop.

"There is one thing more you must see," Daniel says. "I have sent to Dubrovnik, but it is not yet here. We will eat something first."

But how am I supposed to eat when every hour I sit here is one hour Luka gets closer to death?

Daniel locks up the archive and the corridor behind us. Emerging into the courtyard, I'm stunned to realize it's late afternoon.

One more day gone.

I pick at my food and then give up the charade of eating altogether. Making some excuse about a restroom, I stride out of the dining hall, needing air, unable to breathe. But unlike earlier, the courtyard is now occupied by a nun tending several young children.

I decide to visit the chapel instead, but just as I turn, I catch sight of the nun's face.

And she has caught sight of me. She gazes across the courtyard, unmoving, and I know her hair is blond beneath that habit, the same way I know the angle of her brows.

And that her name is Clare.

She is balancing a baby only a few months old in her arms. My heart begins to hammer; I have seen that face before, in the pile of my things. She is the twin image of the child in my baby picture tucked within my journal, a last gift from my mother to me.

Forget the diary, and the archive. I am staring at the secret I died to protect.

She has Luka's eyes.

My name is Audra Ellison and I am twenty-one years old. I am Utod, from the noble and long line of Bathory. I remember who I am . . . those I died for, those I love.

And I am ready for the fight of my life.

ACKNOWLEDGMENTS

I've said before that every book is a journey of a thousand thank-yous and amazing companions— one that leaves me humbled and changed, each time.

Thank you to my readers for your voracious imaginations, intrepid souls, and devoted companionship. The author is only half the story-telling equation, after all, which is a collaboration between two souls. It was one of you who first asked me to write something about Elizabeth Bathory a few years ago. (Keith Moulton, here you go.)

Thank you to my agents, Meredith Smith and Dan Raines of Creative Trust—you are world-class.

Amanda Demastus, Ami McConnell, and the entire team at Howard Books, for your excellence and innovation in an ever-changing industry.

Stephen Parolini, who mucked through ideas with me and, along with Becky Nesbitt, braved my early drafts.

"Asylum Warden" Cindy Conger and Lisa Riekenberg, keepers of my sanity.

Barbara Bocz, Nikola Špehar, and Agi Salgo, who accompanied me throughout Hungary and Croatia, patiently answering my oddball questions as I systematically veered off the beaten path.

Amy Lee, Meredith Efken, Jeff Gerke, Kate Brauning, and the ladies of the YA Launch, who brainstormed with me early in the process and late in the evening.

Kerry Nietz and Perry Marshall, who opened my eyes to the fascinating topic of epigenetics.

My family and friends, who keep me fed and put up with my eccentric hours and unwashed ways. Wynter, Kayl, Gage, and Kole, who remind me daily what life is really about.

Bryan, my love, integral to this story and my own. I am so happy to embark on the adventure of a lifetime with you.

And always, the One That Is, who amazes me time and again with plot twists I never saw coming. I am and will always be grateful till the very last line.

ABOUT THE AUTHOR

TOSCA LEE is the award-winning and *New York Times* bestselling author of *The Legend of Sheba*; *Iscariot*; *Demon: A Memoir*; *Havah: The Story of Eve*; and the Books of Mortals series with *New York Times* bestselling author Ted Dekker. She received her B.A. in English from Smith College. A lifelong world-adventure traveler, Tosca makes her home in the Midwest with her husband and children. You can visit Tosca Lee at www.ToscaLee.com.

Center Point Large Print
600 Brooks Road / PO Box 1
Thorndike, ME 04986-0001 USA

(207) 568-3717

US & Canada:
1 800 929-9108
www.centerpointlargeprint.com

6/2018